THE LIFE
OF LORD WOLSELEY

FIELD-MARSHAL THE RIGHT HON. VISCOUNT WOLSELEY, K.P., 1897.

Frontispiece.

THE LIFE OF LORD WOLSELEY

BY

Major-General Sir F. MAURICE

and

Sir GEORGE ARTHUR

with a Foreword by

General Sir R. WINGATE, G.C.B.

GARDEN CITY   NEW YORK

DOUBLEDAY, PAGE & COMPANY

1924

Printed in Great Britain

PREFACE

A WORD of explanation is due as to the reason for our collaboration. The late Viscountess Wolseley requested one of us to write the biography of her husband, and placed at the disposal of that one Lord Wolseley's official papers and such correspondence as related to his public life; to the other she entrusted for publication at discretion a large number of social letters, together with those which passed between herself and her husband. We seemed therefore to be well advised to pool our resources in a joint effort to produce a faithful portrait.

Lord Wolseley wrote an autobiography taking his life up to the end of the Ashanti War, while the campaigns which he conducted have been adequately described in official and other accounts. We have therefore dealt briefly with his early life, seeking rather to say what he would not say of himself than to describe its events fully; and of the little wars in which he was in command we have attempted no detailed description, but have

v

used our material to show what were his thoughts and feelings during their progress.

On the other hand, we hope to have been able to throw fresh light upon Wolseley's share in the great expansion of the British Empire, which marked the latter half of the reign of Queen Victoria ; upon his relations with Charles Gordon, both immediately before Gordon left for Egypt and while he was shut up in Khartoum ; and upon the part Wolseley played in the preparations for the South African War. But our chief purpose has been to demonstrate how much the Army and the Nation owe to Wolseley for his work as a military organiser, work which has a direct bearing upon many questions still at issue.

The maps which accompany this volume have been prepared from contemporary maps used by Wolseley during his campaigns, and the spelling of names of places has been made to conform to these.

For much valuable assistance in the selection of the illustrations we are indebted to Lt.-Col. Sir Arthur Leetham, K.C.V.O., Secretary of the Royal United Service Institution. We are also under obligations to the Council of the Institution for many facilities and much help.

Our grateful thanks are due to Her Majesty the Queen of Roumania for her gracious permission to make use of Lord Wolseley's correspondence with her mother, H.R. and I.H. the Duchess of Edinburgh, to all those who have kindly supplied us with letters, and to Colonel Lewis Butler for material for the earlier chapters.

BUTTON, THE 90TH L.I.

CONTENTS

LIST OF ILLUSTRATIONS

I. FULL-PAGE ILLUSTRATIONS

List of Illustrations

II. Illustrations in the Text

FOREWORD

By GENERAL SIR R. WINGATE, G.C.B.

I T was in vain that I pointed out to the joint authors, when they approached me to write this " Foreword ", that I could not lay claim to great personal knowledge of Lord Wolseley—it was confined, I said, to a year's service on the Staff of the Gordon Relief Expedition (as A.D.C. to Sir Evelyn Wood), service which often brought me into contact with the Chief, — to correspondence with him regarding certain episodes connected with the fall of Khartoum and the death of Gordon, and to occasional meetings which took place during my brief periods of leave from Egypt and the Sudan. I had then gradually risen from a very junior rank to be Director of Intelligence and eventually Sirdar of the Egyptian Army and Governor-General of the Sudan. Through these meetings and Lord Wolseley's letters to me, I had opportunities of appreciating his geniality and kindness to one so far his junior in rank and age. These were amongst the most attractive qualities of his many-sided character, and of them almost all those who had the privilege, as I had, of his friendship and unvarying support have had experience.

In reply to my protest that there must surely be others far more competent than myself to call the reader's attention to the salient features of the life-story of the hero of these pages, the authors affirmed that they had selected me because I had

xiii

been actively astride of the Army of yesterday and to-day (1880–1916), was cognisant of Lord Wolseley's superhuman efforts to revive or re-create that Army in the face of incredible opposition, and could witness as a commander in the field in the Great War both to the result of those efforts and to the part he played in the great expansion of the Empire which marked the last half of the nineteenth and the beginning of the twentieth century.

The dominant characteristics of the gallant Field-Marshal whose life-story is portrayed in the following pages, may be summed up in a sentence : " A heart to resolve, a head to contrive, and a hand to execute ".[1]

That Wolseley was born with the heart to resolve is shown in many of the episodes of his early military life. He then acquired that experience of men and things which was to prove so invaluable as his subsequent career developed. Speaking of this period his old friend Wood writes : " His courage and presence of mind in the face of death were remarkable in the outset of his campaigns ". He describes how, in an attack on a Burmese stockade, Wolseley fell with " a stone as big as a plover's egg " in his thigh, but when one of the storming party tried to carry him into safety he yelled, "Leave me alone! get into the stockade before they can reload ". Of the Redan in the Crimea he writes : " A 42-pounder shot passed over Lieutenant Wolseley's head—he lay as if dead ; he had lost an eye, a big stone had gone through his face, a part of the shin of his sound leg had been torn away, and a large piece of wood had been driven through his wrist, yet in three months he was out of hospital, joined the Staff of the Quartermaster-General, and was one of the last to leave the Crimea ".

[1] Cf. Gibbon's *Decline and Fall of the Roman Empire*. Written of Andronicus Comnenus, the Eastern emperor of the twelfth century.

Foreword

These examples show what was the calibre of
his personal courage, and, whilst displaying the
greatest intrepidity and fearlessness in the face of
death in those earlier years, he seems forever to
have been feeling his way towards an ideal.
Having found that ideal when, in Canada, he had
time to reflect on his experiences, he was at once
thrown into revolt against his environment. The
earliest wish of that resolute heart was to live a
life of active usefulness, to become an administrator
and reformer, and to live to be of permanent service
to the Army he served so loyally and the country
he loved so patriotically.

To help him in his struggle nature had endowed
him with a clear brain, goodness of heart, strength
of character, and as much adroitness as simplicity.
Possessed of unusual personal charm, he had the
faculty of gaining the close affection of his many
friends, and even sometimes of his official enemies ;
imbued with strong religious convictions and endowed
with a firm faith in the power of our national man-
hood to rise to any effort, he was exceptionally
successful in calling forth the best in his subordinates
and was an excellent judge of men.

Wolseley in the campaigns in Burma, in the
Crimea, the Mutiny, and the China War of 1860–61,
as a regimental officer and on the Staff, learned, in
the first years of his career, that there were many
glaring defects in the organisation of our Army in
the field, whilst the ignorance and lack of military
education amongst the bulk of the officers appalled
him. Further service on the Staff seems to have
strengthened his resolution to grapple with and
remedy these defects. The success of his new
methods, first when in independent command of the
Red River Expedition and later on in the Ashanti
Campaign, gave him confidence and he was soon
singled out as the coming man.

He gained further valuable experience in Natal in 1879–80, and the administrative appointments which he held in that colony, followed by the closing operations of the Zulu War and the capture of Cetewayo, prepared him for the Egyptian Campaign of 1882, where the immediate success of his carefully laid plans resulted in the complete victory of Tel-el-Kebir and the capture of Cairo. These successes marked the turning-point in his brilliantly rapid career, and, although chaffingly described as " our only General " and decried in unmeasured terms by the anti-Reform party, he persevered unswervingly towards the attainment of his ideal of a modernised Army.

A deep student of military history and a voracious general reader, he was perhaps somewhat impatient of those less keen and well-read than himself who stubbornly resisted his efforts to improve efficiency, and he never tired of urging upon officers the importance of fitting themselves for the duties they would have to perform in war. A serious soldier himself, he demanded that they too should take their profession seriously ; but it was not till after many years of self-sacrificing exertion that the soundness of his teaching was to bear fruit.

The story of the opposition he encountered—even in the highest quarters—is told in detail for the first time in these pages, and one cannot but sympathise profoundly with the far-seeing, able, and energetic administrator at the War Office, who found himself faced at the outset with a weight of opposition which wellnigh crushed him, on the part of those to whom he looked for support and help in the Sisyphean task of abolishing the antiquated system which even the Crimean War had failed to modify. The Duke of Cambridge—then Commander-in-Chief,than whom no one had greater love of country nor was a stronger supporter of the prerogative of the Crown—took special pride in parade-drill and set field days; he strongly deprecated promotion except by seniority, and to him "long-service" was synonymous with efficiency for an Army on a battle footing. On the other hand Wolseley urged, in season and out, that with the abolition of the purchase-system merit should be the passport to military advancement; that important appointments as well as nominations to command in the field should be by selection, while he insisted that "short-service" and the creation of an efficient Army Reserve were the means by which our future battles would be won. Yet in spite of this antithesis of view on official matters, the Commander-in-Chief and his revolutionary Adjutant-General had each a respect and esteem for the other which in the end ripened into friendship, if not affection.

The path to reform was a thorny one indeed, and it was inevitable that these years of unremitting labour, and the hard knocks which had come to Wolseley both in peace and in war, should eventually have worn down his indomitable spirit, and brought on the ill-health which clouded the last years of a life of marvellous physical and mental activity— causing the partial loss of memory from which he suffered towards the close of a great and useful career. Writing to his wife shortly before his end he said: "I won the game I played at, but it cost me dear. But I say with all my heart, 'God's will be done'. I have been greatly favoured by the Almighty, and I should indeed be ungrateful were I now to cavil at my small misfortunes."

In briefly reviewing the salient points of Wolseley's career, I have no hesitation in saying that, to me, the chapter dealing with the attempt to save Gordon is of special interest, as I am sure it must be to all who were concerned in the splendid effort which ended, alas! in failure — a failure undoubtedly attributable to the delay in starting the expedition, for which Wolseley was in no way responsible. The misunderstanding which arose between the politicians and Gordon as to the exact meaning of his instructions with regard to the evacuation of the Sudan was, as the authors clearly show, "the prime cause of Wolseley being agonized and Gordon sacrificed". I may say that this conclusion is fully confirmed by my own investigations, and the story may be retold in a few words. Gordon when in London and Cairo believed that evacuation was the soundest policy, and left for Khartoum with the intention of corroborating that view and giving effect to that policy; but once in the Sudan, where he was surrounded by those who believed implicitly in the capacity of the great Englishman to save the country in which their vested interests lay, and who not unnaturally tried to minimise the Mahdi's power and influence, he, in the light of information obtained on the spot, abandoned the policy of evacuation as impracticable, and resolutely set himself to defend Khartoum—a defence which must go down to history as an achievement almost without parallel in our military annals. He was soon to realise that, without external aid, the whole Sudan and those he had been sent to save must fall into the Mahdi's clutches. To abandon them to their fate was inconceivable to such a nature as Gordon's—and he was unable to recall the evacuation proclamation which, on his way to Khartoum, he had given to the Governor of Berber, who promptly published it. With the terms of this proclamation the Mahdi twitted him when Stewart's murder placed the Dervish leader in possession of the actual document, of which Gordon would fain have believed that his opponent had no certain knowledge.

The tardy despatch of the relief expedition;

Wolseley's tense struggle to stretch out a helping
hand to his old comrade hemmed in on all sides ;
his belief, fully confirmed at a later date by the
European prisoners in the Mahdi's hands, that had
but one steamer with a handful of British soldiers
appeared at Khartoum before the fatal morning of
January 26th, 1885, the Mahdi would have retreated
without attacking ; the long suspense awaiting
news ; the deadening shock when at last it became
known that the town and its gallant defender had
fallen only two days before the battered relief
steamers sighted the ruined town and the flagless
Palace ; the terribly depressing reaction which
followed the weary months of ceaseless toil, spent
in conveying an expedition through boiling cataracts
and across burning deserts — feeling that every
moment of delay was fatal—only to find at the end
that we were " too late " ; all indeed that passed
during those thrilling and anxious days is burnt
deep into my memory. Our hearts went out in
speechless sympathy to our gallant Chief, over-
whelmed by the tragic death of his old friend Charlie
Gordon, shocked by the fall of the Sudan capital,
which he had left no stone unturned to avert, and
depressed beyond measure with the magnitude of
the failure when brilliant success seemed almost
within his grasp.

I must not, however, be drawn by these personal
reminiscences into anticipating the contents of these
pages ; it will be sufficient for me to say here that
I think that those portions of the volume will be
perused with special interest which deal with
Wolseley's troubles at the War Office, on which I
have already touched ; they are concerned not only
with the gallant old Duke whom he eventually
succeeded as Commander - in - Chief, but with the
various Secretaries of State for War, and other
civilian members of successive Cabinets, who con-

trolled the Empire's destiny during those eventful years. His own experiences led Wolseley to believe that " the Army suffered greatly from civilian interference ", and although he rightly excluded Lord Cardwell—to whom generous and well-deserved praise is accorded—from this sweeping condemnation, he complained that the soldiers " though in office are never in power ". It is, I think, now generally conceded that Wolseley was right in contending that the functions and responsibilities both of the highest military and civilian administrators should be as clearly defined as possible. On the other hand, the assumption, not infrequently made, that any ordinary civilian of common sense cannot form a proper opinion on many important questions affecting military organisation and the conduct of military affairs —which require little or no technical knowledge for their solution—seems to me erroneous.

After all, the main quality required to meet and overcome the difficulties connected with the supply and transport of troops in the field, is a good head for business—and I think it will be admitted that any commander of marked military and administrative ability will feel that general civilian control, far from exercising any detrimental effect, is on the whole beneficial. This fact was abundantly exemplified in the Great War. Wolseley admits that Lord Cardwell, " though absolutely ignorant of our Army and of war, readily responded to the demands made on him by his military advisers and gave new life to our old Army ", and he adds that in doing so he even incurred " the fierce hatred " of the old school of soldiers. Is the system wrong then which gave birth " to that clear-headed, logical-minded lawyer " who so greatly aided Wolseley in the work of Army Reform, as it gave birth many years later to another eminent lawyer—Lord Haldane—to whom the modern Army is under a deep debt of gratitude for the reorganisation he effected whilst War Minister, whereby we were enabled to despatch to France, in an incredibly short space of time, that magnificent Expeditionary Force which so effectually barred the German rush to the Channel ports in 1914 ?

There are powerful advocates, it is true, who consider that the Secretary of State for War should always be a soldier, unconnected with politics, but there are probably a preponderating number of others who aver that it will be an evil day for the Army when it is established, as a system, that no civilian should be War Minister. In the great world convulsion which brought that very distinguished soldier and capable administrator—Lord Kitchener—to the War Office as Secretary of State, it is probable that the interests of the country were best served at so critical a juncture of our national existence by appointing a well - known and experienced soldier-administrator to supreme control, thus eliminating as far as possible the dangers and objections to anything in the nature of a division of responsibility whilst critical military operations were in actual progress. But on the other hand it may be remembered that this same distinguished Field-Marshal, my predecessor as Sirdar, during the eventful campaign which resulted in the reconquest of the Sudan, was the first to admit the invaluable assistance given to him by Lord Cromer throughout those difficult and protracted operations, and the reason is not far to seek : Cromer, who was almost in the position of Secretary of State for War *vis-à-vis* the Commander-in-Chief in the field, abstained from mischievous activity and acted as a check on the interference of others ; he had full confidence in the abilities of the Commander whom he had chosen, and unless the latter sought his assistance, he left him entirely alone ; " red-tape " was in abeyance, but he exercised some slight control over the demands

for stores which were sent to the London War
Office.

During the many years of my tenure of office in
the Sudan, both as Sirdar and as Governor-General,
I received similar treatment at the hands of Cromer,
and of Kitchener himself when he took Cromer's
place, and I attribute much of the success which
has attended the British administration of the Sudan
and of the Egyptian Army to the system inaugurated
by the wisdom and foresight of one of our greatest
British Pro-Consuls.

In no small degree was Wolseley responsible for
the creation of an entirely new spirit in the Army,
which has resulted in stimulating progress in every
direction, and in producing that type of officer who
is now to be found in various positions of major
and minor responsibility throughout the Overseas
Dominions, Colonies, and Protectorates which constitute our Empire. No one, I conceive, was more
prompt than Wolseley to realise that the British
nation could not shirk its responsibilities without
the degradation of its moral life, and that the truest
national well-being lay in great tasks and grave
difficulties honestly and fearlessly faced—in other
words, he was a constructive Imperialist, and he
sought with considerable success to inculcate the
doctrine throughout the Army that, the foundations
once laid, it was the distinctive work of the century
to look to the building of the superstructure on the
solidity of which must depend the future not merely
of the British Empire but of British democracy and
the world's civilisation. Wolseley, moreover, had
ample opportunity of appreciating that capacity for
government for which the British public - school
training is so largely responsible, a training which
induces a tacit recognition that the right of the
British to rule is by virtue of their justice in dealing
with subject peoples, and encourages inherent ability

to wield authority fairly and firmly. It was his persistent endeavour, as it was that of Roberts in India and of Wood in Egypt, to make his subordinates feel that their own individual share in the general success was known to him and that the credit should be theirs.

The methods of those three pioneers of the saner system of Oriental government, methods which their successors have tried to follow, was invariably to treat their native subordinates with such confidence and goodwill as could not fail to engender in their minds a feeling of trust in and dependence on their British leaders. At the same time they never forgot that the true secret of success in dealing with backward peoples is that progress should be steady and continuous, but that the pace should never be unduly forced.

Such were the lessons learnt by those who were privileged to come within Wolseley's purview, and it behoves us all, in the interests of the Empire, to hand on the torch to those who come after us, to be carried by them high and gloriously towards the consummation of those ideals which he and the group of patriotic and progressive officers by whom he surrounded himself, strove with no small measure of success to attain.

REGINALD WINGATE.

DUNBAR,
  September 1924.

CC
P. 88, line 17 from top,
P. 92, footnote, *for* "Ea

CHAPTER I

IT was in the natural course of events that Garnet
Wolseley became a soldier. His father and uncle
had served in the King's Own Borderers during
the French wars ; both had filled the boy with
stories of their own fighting adventures in the
West Indies ; both had added tales of the doings
of their father, who had fought with the 8th
Hussars during the Seven Years' War, and of
their uncles, who had distinguished themselves in
the Dragoons. Military service was a tradition in
the Wolseley family, and the Irish branch may be
said to have sprung from the sword. Midway in
the seventeenth century Garnet's great-grandfather,
Richard Wolseley, a younger son of a Staffordshire
Baronet, crossed the Irish Channel to claim land
allotted to his uncle by William III. Brigadier-
General Wolseley had defeated the Duke of Berwick
at Cavan, had ridden beside William at the Boyne,
had raised from the lads of Inniskillen " Wolseley's
Horse ", later to become the Inniskilling Dragoons,
and had been made Master-General of the Ordnance.
With such a strain in his blood, there could be no
hesitation as to his future in the mind—so soon as
he had a mind of his own—of a physically active,
mentally alert, and ambitious boy. If Garnet's
father had lived, the British Army might have had
to look elsewhere for its re-creator. Major Wolseley,

who died when his eldest son was but seven years old, had sold out because he was sick of garrison duty in the West Indies, and had no money to buy promotion. The outlook in the Army for a penniless officer was, at that time, not rosy, and a disappointed father might well have discouraged his son from following in his own rather dusty footsteps.

It was the gay Captain of Hussars who plunged his family into poverty ; having spent what he had in a crack cavalry regiment, he married a lady whose pretty face was her only fortune, sold his commission, took holy orders, and became the father of fourteen children. Small wonder that his fifth son, Garnet's father, lived and died in narrow circumstances, and could bequeath next to nothing to his wife and children. His widow, a daughter of Mr. Smith of Golden Bridge House—where on June 4th, 1833, Garnet Joseph Wolseley was born, and where he was brought up—was a woman of quick sympathies, well read and well informed; she exercised a constant influence over her eldest son ; she taught him how to teach himself, and began by imparting to him the implicit faith in God's providence which largely ruled his character and regulated his career.[1] A day school at Dublin was all she could afford for Garnet and his brothers, but at home every encouragement was given to his inherited love of books and his natural aptitude for drawing and mathematics. To acquire some knowledge of the intricacies of surveying without cost to his mother, he took service as a draughtsman in a surveyor's office in Dublin. This experience in the undemo-

[1] " I came down here on Sunday to see my mother, and found her dying. Although eighty-two years old, she was a vigorous woman, and had never been ill in her life. Her death makes a gap in my existence, in my thoughts, which can never be refilled ; it is a blow to me that I reel under, feeling that the world has now lost its greatest charm to me ; I cannot put my feelings into words, and would not if I could. My sorrow is too deep for them."—Wolseley to the Duchess of Edinburgh, Oct. 1883.

cratic 'eighties formed the loose peg on which to hang the fable that the man who was setting Society by the ears was the son of a Dublin shop-keeper, or, as some preferred to describe him, a Dublin corner-boy. Thus slenderly equipped, Garnet Wolseley received, on the 12th March 1852, without

GOLDEN BRIDGE HOUSE, COUNTY DUBLIN
Where Sir Garnet Wolseley was Born, June 4, 1833

purchase, and in recognition of his father's services, an ensign's commission in the 80th Foot.

It was probably just before the Duke of York took over the command from Lord Amherst that the British Army touched bottom in the matter of inefficiency, but in 1852 it was nearing the end of a long level of dullness and incompetency. After Waterloo, the Duke of Wellington had predicted a protracted peace, and had agreed to, or rather urged, drastic reductions in military establishments in the

3

interest of national finance. The regiments and battalions with their fine records must, he determined, at all costs be kept alive, because they were of vital importance, and would be difficult to re-create ; the scraping and scrapping had to be applied to the administrative services, the favourite target of parliamentary economists. Thus the organisations which had served his Army so well found their way to the scrap-heap, without even a framework being left to show how armies might in the future be moved and supplied. And to keep them in being at all, the Duke had to see many of the battalions which, under his orders, had made themselves respected and feared from Lisbon to Antwerp conserved in the " Sugar Islands ", which had fallen to Pitt's strategy, or consigned to other distant parts of the British Empire.

In 1854 the total strength of the Army was 140,143, and of these, 39,754 were tucked away in fourteen colonial stations, the Ionian Islands absorbing 3354, Ceylon 3448, the islands of the West Indies 5338. These troops, scattered in small detachments, and without any opportunity for serious military training, quickly degenerated. There was no regular system of change of stations, for transport was too expensive, and with long service there was no ebb and flow of time-expired men and recruits between the Mother Country and the out-stations. Many of the battalions abroad became dug in to the soil ; the men married and grew fat, did a modicum of drill and a few guards, and otherwise grew potatoes or fed chickens. The story ran that a battalion of Light Infantry, stationed for eleven years in an island garrison, was startled one morning to hear that a General Officer was about to inspect them. Surprise turned to dismay when it was found that less than half the men could button their tunics, and that there was no time to obtain sufficient cloth to cover the expanded chests of an infantry light in

4

nothing but name. In a word, the Army was packed away in small pieces, and Wellington, becoming later absorbed in politics, forgot that they were rusting ; when the time for action came the pieces were laboriously patched together, only to make a some- what sorry and loudly creaking machine.

With Napoleon finally disposed of, the Prince Regent had quickly reasserted the Royal prerogative in army matters, which in war had fallen into disuse, and begun a trial of strength to last until Wolseley had almost ended his military career. The Regent, eager to obtain direction of the personnel of the Army, and little interested in its business, found Ministers whose chief concern with the War Department was to reduce and control expenditure and to curb the power of the Crown. Both Crown and Ministers, each for their own purposes, agreed to govern the Army on the principle *divide ut imperes*, a principle developed by William IV. and not discouraged by Queen Victoria, until Prince Albert drew her attention to the absurdities in its train.

It had resulted by 1850 in there being seven independent Government Departments responsible for the well-being and control of the Army :

(1) The Secretary of State for War and the Colonies, to answer for the size of the Army, the strength of the overseas garrisons, and the selection of officers for Command-in-Chief.

(2) The Commander-in-Chief, generally respons- ible for discipline and efficiency in the cavalry and infantry, but not in the artillery and engineers. He could not move a man without the sanction of the Secretary at War, and had no voice in the supply of arms, equipment, ammunition, food, or clothing, nor as to fortifications. He commanded the troops at home, but was unrecognised by those abroad.

(3) The Secretary at War, with control of finance

and the pay of the Army, and of the movements and quarters of troops.

(4) The Treasury, in direct management of the Commissariat Department and of contracts for supplies.

(5) The Master-General of the Ordnance, charged with the efficiency, discipline and pay of the artillery and engineers, and with the construction and maintenance of fortifications and the provision of all arms and equipment.

(6) The Home Secretary, who looked after the militia and yeomanry when not embodied, and was the responsible Minister for military questions relating to Great Britain.

(7) The Board of General Officers, to deal with questions relating to the clothing of the infantry and cavalry.

These seven authorities never met officially to regulate the business of the Army ; they communicated with each other by letter, and there was no one to co-ordinate their functions. Doubtless it had been intended that the Sovereign should exercise general supervision over the military machine, but when a young Queen was surrounded by Ministers with little appetite for military affairs, all higher direction ceased, and the seven went their several ways. The wit of man could hardly devise a system better calculated to disarm an army, and the qualities of the British soldier alone served to prevent the total paralysis of the forces of the Crown. In 1842 Wellington retired from politics to resume his seat at the Horse Guards. He could not fail to be alarmed at the state in which he found the standing army,[1] but he was seventy-two years old, and his day was past to restore what he had built up in the

---

[1] In 1847, to expose our defensive weakness, he wrote a letter subsequently published in *Life and Correspondence of Sir J. Burgoyne*, vol. i. p. 444.

Peninsular War, especially at a time when men's minds were lulled by the prevalent peace and turned to International Exhibitions.[1] For close on forty years, from 1816 to 1855, the tangle of disorder had increased, and it required the next forty years, which covered almost the whole of Wolseley's active service, to unravel the complex web.

While the organisation of the Army was in a state of confusion and inefficiency, the training of the officers and men for war had ceased almost entirely. If a battalion could turn out smart and clean on parade and perform the drill-book movements with reasonable precision, no further questions were asked. The officers who had private means did their so-called soldiering at home ; those who had none must be content to serve abroad. The purchase system, which had to some extent lapsed in the field, was again in its full maleficent swing.[2]

It is difficult to understand how and why a régime, which had its roots in mediæval feudalism and its early results in proportionate booty, should have persisted until the seventh decade of the nineteenth century. There was just this to be said for it. By putting down their cash on the military counter, many officers rose to high ranks in comparatively early life; the sale of their commissions sufficed to keep them off the pension list, and of course a class of men who often proved admirable leaders was attracted to the Army. This latter was Wellington's main argument when he urged that " the description of gentlemen of whom the officers of the Army were composed made, from their education, manners, and habits, the best officers in the world, and that to compose the officers of a

---

[1] The Great Exhibition was held in Hyde Park in 1851.
[2] Vacancies caused by death in the field were filled without purchase.

7

lower class would cause the Army to deteriorate ".[1] Palmerston, with his War Office experience behind him, thought it was desirable to connect the higher classes of Society with the Army, and that it was " only where the Army was unconnected with those whose property gave them an interest in the welfare of the country, and was commanded by unprincipled military adventurers, that it could ever become formidable to the liberties of the Nation ".[2] Just when " Pam " was delivering himself of these rotund phrases, two young men, Garnet Wolseley and Frederick Roberts, both to become Commanders-in-Chief of the British Army, were preparing to enter that army without purchase. Neither of these was blessed with any estate or property, and one of them was not infrequently to be styled an " unprincipled military adventurer ". At no time was there any purchase system in the Royal Navy, and this fact was seriously adduced as a reason to esteem the officers of the senior service less highly than their military colleagues whose gold had secured their commission.[3]

Whatever benefits the purchase system could boast, its defects were gross and glaring, and its inherent vice was that it tended to make the Army the property of the officers. Amongst them there were an honourable few who showed keenness and sighed for efficiency, but for the most part they treated the Army as a sort of lounge they had taken on lease, and seemed to think the State ought to be grateful to them for the investment of their money. Their gallantry in the face of the enemy was never in doubt, but in 1794 General Craig, the Adjutant-General to the Army in Flanders, wrote that there was not a young officer who cared one farthing what his colonel, his brigadier, or the Commander-

[1] Evidence before Finance Committee, April 15, 1828.
[2] Clode's *Military Forces of the Crown*, vol. ii. p. 86.
[3] Adam Smith, Book I. p. 180 (1828 edition).

in-Chief thought of his conduct, and that out of the forty-one regiments in the field half were commanded literally by boys or idiots.

In 1856 it was stated before the Commission on the Purchase of Commissions in the Army that the common price for a Lieutenant - Colonelcy in the Cavalry was £14,000, although as much as £18,000 had been charged; that a Lieutenant-Colonel in the Foot Guards usually paid £13,000, and in the line £7000.[1] Often, it was alleged, the pay of officers was less than the interest they would have received had they invested in the funds the capital with which they had bought promotion.[2]

In 1871, when purchase was abolished, its incongruities had reached their high-water mark. In the 15th and 16th Foot the senior lieutenant had longer service than ten of the captains. In the 41st Foot one of the lieutenants was senior to every officer above him from the lieutenant-colonel downwards. In the 87th Foot two captains had six years' service, while two lieutenants had thirteen and fifteen years respectively, the lieutenant-colonel having joined the army two years after the senior subaltern. In another regiment three captains of nine years' service were senior to one of thirty-two years' service, and a regiment serving in India boasted a captain of forty-seven years' service who had been at Waterloo, at which time no brother officer, except the lieutenant-colonel, was born. On one occasion, in the 24th Regiment in 1846, a father and son were serving as captains. A majority was

[1] Report of the Commissioners appointed to enquire into the System of Purchase and Sale of Commissions in the Army, 1857, pp. 49 *et seq.*

[2] Cf. *History of the British Army*, Fortescue, vol. xi. p. 31. These high prices were due to payments over the rate fixed by regulation. An officer could only recover these "over regulation" payments by private sale to another officer. Lord Cardigan is reported to have said as he led the Light Brigade at Balaclava that he carried £10,000 on the point of his sword.

for sale, and the father, with nearly forty years' service, allowed his son to purchase over his head. The story had a tragic sequel. Two years later the regiment went on active service, and the son was killed, when the father became a major without purchase.[1]

It was not merely these anomalous situations within the regiments which were subversive of discipline; the whole system was based upon an open breach of regulations, and was therefore little calculated to inspire respect for authority. Though the prices of commissions were officially fixed, there was considerable traffic at profit figures, and dealings in the auction-room in Charles Street were as familiar to the officer as the Exchange was to the stockbroker. When authority shut its eyes to these goings-on, it was natural for the wealthy officer to regard himself as reasonably immune from discipline, if it proved to be irksome. While he had no inducement to take his profession seriously, his impecunious brother-officer had little hope of promotion.

A few well-to-do men used their means to further their careers, and would change their regiments so constantly as to have little interest in the unit which happened to be their temporary lodgement. Wolseley spoke of a staff officer in Dublin who had to ask his soldier servant for the name of the corps to which they then belonged. These ambitious migrants, however, were rare, and usually the regiment or the battalion was the officer's home. In every mess there were stories galore of regimental heroes in the Peninsula or at Waterloo, but there was no thought of the years of patient organisation and training which went to create the Army of Vittoria and of the Pyrenees. And if the long isolation of battalions at distant stations fostered regimental *esprit de corps*, it killed any interest in the larger formations or in

[1] Cf. *Lord Cardwell at the War Office*, Biddulph, p. 77.

the Army as a whole. Internally, except in the regiments of the Light Division, which retained the tradition of Moore's teaching, there was little inter-course between officers and men in the battalions at home. The drilling of the battalion and the training of the recruits were left to the adjutant and the sergeant-major ; the other officers were only expected to know the words of command and their places on parade. The commander of a company of Guards, who, as such, ranked as lieutenant-colonel in the Army, rarely went into the barrack-rooms except for inspection ; he drove down to parade in Hyde Park in his cabriolet, which waited to take him back to his lodgings when parade was over ; and what the Guards did to-day the Line were prone to do to-morrow.

Worst of all, service in the ranks had, during the long peace, taken on a character which was almost penal. From 1826 to 1847 enlistment was for life, and magistrates and judges would offer the criminal the alternative of military service or gaol. Hence the vulgar notion, which hardly died with the nine-teenth century, that to enlist was to be disgraced. Discharges were occasionally permitted as a reward for good conduct or ordered in case of extreme mis-conduct, but there was no middle door of exit. So while amongst the population there was no reserve of men trained to arms, many soldiers in the ranks, enervated by long years of service in a hot climate, were unfit for active service. On the outbreak of the Crimean War the only reserve consisted of 10,000 pensioners, who, if they chose to volunteer, might be accepted for garrison duty at home, while seventy field guns was the full quota available for Great Britain to take the field.

So—and so lamentably—did the military forces of the Crown drift to the close of the long peace.

Wellington was right when he said that the

British regimental officer was the best in the world, but wrong in ascribing his excellence to the purchase system. The gift for leadership ingrained in the British gentleman, and stubborn valour, the hall-mark of the British soldier, shone on active service and were to pull us through the troubles of the Crimea; but success was secured, despite neglect of administration; despite the absence of what goes to compose an army from a congerie of regiments, battalions, and batteries; despite the lack of military education and of encouragement to study which issued in inefficient and ignorant staffs; and despite commanders who, with a few notable exceptions, owed their advancement to the length of their purses and were wholly unfitted for the stern test of war. The British Army was still made up of the old fine material; it needed imagination, conviction, courage, and energy to cut that material into its former invincible shape.

Such was the Army which young Wolseley joined in 1852. The second Sikh War had not long ended ; stories of Sobraon, Chilianwalah, and Gujerat were circulating in the messes. Pennyfather's address to the 22nd after Meeanee was still ringing in every one's ears : " I can't make you a speech, my lads, but, by God, you are all gentlemen ".

One of Garnet's first companions on joining at Chatham was an officer who had been wounded at Chilianwalah, after a bellyful of Indian fighting, and had much to tell the young recruit.

Wolseley could not afford to serve at home, and, fired by all he heard, he decided that India was the country in which to seek his fortune. With high hope and a heart as light as his purse, he left England for the East to join the 80th Foot, which was employed in the second Burmese War. Towards the end of October 1852 he was sailing up the Hooghly on his way to his new station, and as he

ENSIGN WOLSELEY, 80TH FOOT.

From a Miniature in the Wolseley Collection, R.U.S.I.

To face page 12.

neared Calcutta he heard the minute guns from Fort William firing a last salute to the Duke of Wellington. Thus the young soldier who was to re-create the organisation and renew the fighting power of the British Army entered on his active career as the great leader of the previous epoch passed to his rest.

BUTTON, THE 80TH FOOT.

CHAPTER II

FROM Calcutta Wolseley was sent across to Burma. At the end of 1851 the King of Ava had insulted a British flag at Rangoon, and opened fire at H.M.S. *Fox*, which had been sent to the Irawaddy to obtain an apology. So began the second Burmese War, to follow the course common to every campaign in that province of the Indian Empire up to its final pacification. Organised resistance was soon overcome. Martaban, Rangoon, and Bassein were taken in April 1852, but terms offered were contemptuously rejected, and local chiefs sallied forth defiantly from their stockades to raid our friendlies and loot our lines of communication. The minor expeditions required to reduce these raiders to order enabled junior officers to show their mettle, and the wars in Burma were nicknamed "Subalterns' Wars". No subaltern was more eager to seize his opportunity and win the bubble reputation than young Wolseley ; but, though his regiment was up in the jungle at Pegu, he was kept kicking his heels at Rangoon, on tenterhooks lest the fighting should finish without him. But while waiting, he was busy with his miniature military library, intent on his surveying, and for his recreation rode about the country making notes of the ways of the Burmese, of the lie of their land, and even of the tenets of their religion. " The Buddhist priests ", he wrote

14

appreciatively, " are not only priests, but secular schoolmasters, and one seldom meets a Burman who cannot read, write, and do simple arithmetic."

His first opportunity was nearer than he had begun to believe. One Meeah-Toon, a chief whose headquarters were a stockaded village in a fever-stricken jungle on the Irawaddy, had been having a royal time capturing boat-loads of our supplies between Rangoon and Prome, and in February 1853 an expedition under a naval officer, chiefly composed of sailors and marines, was sent to rout him out. But sailors were sadly out of their element in the jungle ; the tactics were faulty, and the enterprise was a failure. A military force from Prome was at once ordered to tackle the truculent chief, now swollen with pride at his success, and to Wolseley's delight orders arrived at Rangoon that the recruits of the 80th were to report to Brig.-General Sir John Cheap, who commanded the force.

A difficult march through the jungle brought the expedition within reach of the stockade on March 18th ; the next day the 80th were to be the advanced guard with Wolseley in charge of its " point ". This meant that he would be well ahead on the move to the stockade, and might be the first into it. With a prayer to God for His protection on the morrow, a happy lad rolled himself in his blanket and went to sleep. During the advance there was some confused fighting in the jungle, and eventually Major Holditch, who directed the right attack, called for a storming party. The chance had come. Young Garnet impetuously volunteered ; he led his party through the prickly pear, fell into a cleverly prepared man-hole, met with a nasty check, rallied his men, returned to the assault, and at the very foot of the stockade received a bullet in the upper part of his thigh, the effect of which did not wholly disappear to his last day. The hurt was so severe that he was invalided home, but not before he had heard that he, the junior officer, would be mentioned in the official report—a mention to be confirmed in Despatches.[1] Early impressions count for much, and two things were burnt into Wolseley's mind. He had been asked to fight in the steaming jungle, clad in a scarlet cloth jacket buttoned up to the chin, and in white buckskin gloves. The discomfort he suffered in this absurd uniform spurred his efforts, when in authority, to give to soldiers fighting in hot climates a serviceable and comfortable kit. Then he never forgot that his first chance of distinction came to him as a volunteer, and that the gallant fellows who had rushed the stockade with him were in the same category. Hence, his strong predilection for volunteers for active service up to the time when he became Commander-in-Chief of the British Army, a predilection to bring him more than once into sharp conflict with the temper of the Army.

Garnet Wolseley was promoted Lieutenant and transferred to the 90th Light Infantry which he joined in Dublin, where he was immediately initiated into Masonry in a lodge of which, thirty-six years later, when Commander-in-Chief in Ireland, he became Master. After war was declared on Russia he was to pass many months in Dublin, as in Rangoon, panting for active service, and feeling sure that Sebastopol must fall to an attack from the land side. It was not until after Inkerman that the authorities rubbed their eyes and realised that the campaign in the Crimea was to be a good deal more than a military parade. The 90th was on the roster for India, but the roster went by the board, and the battalion embarked for the Near East on November 15th, 1854, armed with the old Brown Bess musket.

[1] The report recorded that he had not only distinguished himself by his gallantry in leading the storming party but by his judgement in marking the weak part of the stockade, whereby the breach was effected.

Earlier in the year, the new Minie rifles had been served out to them, but the Government withdrew these to furnish the original expedition, having thrown down a challenge to a Great Power without sufficient rifles to arm a modern division.

When the 90th landed in Balaclava, the lines of investment had been drawn tight about Sebastopol, and trench warfare was the vogue. The miseries of that first winter have been described in all their gruesome details. What Garnet Wolseley thought most miserable was that the suffering of the soldiers could have been infinitely lessened if the most ordinary forethought had been shown by the politicians at home. Parsimony and procrastination in the Cabinet had to be atoned for by bitter endurance in the camp.

The indignation of a regimental officer was naturally aroused against the staff, whose work certainly left much to be desired, for staff appointments in the Expeditionary Force had been largely due to family influence. "I don't know what our Brigade-Major knew," Wolseley wrote, "but he certainly did not evince any intimate acquaintance with the duties of his office"; and again, "I knew the officers well who were, as late as the fall of Sebastopol, the Quartermaster-Generals of two of our five divisions; they were not men whom I would have entrusted with a subaltern's picket in the field; had they been private soldiers, I don't think any Colonel would have made them Corporals". But perhaps the bitterest drop in the cup of a subaltern whose diligent study of the Peninsular War had persuaded him that one English soldier is worth two French conscripts, was to find that the French army at our side was well equipped where we were lacking, that many more French officers knew their business than did British officers, and that their army was well supplied with drafts to make good the losses of war, while we were sending out immature, un-trained lads, bribed with bounties, to die far more often from exposure and disease than from the Russian bullets. "The French", he noted rather gloomily, " were able to end the war in triumph and with credit, whereas at the end of the war our battalions carried with them to the remotest pro-vinces of the Empire, where we maintain garrisons, the sad story of failure for which the British Ministers, not the British soldiers, were directly responsible."

The lessons in surveying were now to stand him in good stead. Among other deficiencies, engineer officers were badly wanted for the conduct of the siege, and Wolseley was made an assistant engineer just when a run of promotion gave him his captaincy—and this without purchase, as the regiment was on active service. In the lines, in which during the winter there was little that could be done beyond keeping the trenches in repair and clear of snow, he found the man with whom—although they seldom met—he was to be linked by a common and lively religious faith in constant friendship for over thirty years. "Charles Gordon", Wolseley wrote, " was one of the very few friends who came up to my estimate of a Christian hero. When I first met him in the Crimea he was a good-looking, curly-headed young man of my own age ; his clear blue eyes seemed to court something, while at the same time they searched your inner soul. His absolute single-mindedness of purpose startled one at times, making one feel how inferior one was to him in all the higher qualities of character."

In the spring of 1855 came the active pro-secution of the siege, culminating in the assault on the Quarries on June 7th, where Wolseley, who in the preceding months had already been hit twice, received a nasty flesh-wound from a round of grape-shot. To this he paid no attention, but spent

a long night of toil consolidating—to use a term
which became hackneyed in a later and greater war—
the ground won, and at dawn perceived a column of
Russians coming up to retake their lost trenches.
His own regiment, the 90th, was near by, and with
the Colonel he rallied and, by his personal example,
kept together a handful of sleepy and all but
exhausted men to beat off the attack. That done—
and it was a tough job—he himself was so played out
that he fell down from sheer exhaustion and lay like
a log until he was roused by a voice regretting that
" poor Wolseley had been killed ".[1] The flesh wound
healed quickly, but three months later he was more
seriously injured in the face, as well as in the leg, by
a bursting shell, and the sight of one eye was
practically destroyed.[2] This served to keep him out
of the unsuccessful assault on the Redan on September
8th, when he compared our blundering effort with
the French success at the Malakhoff, which forced
the Russians to abandon Sebastopol. The French,
he insisted, had made more thorough preparation
than had we; they displayed greater dash and
imagination in leading, and had made better provision of support for the assaulting troops. " No
appeal ", he said, "was addressed to the imagination
or to the fighting instinct of our men. Had volunteers
been asked for, a forlorn hope of say 200 dare-devil
men and officers would have given a chivalrous, an
infectious interest, energy, and dash, and a reckless
and romantic spirit to the whole affair that was
a sadly wanting element in all the plans for the
operations which culminated in our defeat that day."
His eye gave him considerable trouble, and he was

[1] For his conduct on this day he was recommended for the V.C.
[2] How constantly he exposed himself in the trenches is shown by
the fact that he was wounded slightly on April 10th, June 4th, and
June 7th, severely on August 30th, while on February 15th his coat
was pierced by a bullet, on April 10th his trousers were cut by a
round shot, and on June 7th a ball lifted his forage-cap from his head.

on the point of going home to consult an oculist when the Quartermaster-General, Sir Richard Airey,[1] who had been busy shedding incompetents and replacing them by officers who had proved their worth, offered him the position of Deputy-Assistant Quartermaster-General on the staff of the Light Division. This was too tempting an offer to be refused, and he remained in the Crimea, a second winter being very different from the first. The public had been thoroughly stirred by Sir William Russell's letters to the *Times* ; reinforcements and stores were poured forth, and when fighting died down, the Army in the Near East was as it should have been at the beginning of the campaign. Wolseley went home in the autumn of 1856 to rejoin the 90th at Aldershot, and to ponder war lessons which threw a lurid light over the defects of our military administration.

A few months of service at Aldershot and Portsmouth and a new excitement broke the monotony of garrison life. Repeated infractions of treaties and assaults upon British traders had decided Palmerston to try to teach China how to behave herself, and the 90th Light Infantry went overseas in April 1857 to take part in a punitive expedition.

Her Majesty's troopships of those days were a by-word in the Army, and not even the scandals of the Crimean War had roused the Transport Department of the Admiralty, which considered any rotten old tub good enough to carry troops. On this occasion My Lords surpassed themselves in the selection of a transport for three companies of the 90th, of which Wolseley's was one. H.M.S. *Transit* was known as an unlucky ship, and she at once reaffirmed her reputation. The first night, while riding at anchor off the Isle of Wight, the tide receded and the fluke of the anchor pierced her bottom ; the vessel was barely saved, but after

---

[1] Later Lord Airey.

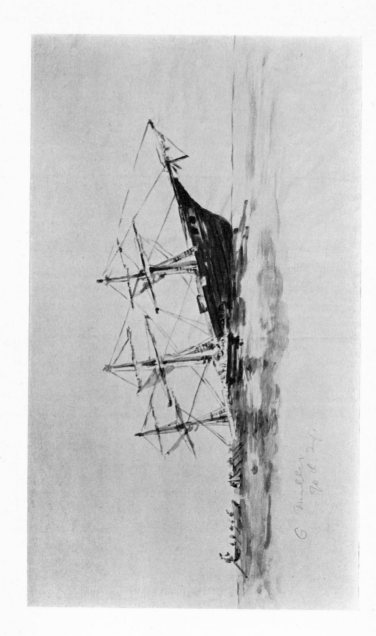

THE SINKING OF H.M. TRANSPORT *TRANSIT*, JULY 1857.

From a contemporary Sketch.

To face page 21.

a few days for repairs made a fresh start. Storms in the Bay so strained her masts that she put into Corunna to refit—a welcome relief to the sea-sick soldiers, and for Wolseley an opportunity to visit the scene of Moore's victory and death. With calmer weather reading was possible, and Wolseley, with the expert help of Major Barnston, also of the 90th, was absorbed in Jomini's *History of Napoleon*. The remainder of the voyage to Cape Town passed without adventure, but in the Indian Ocean the ship was struck by a cyclone, sprang a leak, and nearly foundered. The crowning calamity was, however, to come, for while threading the Straits of Banca, off Sumatra, the *Transit* struck a rock. Wolseley's company fell in on the lower deck, where it remained for several hours in almost total darkness, and only aware that the vessel was sinking by the stern. The discipline of the *Birkenhead* was happily the discipline of the lower deck of the *Transit,* and the tension was at length relieved by a welcome summons to the main deck. The weather was calm, and the troops were landed without loss of life on a barren coral reef under a grilling sun. Thence they were later rowed across to the more hospitable Island of Banca, while the ship went to the bottom unmourned by any of her passengers. Ten days later came a gunboat from Singapore with the news that the native army in India had mutinied, and that the 90th were to proceed to Calcutta. Then H.M.S. *Actaeon* arrived, and took Wolseley and his companions to Singapore, Calcutta being eventually reached after a journey of 133 days crowded with sufficient incident to satisfy the veriest glutton for adventure.

The situation in India was critical ; Delhi was besieged by a force in numbers barely one-fifth of the garrison ; the tragedy of Cawnpore had been enacted ; the Residency of Lucknow had been reached by General Havelock, but his own force had been surrounded, and his arrival meant the reinforcement, not the relief of the garrison ; Meerut and the forts of Allahabad and Agra were in our hands, but the North-West Provinces generally were held by the mutineers.

With the first news of the Mutiny the British Government turned to Sir Colin Campbell, probably the best soldier available, to take command in India. He arrived in August and at once bent himself to relieve Lucknow. The headquarters and seven companies of the 90th, who had travelled more happily to India, had already been sent forward to join Havelock ; the three remaining companies, under Wolseley's close friend, Major Barnston, marched from Ranegunge, then the railhead, by the Grand Trunk Road connecting Calcutta with Lucknow, Delhi, and the North-West Provinces. After halts at Futtipore and Cawnpore, where there were hideous traces of the recent massacre, they reached, late in October, the Alum Bagh, a palace near the suburbs of Lucknow held by a detachment, which had been dropped by Havelock before he advanced to the Residency. The Alum Bagh was to be the headquarters of Colin Campbell's army of relief, and from it he moved on November 14th towards the Residency. He skirted the southern and eastern suburbs, and arrived at the Dil Khoosha Palace, about three and a half miles south-east of the Residency, and seized the college known as La Martinière, three-quarters of a mile to the north.

The next two days Wolseley was to the fore in capturing some fortified buildings, and on the 17th was told by Sir Colin in complimentary terms that he had been selected to attack the building which had been the Officers' Mess of the 32nd Regiment. The mess-house was skilfully and gallantly seized, Wolseley planting the British ensign on the roof. His allotted task was then completed, but his men's

blood was well up ; the mutineers were yielding,
and he decided to attack the Motee Mahal Palace.
The gateway of the palace was built up and loop-
holed ; by hard fighting the enemy was driven from
the loop-holes, and Wolseley sent for picks and crow-
bars to knock in the newly-built brickwork closing
the gate. Private Andrews, his servant in the
Crimea, was shot down as he was guiding the party
with the tools, and was lying in the open street
under heavy fire when his former master sprang
out from cover and carried him to safety, but
not before the soldier was again hit by a bullet
intended for the officer. Mr. Kavanagh, who had the
distinction of winning the Victoria Cross as a civilian,
offered to guide the party to other entrances to
the palace, but they were all found to be heavily
barricaded, and Wolseley, returning to the working
party, found that it had managed to knock a hole in
the wall. Squeezing themselves through this narrow
approach, Wolseley's company drove the mutineers
from room to room of the palace, and out of it into the
Gomtee, in which many were drowned or shot. He was
just taking his men towards the Residency itself when
the defenders made a sortie, and the first encounter
between relievers and relieved was that of Captain
Wolseley and Captain Tinling of the 90th, who had
been separated by the vagaries of the *Transit* ; a
few minutes later, in the courtyard of the Residency,
occurred the meeting of Campbell, Outram, and
Havelock, the subject of the well-known picture.
Wolseley was told that Sir Colin was furious with
him for having pushed beyond the mess-house, and
shrewdly suspected this was due to the 90th having
done what the General had intended that his beloved
Highlanders should do. He had, however, exceeded
his orders, and taken perhaps an undue risk, so was
probably relieved when, the next morning, the Commander shook his fist and cried out laughingly—

"If I had caught you yesterday!" proceeding to make some flattering remarks.

Sir Colin had secured his immediate object, but was not strong enough to take the whole city, and had to content himself with the withdrawal of the garrison from the Residency. There was other work to be done quickly; the lines of communication were in dire peril, for General Wyndham, left in command of Cawnpore, had been driven by the Gwalior force within his entrenchments. For the moment it was chiefly necessary to reinforce Wyndham and safeguard the sick and wounded soldiers of the garrison, as well as the flock of women and children who were too stunned by what they had endured at Lucknow even to be grateful to their rescuers. Sir Colin himself went off to Cawnpore to help out Wyndham, whom he found in sorry plight, leaving Sir James Outram at the Alum Bagh with a mixed Division, which included the 90th. For Outram Wolseley conceived an admiration which soon deepened into reverence. "He exercised", he wrote, "a great spell over me, and upon each and all of us he made a deep impression. His presence anywhere made others bold and daring, and seemed to stiffen any weak knees. There was something positively magnetic about his high courage."

Before Sir Colin could reach Cawnpore the mutineers had taken and burnt the cantonment, and for the second time Wolseley lost his kit, which had been left there on the way to Lucknow. He seemed to be hunted by bad luck of this kind. One lot of baggage had gone down in the *Transit*; a second instalment, which included his Crimean decorations,[1] was burnt in Cawnpore; and, on the day of his return home from Ashanti, his furniture and papers were destroyed in the great fire at the Pantechnicon.

[1] These were afterwards found upon the dead body of a Pandy. It was three years before compensation for loss of kit was granted.

Outram's defence of the Alum Bagh kept the garrison on the stretch from the end of November till the spring. Late in December, Wolseley had a change from constant picket duty, and almost constant skirmishes, by escorting a convoy to Cawnpore, where he learnt of the death from wounds of his comrade and first military mentor, Major Barnston. In March 1858 Sir Colin was ready to take Lucknow, which fell to him more easily than had been anticipated. On the 14th the Kaiser Bagh was stormed, and Wolseley had his first experience of the lust of loot. Priceless treasures were destroyed and much rubbish appropriated by the soldiers, who thought they had secured rich booty. One man sold for £10 jewels which afterwards fetched £7500, and many others refused offers for bad paste and glass, believing that they had found some of the King of Oudh's state treasure. Wolseley's own share was a Cashmere shawl, which he used one night as a blanket, and of which he was robbed next morning.

Lucknow was cleared of the mutineers a week later, and at the end of the month Garnet Wolseley was chosen to fill a vacancy on the Quartermaster-General's staff, caused by the invaliding home of Lieutenant Frederick Roberts, V.C., who had aggravated the wound received before Delhi by incessant work during the relief. Thus occurred the first link between the two leading soldiers of the Victorian era, though they do not seem to have actually met at the time. So Wolseley joined the staff of Major-General Sir Hope Grant, who took over the Oudh Division, and with Grant he remained until the close of the campaign. He had completed the six years' service which qualified him for the Brevet Majority earned in the Crimea.[1] This step came in the nick of time for further preferment. The young staff

---

[1] The regulations required a minimum of six years' service before a Brevet Majority could be awarded.

officer won the entire confidence of Hope Grant, who in 1858 hunted the mutineers of Oudh into the Forests of Nepal. Wolseley was mentioned five times in Despatches, and in 1859, for his services in the Mutiny, received the Brevet of Lieutenant-Colonel just before his twenty-seventh birthday.

While the Indian Mutiny was raging, China was left to the diplomats. Palmerston appointed as British High Commissioner Lord Elgin, who, with his French, American, and Russian colleagues, concluded a treaty in June 1858, with a rider that resident diplomatic agents should be properly received at Pekin. This provision was resented by the Chinese, and when the Ambassadors arrived with a British naval escort off the mouth of the Pei-Ho, they were roughly told to land elsewhere. The British admiral sought to force a passage, but found the Taku forts at the mouth of the river too strong for him. Such a rebuff had to be redressed. An Anglo-Indian force was put together in India, and Napoleon III. readily agreed to back it up with an expeditionary force under General Montauban, later known as Count Palikao, the unhappy War Minister of August 1870. Wolseley rated Montauban's military merits very cheaply,[1] but had unbounded belief in the British Commander, Sir Hope Grant. Grant had wished to make him the Quartermaster-General of the expedition—a post akin to that of the modern Chief of the General Staff. Grant was only dissuaded from this idea by the representations of Lord Clyde that so junior an officer would be out of place in so prominent an office. Accordingly, Col. Kenneth

---

[1] " It is all up with France ", he remarked on the Red River in 1870, when he heard that Palikao had been given the portfolio for war. A month later Palikao had pushed MacMahon into the march which ended at Sedan.

McKenzie was named Q.M.G., with Col. Ross as his deputy, Wolseley receiving the third place on the staff for a campaign which he always alluded to as the best-managed within his experience.[1]

General Headquarters reached Hong-Kong on March 13th ; there the expedition assembled, but it was not until August 1st that the Allied Forces landed at Peh-Tang. Three weeks later the Taku forts fell after some stiff fighting, when the Allies marched on Pekin and occupied Tientsin on the 25th. Elgin and the political officers of the Army fondly thought the Chinese must now accede to our demands, especially when two Imperial—but irresponsible — commissioners from Pekin made their appearance. Nothing, however, happened to give pause, and Chang-Kia-Wan was reached on September 18th.

All the while the Pekin Government was parleying with our diplomatists ; but Grant had no illusions as to the good faith of the Chinese, and the political officers were to be quickly undeceived. For on the 19th Mr. Parkes and Mr. Locke, who were conducting negotiations at Tung-Chow, some miles in advance of the Army, were with their escort ambushed, imprisoned, and tortured. On this day Wolseley nearly went to his death. Mr. Locke had returned to report a situation which was rapidly becoming acute, and volunteered to return to Tung - Chow and bring back our advanced guard. Sir Hope consented, and said he would send Col. Wolseley with him. Wolseley was for the moment not at hand, and Captain Brabazon, a staff officer,

---

[1] Wolseley spoke of Grant as " a soldier and a daring leader, with keen bright views upon war in all its phases—a man of strong opinions and with plenty of good ideas, who could not always describe to others what he wanted to be done. His faith in an all-seeing God who watched over soldiers was as the very life within him, and his religion a powerful force that influenced him through all that he did and said".

asked to go instead ; he started, and within an hour was caught and cruelly beheaded. Before noon that day our vedettes galloped in ; they had been fired upon by Chinese troops, massed north of Chang-Kia-Wang, and there was no further doubt as to the temper of the Chinese. Two days later Grant attacked the enemy drawn up on the farther side of Tung-Chow, and again defeated him. Once more the Chinese tried to negotiate, to be told that, in default of the immediate release of the prisoners, the Allies would occupy Pekin. The prisoners were not released, and on October 6th the Army bivouacked inside the ramparts of Pekin. The next day the French seized the Yuen-Ming-Yuen Palace—popularly called the Summer Palace—and Wolseley, riding on to communicate with them, found them busily intent on loot. "Imagine", he wrote, "some three thousand men let loose into a city composed only of Museums and Wardour Streets, and one has some faint idea of what Yuen-Ming-Yuen looked like after it had been about twenty hours in the possession of the French. Officers and men seemed to have been seized with a temporary insanity ; in body and soul they were absorbed in one pursuit, which was plunder, plunder. I stood by while one of the regiments was supposed to be parading, but although their fall-in was sounded over and over again, I do not believe there was an average of ten men a company present."

One of a band of French soldiers, laden with silks, porcelain, and ivory, handed him a small miniature : " Mon camarade, voici un petit cadeau pour vous ". It was a portrait of Boileau by Petitot.

The French began the looting only because they were first on the spot, and British officers were soon equally busy. Grant would have none of this ; he appointed prize agents, ordered all loot to be given up to them for sale by auction, and the proceeds to be distributed on a fixed scale to all ranks.[1] Wolseley had hated the pillage of the Kaiser Bagh; what he saw at Pekin decided him that indiscriminate looting is demoralising, destructive of discipline, wildly wasteful, and grossly unfair to those whose duty kept them away from the plunder. He himself copied Sir Hope's order in respect of King Koffee's treasure at Kumasi, and at Cairo sternly forbade any looting whatever.

On October 8th the nineteen survivors of the thirty-nine prisoners taken by treachery were given up, and on the 13th the city surrendered at discretion. Peace was quickly concluded, and at the end of November, Grant and the Headquarters Staff embarked at the mouth of the Pei-Ho for Shanghai. Wolseley then betook himself to Japan, and to Nankin, the old capital of China (then occupied by a rebel who styled himself Tiew-wan, or " heavenly king "), and was back in England in the spring of 1861.

China and the Chinese had deeply impressed him. Once released from the tyranny and rapacity of the Mandarins, he believed the country would flourish and the people become a virile and greatly capable race.[2] Later, as the mediæval Japan he had visited emerged into a great modern Power, he would say that if China did likewise the struggle for supremacy must eventually lie between the Chinese and the Anglo-Saxons. Such an Armageddon would best be averted if an Englishman were to lead reform in

[1] Wolseley bought the miniature back at the sale, and also a valuable screen which is now in his collection at the Royal United Service Institution.

[2] Mr. Edmund Gosse remembers how on one occasion, when dining with Wolseley at Ranger's House, Sir Francis de Winton expressed some views over-indulgent to the Turks; his host turned on him indignantly, and swore that no Turk could hold a candle to a Chinaman, who was the cleanest, the most temperate, and the most philosophical creature in the world.

29

China; and his dream was to be that Englishman.
A few years later it was a question whether Garnet
Wolseley or Charles Gordon should be sent to help
China in dealing with the Tai-Ping rebellion. Gordon
was chosen, and no one more heartily approved the
choice than Wolseley. When Gordon returned, his
friend said to him : " How differently events might
have turned out had I been sent on this mission
instead of you. I should have gone there with a
determination of wiping out the rebellion, and of
becoming myself Emperor of China." Gordon,
Wolseley admitted, had played the much nobler part
of " a great Christian hero without earthly aspirations
or ambitions ".

The close of the China campaign was the end of
a chapter in Wolseley's life ; he would no more serve
as a subordinate in the field; for the future it would
be for him to command in war.

At the age of twenty-seven he was a Lieutenant-
Colonel ; he had served with distinction in four
campaigns, he had been wounded four times, and
nine times mentioned in Despatches ; he had shown
himself a gallant and cool-headed leader of men,
full of initiative and resource, and what was far
rarer in those days—a student and thinker no less
than a man of action. He had the good fortune to
enter the Army at an hour rich with opportunity ;
he had the enterprise to reach out eagerly to every
opportunity which came near ; in eight years the
penniless lad from Ireland had made himself a man
of note, upon whom the chiefs of his profession
kept watchful eyes.

APPENDIX

LORD WOLSELEY'S VIEWS OF THE CRIMEAN WAR IN 1899 [1]

LORD RAGLAN, as a brave soldier and a perfect gentleman in thought, word, and deed, deserves every praise—but he was not born of God to begin commanding an army when already an old man.   His one great mistake was his acceptance of that command.   He had been for nearly forty years leading a sedentary life in London, and I do not think he ever knew anything of war as a science.   At least he had forgotten anything about it long before 1854.   The Government sent him a very clever old man, Sir John Burgoyne, to coach him. But the latter was on engineering points too wedded to the ideas which held good in the days of Badajos and the Peninsula. To what extent Raglan was responsible for the selection of the Generals and Staff sent to Turkey in 1854 I know not.   I was a young man in that year—just twenty-one—and in every sense one of the new school who believed in military education. We—our number was small at first—believed thoroughly in Sir Richard Airey—the ablest of the Quartermaster-Generals —in Sir Colin Campbell, in General Eyre, and a very few others of the same kidney, but we had a very low opinion of Lord Raglan and most of the Generals.   The Staff was mainly composed at first of very ignorant London " flaneurs ", almost all useless.   Lord Raglan, ignorant of war both in practice and in theory, was consequently very seriously handicapped.   The expedition to the Crimea was one of very great risk, and to have embarked in it, as we did, without any land transport was an act of criminal folly.   The few ponies we bought in Turkey were a laughable substitute for the organised transport without which the attempt on Sebastopol was a truly dangerous undertaking.

All this is, however, to be found in the pages of the Report of the Parliamentary Commission which enquired into the causes of our disasters, and which recorded so scathing a condemnation of the Government of the day.

[1] A letter written to the Duke of Argyll, then the one survivor of the Ministry which embarked on the Crimean War, in reply to a request for his views of Lord Ellenborough's criticisms of Lord Raglan.

31

But the knowledge of a Government is almost always what the knowledge of the educated classes is, and of war and its science no one in England knew anything. It is easy to abuse the Cabinet for going to war, when England had *no* army; but the people of England foolishly thought they had an army, and from that mistake arose all our troubles in the Crimea.

The conduct of the war was very bad. The Alma was a badly delivered battle, and when the pluck of the Regimental officer and the private soldier won it for us, we lacked both the military knowledge and the nerve to take advantage of it. We were surprised at Inkerman, and, having embarked upon a siege, we did not possess either the troops or the transport or the stores such a great undertaking demanded. Of course our having done all this is a proof that Lord Raglan was not a great general, in fact, that he was ignorant of a trade he had never learnt, indeed, I believe had never studied. He had very many fine characteristics, and I hate finding fault with him when I know how much the blame for all that took place in 1854–5 lay equally at the door of the Cabinet that urged the Crimean campaign upon him.

The fact that Lord Raglan went to the Crimea at all is to me sufficient proof that he was not fit to command an army in the field. But some of the points for which he is condemned by Lord Ellenborough cannot be directly charged against him. Indeed, Lord E., apparently anxious to find fault, has not examined his maps with sufficient care. Had he done so he would not have made the Warenzoff road run to Balaclava.

What killed our Army was want of land transport. The men who might have made a road from Col to Balaclava were employed in bringing up stores and food, and in digging up roots near Inkerman to cook that food with. I quite agree that we originally occupied too great an extent of front, but the whole expedition was a game of " Brag ", and we played it as long as we had any counters left.

Sir John Burgoyne and the other Engineer officers of rank misled Lord Raglan as regards what he could do before Sebastopol, and he was too ignorant of his trade to judge the question soundly for himself. Our victory at Inkerman— we won it, thanks to the French—destroyed all our chances of taking Sebastopol in 1854. The Russians were horribly defeated there, but their defeat secured them what they wanted, namely, either to raise the siege or to prolong it indefinitely. We very nearly did raise the siege, and it was Lord Raglan's firmness that saved the Army from embarkation after that battle. Whilst therefore I cannot endorse Lord Ellenborough's sweeping condemnation of Lord Raglan as a general, I feel that he was entirely unsuited either by experience or knowledge of war for the position the Cabinet of the day selected him for. I think he ought not to have accepted it, and that under no amount of pressure from home should he have attempted a landing in the Crimea without an ample and thoroughly efficient Land Transport service.—His only chance of effecting the object aimed at was by a victory, and then a very rapid pursuit which would have delivered Sebastopol into his hands ; but he could not hope for this unless he was provided with a well-organised Land Transport service of sufficient size.

I hope you will publish your views upon the story as told in that very long work of Kinglake. We have never yet had any official answer to the many serious charges he makes against Lord Aberdeen's Government.

BELT PLATE, 90TH LIGHT INFANTRY.

CHAPTER III

BEFORE leaving China, Wolseley had heard that the first shots had been fired in the American Civil War; and early in December 1861 he received a telegraphic order to embark immediately for Canada as Assistant Quartermaster-General. The hurried summons was due to difficulties which had arisen with the United States when one of their naval captains had boarded our mail steamer, the *Trent*, and carried off Messrs. Slidell and Mason, envoys of the Confederate States to Europe. Feeling in England was inflamed by the insult to our flag; an angry protest was drafted, to be toned down at the intervention of the Prince Consort before being despatched to America. Eventually an incident which was handled by our Government with some excess of bluster was composed by the wise discretion of Abraham Lincoln, but for a time the danger of war was acute. To meet the possibility of hostilities a few regiments had been sent across the Atlantic to guard the Canadian frontier, and it was at the same time decided to increase the staff. Wolseley found himself once more under his old chief, Colonel Kenneth McKenzie, and sailed with him on board s.s. *Melbourne*, a transport only one degree better than the *Transit*. McKenzie knew her to be a very bad sea boat, as slow as a coach, and to have been condemned as useless during the

34

Crimean War. He urged that another steamer should be chosen so that he and his department might be in Canada in time to arrange for the arrival of the troops. The Government, however, was more concerned with his departure than his arrival, and, so long as an excited Parliament could be informed of his actual embarkation, was apparently content that the Quartermaster-General and his staff should reach Halifax long after the Expeditionary Force. By this time all fear of trouble had evaporated, and it only remained for the staff officers to travel to Montreal through Boston by the courtesy of the nation which they had crossed the Atlantic to fight. At Montreal, Wolseley first met, to form a lifelong friendship with, Mr. George Stephen, afterwards Lord Mountstephen, one of the pioneers of Canada, and perhaps the first to see the vast development which lay ahead.

From 1861 to 1865 the world was watching the struggle between North and South, and Wolseley did not neglect the opportunity of studying a war which was being waged almost at his door. He obtained, late in August 1862, six weeks' leave, and, without saying what his purpose was, arrived in New York just when Lee had launched his first great offensive, had seized Harper's Ferry, crossed the Potomac, and was marching on Washington. Wolseley, who already rated Lee's military merits very high, was eager to get touch and word with the Confederate General, and chance favoured him. He was travelling so far with his friend Inspector-General Muir, head of the Canadian Medical Service. The two tossed up which should join the Northern and which the Southern Army ; Wolseley won and elected to go to the latter. He expected to find Lee in Maryland, or to meet him in Washington, which he thought would surely fall to the Confederate chief, but a copy of Lee's orders had come into the hands of his opponents. General McClellan learned that the Confederate forces were divided, forced Lee to fight on the Antietam, and to fall back across the Potomac. Wolseley had therefore to pass into Virginia by what was known as the " underground route ", by which friends of the Confederates in Maryland communicated with Richmond. The journey, made in company with Mr. Lawley, the correspondent of the *Times*, was not easy, and the crossing of the Potomac was only accomplished by means of fair words and forty dollars in British gold expended on a fisherman on the bank, together with a large cigar and a specious story complacently smoked and swallowed by a Federal officer, who most inopportunely strolled into the fisherman's hut just as Wolseley and his companion were making their arrangements.

The trip and his conversation with Lee induced Wolseley's first literary effort. He described it in an article over the signature of " An English Officer ", and sent it to Mr. Blackwood, who gave it pride of place in the issue of January 1863, and forwarded a cheque for £40, covered by a highly appreciative letter. Wolseley had immediately succumbed to the influence of Lee, and evinced the strongest sympathy with the South. " Lee", he wrote, " is a person who must at once attract attention as a splendid specimen of an English gentleman, with one of the most rarely handsome faces I ever saw ; while all honour and place implicit faith in his courage and ability, those with whom he is most intimate feel for him the affection of sons to a father. Old General Scott rightly said that when Lee joined the Southern cause, it was worth as much as the accession of 20,000 men to the rebels."

With subsequent closer study of Lee's campaign, Wolseley's opinion of him waxed higher and higher, and he said deliberately that there was quite as much military knowledge to be gained from the American General's operations of 1862 as from Napoleon's campaign of 1796, which " we all read so attentively ". A voracious reader of everything worth reading on the Civil War, he wrote an essay, in 1887,[1] when his judgement was mature, under the title " Military Genius ". In this he gave to Lee a place as a soldier only after Napoleon, Caesar, and Marlborough. " Lee's strategy in this year," he wrote, " when he fought in defence of the Southern capital and threatened and finally struck at that of the United States, marks him as one of the greatest captains of this or of any other age. No man ever fought an uphill and a losing game with greater firmness, or ever displayed a higher order of military genius than he did in command of the Confederate Army." Stonewall Jackson he also met, and was only less impressed by him than he had been by Lee : " With him we spent a most pleasant hour, and were agreeably surprised to find him very affable, having been led to expect that he was silent and almost morose. Dressed in his grey uniform, he looks the hero that he is, and his thin compressed lips and calm glance which meets yours unflinchingly give evidence of that firmness and decision for which he is so famous. Altogether, as one of his soldiers said to me in talking of him, ' he is a glorious fellow ', and after I left him, I felt that I had at last solved the mystery of the ' Stonewall Brigade ', and discovered why it had accomplished such almost miraculous feats. With such a leader men would go anywhere and face any amount of difficulty, and, for myself, I believe that inspired by the presence of such a

[1] " 26 Feb. 1887. . . . I have just written a little article for the March number of *Macmillan's Magazine* which I shall feel very flattered if you will glance over. It is about one of the very greatest and most remarkable men I have ever met, General Lee, who commanded the Confederate Armies. . . ."—Wolseley to the Duchess of Edinburgh.

man, I should be perfectly insensible to fatigue, and reckon upon success as a moral certainty. Whilst General Lee is regarded in the light of infallible Jove, a man to be revered, Jackson is loved and adored, with all that childlike and trustful affection which the ancients are said to have lavished on the particular deity presiding over their affairs." [1] The Southern soldiers he regarded as of a piece with their leaders. " I have seen many armies file past in all the pomp of bright clothing, and well-polished accoutrements, but I never saw one composed of finer men or that looked more like *work* than that portion of General Lee's army which I was fortunate enough to see inspected." [2]

There was no opportunity of meeting any of the Northern commanders, of whom—from all he heard—he judged McClellan to be the best, for Grant had not then leaped into fame. Of Grant he wrote in one of seven articles on the Civil War, which he published in the *North American Review* : " Though not prepared to modify the opinion expressed elsewhere, that General Lee was the most remarkable man the Civil War produced, and though I cannot think that General Grant possessed at all the same genius for command, yet it must be at once confessed that it is an immense relief to turn from the mirage of these indecisive battles and movements in the West to the story of the Vicksburg campaign. It is very natural that General Sherman should rate very highly the military genius of General Grant, for the great services which, in the summer of 1863, Grant rendered to the Union made him tower head and shoulders over all others who could possibly be placed in supreme command of the Federal Armies." [3]

In this series he was outspoken in some scathing

---

[1] *Blackwood*, vol. xciii. p. 21.
[2] *Ibid.* p. 24.
[3] *North American Review*, 1890, p. 454.

criticisms of Mr. Jefferson Davis's political conduct
of the war, which drew from the ex-Confederate
President a spirited reply. " The shrewd, the wise
Mr. Lincoln " excited his admiration in the same
degree as Lee, yet he offended the great President's
most devoted followers by coupling the two as the
outstanding figures of the Civil War.

Wolseley spent nine very happy years in Canada,
years of comparative leisure which came at an
opportune moment. His first nine years of service
had been passed in hurried journeys from one
campaign to another, in the field under violent
variations of climate and country, and against foes
of strongly contrasting characteristics ; he had had
first-hand knowledge of the nature and complexity
of the military problems of Great Britain. In
Canada there was time to ponder over these experiences, to compare the peace training of our Army with
the realities of war, to classify and put away in their
proper places, in a mind naturally orderly, the
lessons learned in Burma, the Crimea, India, and
China ; and this time for reflection and assimilation
came to him when he was living among men daily
engaged in the development of a new country, men
who had to be practical to live, whose minds were
broadened by the vast spaces of their land, whose
continual struggle with nature compelled in them
initiative and common sense. Two of the greatest
of Canada's pioneers, Stephen and Donald Smith,[1]
became his friends and taught him much, but the
keenness and energy of the youth of Canada taught
him even more.

In 1865 the Fenians in the United States,
constantly recruited by emigrants from Ireland and
numbering many who had gained military experience
during the Civil War, planned an invasion of Canada,
under the delusion that they would have the sym-

[1] Later Lord Strathcona.

pathy, if not the open support, of the powers in Washington. Canada, realising at once the weakness of her defensive forces, and urged on by the Governor-General, set to work to reorganise her militia. Colonel Patrick MacDougall, an able and highly educated officer, who had had a long experience of the country, was chosen to direct this reorganisation. Many senior captains and colonels in the British Army of the 'sixties knew little of their work beyond what Wolseley called the " childish manœuvres of the parade ground " ; but others, impressed by the blunders of the Crimean campaign, had learned the need for professional study, and of this school Patrick MacDougall was one of the leaders. His first acts were to create an efficient military staff and military schools at every place where regular troops were stationed. He formed near Montreal a camp of the young officers who had qualified at these schools, and made Wolseley its commandant. Wolseley, proud of his pupils, wrote that " they were thinking and yet practical men, without any of the pedantry which too often clings to the young officers of all Regular Armies " ; and long before Canada made her noble contribution to a noble cause, he said : " My own experience of Canada, and of its own fine loyal, manly people, has taught me that England can always depend upon the Canadian Militia to supply her with a first-rate division, under Canadian officers, who are not to be surpassed in military character-istics of a high order by any other troops. . . . Our young officers of the regular Army are too prone to depend upon regulations which are apt to dwarf their natural military instincts in positions where the Canadian officer would act according to the common sense that is within him."

It was in these surroundings and under these influences that Wolseley set himself to consider how the British Army could be better fitted and furnished to do its duty in time of war. He read diligently and regularly; he started the practice—to be continued nearly to the end of his life—of entering in his diary a brief appreciation of such books as impressed him. He read widely, believing that, if he were called to high administration and command, military knowledge alone would be far from sufficient. " A man who aspires to command men must ", runs a jotting of 1866, " know all about men and their ways, if he means to lead them, and not about soldiers and their ways only, for he will have plenty to do with men who are not soldiers ", and he studied men and their ways not only in life, but in books. He read eagerly because, apart from this objective study, he was drawn by a real love of literature to make a wider circle of friends in print, and he would surprise those whom he met and talked to in later life by displaying tastes which they little thought to find in a soldier. " I would sooner live upon porridge in a book-room than on truffles and venison where books were not ", he said once to his friend Mr. Edmund Gosse, who adds that this meant much from one who was by no means indifferent to the truffles and venison of life.

From the habit of reading sprang the wish to use his pen. In the winter of 1862 he had drawn from his journal and letters a book entitled *The Narrative of the War in China in 1860*. He then gave himself to reflect what guidance and information the soldier had needed, and had not received, through the four campaigns in which he himself had fought. The result was the *Soldiers' Pocket Book*, published in 1869. Hitherto official manuals and regulations had not travelled outside the parade ground and administration in barracks; the *Pocket Book* was devoted to preparation for war and the duties of the soldier in the field. It was the first, but by no means the last, of his publications to embroil him with the

War Office, which looked askance at an officer
daring to make good official deficiencies ; but it had
an immediate success in the Army, and ran to many
editions. It was the forerunner of the modern
Field Service Regulations, and forty years later the
War Office itself produced a Field Service *Pocket
Book*, which was in fact an expansion of Wolseley's
attempt to give the soldier a compendium to which
he could refer the questions which war would bring
to him. And if he kept his mind thus alert, he kept
his body well braced and disciplined to endure
fatigue and possible privation. Games made little
appeal to him, though other forms of outdoor
exercise were delightful, and he rarely spent less
than three or four hours in the day in the saddle.
He wanted no more than six hours' sleep, was up
before the sun, did most of his writing before breakfast, and most of his reading at night.

In 1865 he was promoted full Colonel, and in
May of the following year the long-expected invasion
by the Fenians took place. Their leader, "General"
O'Neil, crossed the Niagara River with some 12,000
men, captured Fort Erie, near Buffalo, and then
advanced towards Ridgeway, where he entrenched
himself. Wolseley at once left Montreal for Toronto,
and started with a column of regular troops for
Ridgeway. Before he arrived the Canadian Militia
had engaged the Fenians, who retreated, many of
them being captured, as they were crossing the
frontier, by troops of the United States. The
Canadian commander in this action was inexperi-
enced, and there was some confusion amongst his
force. Wolseley was constantly impressing on his
Canadian friends, whose military qualities he so
much admired, that the art of command required
something more than courage, initiative, and common
sense. "The weak side", he wrote, "of all militia
officers is that officers accustomed to command or

MINIATURE OF LADY WOLSELEY, BY TURRELL.
From the original in the Wolseley Collection, R.U.S.I.

To face page 43.

even instructed in the art of commanding are but few, though it is difficult to convince the officers themselves of this fact. Any one can learn in a few weeks to shout out the drill-book words of command required for any military movement. That parrot-like accomplishment is easily learnt, but not so the art of commanding men ; for it is essentially an art, and so high and peculiar an art, that many officers even in regular armies never master it. Good pleasant manners, closely allied to firmness, a genial disposition, a real sympathy for the private soldier, and an intimate knowledge of human nature are essential qualifications for the man who would command soldiers anywhere."

On the expiration of his term of office as Assistant Quartermaster-General he, in April 1867, returned to England, where he met and fell in love with Miss Louisa Erskine, daughter of Mr. Alexander Erskine. But it was not long before Canada summoned him back, for in September the appointment of Colonel Lysons as Deputy Quartermaster-General came to an end, and Wolseley was appointed to his place as senior staff officer in Canada, being then the youngest officer — he was thirty - four — who had ever received so high a position on the staff. He managed to snatch two months' leave in 1868, went home, married Miss Erskine, and so began a life of mutual confidence and devotion to which death alone set a term.[1]

Early in 1870 a little cloud which had appeared on the western horizon of Canada rapidly increased in volume. In what is now the province of Manitoba lies the Red River Territory. This territory was, up to 1869, a part of a vast extent of land with ill-defined boundaries, which had been granted by

[1] The relations of husband and wife are portrayed in *The Letters of Lord and Lady Wolseley*, edited by Sir George Arthur. London, William Heinemann.

Charles II. to the Hudson Bay Company. In December 1869 the rights over what was called Rupert's Land were transferred by a tripartite agreement between Great Britain, the Confederation of the North American Provinces, and the Hudson Bay Company to the Confederation in consideration of the sum of £300,000 paid to the Company. The settlers on the Red River, which flows through the modern town of Winnipeg into the lake of that name, were allowed no voice in this arrangement. The Red River had already begun to attract emigrants, whose enterprises were opposed on the one side by the Hudson Bay Company and on the other by the French-Canadian priests, who had established missionary stations in the territory and dreamed of attracting a large French population of their faithful. There were therefore numerous causes of friction, and the French half-breeds in particular were easily stirred to resentment against an attempt to dispose of them without their consent. Towards the end of 1869 a half-breed, one Louis Riel, collected a band of followers, took possession of Fort Garry, close to the present position of Winnipeg, and proclaimed " the Republic of the North-West ". The Canadian Government sent Mr. Donald Smith to Fort Garry as special commissioner, but he was unable to appease the malcontents. Riel imprisoned in Fort Garry a number of English and Scottish settlers, and on March 4th executed a man named Thomas Scott, who had sought to effect their release. This act aroused intense indignation throughout Canada, and the Government decided to send an expedition to Fort Garry. An infantry brigade consisting of the 1st Battalion of the 60th Rifles and two battalions of Canadian militia, aided by detachments of artillery and engineers, with four 6-pounder guns, was placed under the command of Colonel Wolseley. The starting-point of the expedition was

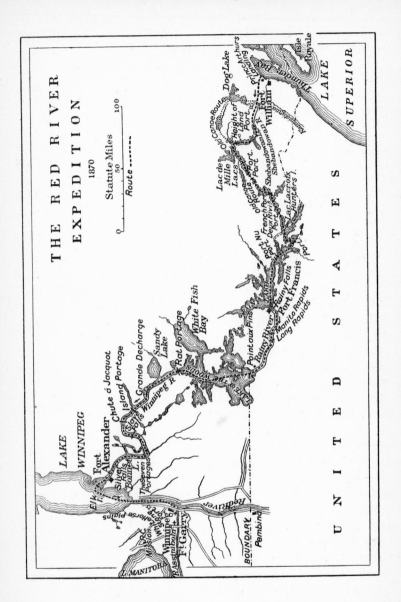

THE RED RIVER
EXPEDITION
1870

Statute Miles

0   50   100

Route ------

LAKE
WINNIPEG

Fort
Alexander

Chute à Jacquot
Island Portage
Sault Grande Decharge
Winnipeg R.
Rat Portage
Sandy
Lake

White Fish
Bay

Elk
Silver Falls
L. Bonnet
The Seven
Portages

Pointoux Pines
Rainy River
Rainy Falls
Fort Francis
Manito Rapids
Long Rapids

Lac de
Mille
Lacs
Old Canoe Route
Dog Lake
Kaministiqua R.
Fort Arthur's
Prince Arthur's
Prince Arthur's Landing
Height of
Land
Port.

Port French
Port Deux Rivières
Port Nu
Port Milles
Shebandowan Port.
Shebandowan
Fort
William

Lac Lacroix
Hunter's I.
Port...

LAKE
SUPERIOR
Isle
Royale

Red River

U N I T E D   S T A T E S

BOUNDARY
Pembina

Red River
Assiniboine
Winnipeg
Ft. Garry
White Horse Plains
L. MANITOBA

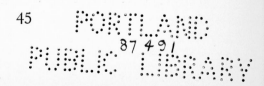

Toronto, and the route was divided into three stages : the first, of 94 miles, from Toronto to the railway terminus at Georgian Bay ; the second, by steamer along Lake Superior to Thunder Bay on the western shore, a distance of 534 miles ; the third, partly by road, partly by river - boat, from Port Arthur on Thunder Bay to Fort Garry, 560 miles distant. Thus the total length of the route to be covered was 1188 miles, of which the last stage was longer than Napoleon's march from the Niemen to Moscow ; while the expedition had to traverse a country unknown and unexplored, except by Red Indians and a few hunters. The period in which to complete the move was strictly limited, for a start could not be made until the ice on Lake Superior had melted, which usually happened early in May, and the return must be before the approach of the October frosts.

On May 25th Colonel Wolseley landed at a small clearing which had been made by the Canadian Public Works Department on the shore of Thunder Bay, where is now Port Arthur. This was to form the base of operations, and a few huts had been run up as store houses at a dreary spot where a forest fire had destroyed all vegetation. A few fish and a little game might be killed on the way to Fort Garry, but otherwise the country could afford no supplies of any kind, and it was necessary to carry with the troops all food, equipment, and requisites during the period, which could hardly be less than four months, between quitting and returning to the base. On the other hand, it was equally necessary to dispense with every pound of baggage not absolutely essential.

The first task was to fortify the base in case of a raid, for the Fenians were still in force and threatening mischief. Of the four guns, two were left there in case of need. From Port Arthur to Lake Shebandowan a road had been begun, and the Canadian Government had promised that it should be open for

46

traffic by the end of May ; but when the time came only thirty out of the forty-eight miles had been completed, and for a large portion of the remaining distance the forest had not been even felled.   Fatigue parties detailed from the troops extended the road ; but time pressed, and Colonel Wolseley sent a Rifle officer to explore the Kaministiguia River, which connects Lake Superior with Shebandowan, and had been said to be absolutely unnavigable on account of its rapids and falls, one of which was known to be 120 feet in height.   The officer reported, however, that it was practicable, and the result proved that he was correct.

Owing to these delays Lake Shebandowan, the advanced base of the expedition, was not reached until the second week of July.   Henceforward the journey was to be entirely by river, but the boats, having been dragged up the rapids and over the rocks of the Kaministiguia River to a height of 800 feet above the level of Lake Superior, required repairs which caused another delay.   Each boat with its crew consisting of eight or nine soldiers and two or three *voyageurs*—Indians or half-breeds—was a self-contained unit. Each contained sixty days' provisions for its crew, the food consisting of salt pork, preserved vegetables, flour, biscuits, tea and sugar.   Alcohol was strictly forbidden.   In addition the boat was laden with entrenching tools, ammunition, tents, waterproof sheets, blankets, cooking utensils, etc., to say nothing of boat-builders' tools, tin plates, white lead, mosquito oil, etc.   The preparations required the most careful forethought, the most accurate calculation : a work which fell principally on the Commander of the expedition.

July 18th had been fixed by Colonel Wolseley as the date of starting, but a strong gale stopped embarkation until nearly sunset, when the advanced guard, consisting of two Rifle companies, a party of

47

Royal Engineers, and two guns Royal Artillery began the voyage. The flotilla of boats moved by sections, and it was not until August 2nd that the last detachment embarked on Lake Shebandowan, the advanced guard being then 150 miles ahead. The local population now presaged every kind of disaster : the expedition would certainly be ambushed if not eaten up by flies or drowned in the waters. Nevertheless, in spite of all such forebodings, progress, and that comparatively rapid, was made. The men were soon in first-rate condition, and became extremely handy as boatmen and lumbermen. Reveille sounded at 3 A.M. ; two halts, each of one hour, were allowed for breakfast and dinner, and the day's voyage was concluded an hour before sunset. The principal difficulty lay in crossing the *portages*, that is, the place where rapids made it necessary to take the boats out of the water and convey them by means of rollers to the next spot where the water allowed of their being again launched. Wolseley found the forty-seven portages, some very steep, some over a mile in length, far more troublesome than those he had to negotiate later on the Nile, where the distances were shorter, the banks lower, and there were no forests. Here is his description :

" On arrival at the portages the boats were at once drawn into the shore as close as possible and unloaded, the stores belonging to each boat being put into a separate pile. These were covered over with tarpaulins, if the time was too late for work ; or if—as was always the case with the leading detachment—the road over the portage had to be opened out, and rollers for the boat laid down upon it. At other times the men began to carry over the stores without delay, piling them in heaps, one for each boat, at the end of the road. The ordinary method in vogue with Indians and experienced *voyageurs* for carrying loads is by means of a long strap, about

three inches wide in the centre, where it is passed
across the forehead, but tapering off to an inch in
width at the ends, which are fastened round the
barrel or parcel to be portaged.   Men accustomed to
this work will carry 400 lbs., and some 500 lbs., across
the longest portage, the loads resting on the upper
part of the back, and kept there by the straps going
round the forehead.   The great strain is thus upon
the neck, which is kept very rigid, while the body is
bent forward.   As it could not be expected that
soldiers untrained to such labour would be able to
carry loads in that manner, short pieces of rope, with
a loop at each end, were supplied to the boats, by
means of which two short poles—cut in the woods as
required—were easily converted into a very efficient
hand-barrow, of just the dimensions required for the
conveyance of the small barrels in which our flour
and pork were packed.   After, however, a little
practice, a large proportion of the men soon learned
to use the common portage strap, their officers setting
them the example by themselves carrying heavy
loads with it.   As soon as all the stores were conveyed
across the portage, the boats were hauled ashore and
dragged over, their keels resting on small trees felled
across the path to act as rollers.   The labour involved
by hauling a heavy boat up a very steep incline to a
height of about one hundred feet is no child's play.
In each boat there was a strong painter and a towing-
line, by means of which and the leather portage strap
a sort of man-harness was formed when required, so
that forty or fifty men could haul together.   Say
the portage was a mile long (some were more), and
that each man had to make ten trips across it before
all the stores of his brigade were got over, he would
have walked nineteen miles in the operation, being
heavily laden for ten miles of them.   At some
portages considerable engineering ingenuity was
required ;   small streams had to be bridged and

marshy spots to be corduroyed over. By the time our men returned many of them were expert axemen, and all were more or less skilled in the craft of the *voyageur* and American woodsman."

At Fort Francis, on the western edge of Rainy Lake, reached on August 4th, Wolseley was met by Lieutenant, afterwards General Sir William, Butler of the 69th Regiment, whom he had sent by another route to learn the state of affairs in the neighbourhood of Fort Garry.

On getting to the north-western corner of the Lake of the Woods, Colonel Wolseley decided, from the reports he received, that the half-made road leading thence direct to Fort Garry was impracticable. Captain Redvers Buller of the Rifles held a contrary view ; and as regards his own party made good his opinion on the return journey, but Wolseley preferred to navigate the Winnipeg River. Local inhabitants acquainted with it, while astonished that the boats should have come so far in safety, said bluntly that none but madmen would attempt to steer what they termed clumsy craft through the fearful rapids of the Winnipeg, and told Wolseley that, if he got there at all, the journey to Fort Alexander would take him a month. He proved right and the inhabitants wrong. Fort Alexander he entered on August 18th, and two days later the 60th was there assembled. But if the route proved practicable it provided plenty of thrills :

"No length of time, nor any amount of future adventures, can erase from my mind", wrote the leader of the expedition, "the arrival at the Slave Falls. I was in a birch canoe manned by Iroquois, one of whom acted as guide. The regular portage for boats was several hundred yards from the Falls, and lay in a slack water bay, reached without any danger as long as the boats kept tolerably well in towards the bank on that side. Our astonishment was great at finding the guide take the canoe out into mid-stream, where the current ran at an exciting pace, becoming swifter at every yard, until at last, as we approached the vicinity of the Falls, it was palpably evident that we were descending a steeply inclined plane. Consoling ourselves at first with the reflection that the guide knew best what he was about, we sat motionless, but, let us confess it, awe-stricken, as we swept into the narrow gully, at the end of which the great noisy roar of falling waters, and the columns of spray that curled up like clouds into the air, announced the position of the Fall. We were close to the brink. We appeared to have reached that point which exists in most falls, whence the water seems to begin its run preparatory to a good jump over into the abyss below ; and we knew from having watched many great cataracts for hours, that it was a bourne from whence there was no return. Quick as lightning the idea flashed across us that the Indians had made a mistake, and that everything was over for us in this world. In that infinitesimal fraction of time a glimpse of the countenance of the sturdy bowsman rather confirmed this idea, his teeth appeared set, and there was an unusual look in his eye. All creations of our own heated fancy ; for in another second the canoe's head swept in towards the rocks, and was turned nose upstream in tolerably slack water, two of the paddlers jumping out and holding it firmly there.''

The excitement of negotiating rapids, the courage and skill of the *voyageurs*, were a real joy to Wolseley, and years afterwards, when he could get a day away from the stuffy atmosphere of the War Office there were few things gave him greater pleasure than to try to recapture the thrills of the Winnipeg by shooting the biggest weirs of the Thames with a trusty friend in a birch bark canoe.

On August 20th Wolseley began to navigate the

Red River; but before he quitted the Winnipeg a valuable reinforcement had joined him in the person of Mr. Donald Smith, and on the 23rd both were received with enthusiasm by the loyal inhabitants of Stone Fort. Here Wolseley lightened his boats of surplus stores, commandeered all the ponies in the district, and mounted a company of riflemen; that night he bivouacked within six miles of Fort Garry. At 6 A.M. on the 24th the advance was resumed, and

FORT GARRY

(from a contemporary engraving)

as the troops neared the English Cathedral, the bishop ran up the Union Jack in honour of the restoration of the Queen's authority. Wolseley's "intelligence" was that Riel had been taken by surprise, but according to the report he intended to fight. At the last moment, however, his heart failed him; the gates of the fort were left open, and Wolseley and the riflemen entered without firing a shot. Riel had made his escape; some sixteen years later he again rose in armed rebellion, was caught, and deservedly hanged. The two militia battalions on arrival were left in occupation of Fort Garry, while the riflemen returned to Quebec well ahead of the winter frosts.

So ended the Red River Expedition, long forgotten in England but in many ways most remarkable. The business capacity and forethought which ensured success at a cost of less than £100,000, for which small sum the riches of Western Canada were made accessible to settlers, the boldness with which an unknown region was penetrated, the splendid toil and versatile qualities of the men engaged, were understood and appreciated in Canada, which received Wolseley on his return with enthusiasm. He left for England in October 1870, the British Government having decided to withdraw the greater part of the regular garrison of Canada.

At home he found much favour. The Commander-in-Chief, the Duke of Cambridge, not scenting the duels which lay ahead, was forward with compliments. The Sovereign was pleased to confer a K.C.M.G. But the *Soldiers' Pocket Book* still lay heavy on the stomach of the War Office, and its unrepentant author was ruefully contemplating inaction on half-pay when Mr. Cardwell, then Secretary of State for War, summoned him to his side as Assistant Adjutant-General.

GENERAL JAMES WOLFE'S SNUFF-BOX.
(Wolseley Collection, R.U.S.I.)

53

CHAPTER IV

CARDWELL REFORMS · ASHANTI EXPEDITION

IN his new post at the War Office, which he took up in May 1871, Wolseley quickly found himself caught in the maelstrom of army reform. In sixty years only two Secretaries of State for War left any permanent mark upon the administration of the Army, and one of these, Mr.—afterwards Lord—Cardwell, was now in office. Only a few months earlier the people of England had been shocked and startled by the rapid and utter defeat of the country which had been regarded as the first military power in Europe. Men uneasily asked themselves and each other what was the secret of the military success of Germany, and the only answer that could be found, preparation and organisation, led to the further question—were we prepared and organised ? One of the by-products of this anxiety was the offer by the second Duke of Wellington of a prize of £100 for an essay on the "System of Field Manœuvres best adapted for enabling our troops to meet a Continental Army". Colonel E. B. Hamley, then Commandant of the Staff College, and the author of *Operations of War*, agreed to be judge, and Sir Garnet Wolseley was a competitor. The prize was awarded to Lieutenant F. Maurice, but Wolseley's essay, in which he insisted that barrack-square drill, then the chief training of the Army, was not sufficient to fit troops for battle and proposed a scheme of training for war, was

54

highly commended and directed to be published with four others.[1]

This general anxiety regarding our readiness for war enabled Cardwell in the teeth of strong opposition to carry through his reforms, of which a number were measures inaugurated or projected by the Duke of York, but left to languish in the piping times of peace. The fight was hottest over the abolition of purchase. Mr. Disraeli, then leader of the Opposition, was himself too shrewd to defend what was indefensible, but many of his party were otherwise minded, and the Bill only passed through the Commons after a stormy debate, to be thrown out by the Lords. Mr. Gladstone, secure in the support of public opinion, at once invoked the Royal prerogative, and purchase was abolished by warrant as from November 1871. " The Army Regulation Bill " then passed through both Houses without further opposition. Its most important provisions were :

1. The sale of commissions was abolished.

2. Power was given to the Secretary of State to make regulations to vary the conditions of service, so as to lengthen or shorten the period of colour service, as might be found expedient from time to time.

3. The jurisdiction of Lord - Lieutenants of Counties in respect of the Auxiliary Forces was re-invested in the Sovereign.

4. The statutory limits to the numbers of the Army Reserves and Militia were removed.

5. The training of Militia recruits was provided for and extended.

6. The Mutiny Act was made applicable to Volunteers called out for training.

7. Power was given to the Government, on occasion of emergency, to take possession of railroads in the United Kingdom.

[1] *Essays written for the Wellington Prize,* 1872.

From the passage of this Act and the Enlistment Act of 1870 may be dated the foundation of the modern British Army. These measures inaugurated a cycle of Army reform which began with the Franco-Prussian War, and had hardly concluded when the greatest conflict in history broke out. For thirty years of this period Wolseley was a vehement and untiring champion of the party of progress, and the struggle, which in the end wore him out, brought him something of disillusionment and disappointment. He entered on it with fiery zeal and fierce enthusiasm. His admiration for Cardwell was profound, a very real tribute from a man none too disposed to admire the activities of Ministers in military affairs. Later, when reviewing his own life, he wrote : " Except those who worked with and for Mr. Cardwell few know the difficulties he had to overcome when all 'Society' and almost the whole Army was against him. Honest, straightforward, clear-sighted, and determined, full of amiable qualities, he carried out the herculean task he had resolved to attempt, but the effort killed him. Never was Minister in my time more generally hated by the Army and by almost all its old-fashioned and unthinking officers. And yet, looking back now over the quarter of a century we have since lived through, I can think of no man whose memory and whose great services entitle him to be remembered with such gratitude by all ranks of the Army, by the nation, the age, and the Empire at large." [1]

Like Lord Haldane, when he sought to fashion the coping-stone of the edifice founded in 1870, Cardwell gathered to his councils many of the younger men who had given proof of their ability. " Committees on matters vital to the very safety of our Empire ", Wolseley declared, " sat daily under Mr. Cardwell's inspiration. The modern school of military thought

[1] *Story of a Soldier's Life*, Wolseley, vol. ii. p. 272.

56

for the first time in the Queen's reign, obtained the ear of the public. Mr. Cardwell asked for and obtained the advice of the young school, sifted it, and finally adopted the most important of their measures. No British War Minister ever responded more readily to demands made upon him by his military advisers." Amongst the young school the three most active members were Colonel Sir Garnet Wolseley, Major, afterwards General, Sir Robert Biddulph, and Captain Evelyn Baring, afterwards Lord Cromer. Without the constant and devoted support of these three the technicalities and complications of his task would have baffled Cardwell, who had little personal knowledge of the British soldier.

The three reforms which Wolseley regarded as cardinal were the abolition of purchase, the establishment of a system of short service, which would make possible the creation of a real reserve, and the organisation of enlistment on a territorial basis, to ensure systematic mobilisation for war. Purchase was dead and damned, and Cardwell had cleared the way for the detailed application of the other two measures to be worked out by a committee [1] of which General Patrick MacDougall was the president, and Wolseley an energetic member.

In 1871 the infantry was organised in three regiments of Foot Guards and 110 of the Line. Of the latter all except the Rifle Brigade were officially known by their numbers. Of the Foot Guards the Grenadiers had three battalions, the Coldstream and Scots Guards two each. In time of peace these seven battalions were quartered in the British Isles. Of the infantry of the line, two regiments, namely the 60th, King's Royal Rifle Corps, and the Rifle Brigade, had each four battalions. The regiments numbered from 1 to 25 had two battalions, and the other eighty-three but one. Foreign service absorbed

[1] The Localisation Committee.

a considerable majority of the infantry; and to
supply them with the drafts required to keep them
up to establishment, depot and provisional battalions
were organised, and at times moved from place to
place. These improvisations were expensive to
maintain, and, being too small to take their place in
the field in time of war, were wasteful, so it was
determined to return to the practice established by
the Duke of York, under which battalions on foreign
service received their reinforcements from a second
battalion at home large enough for training, and in
case of need for fighting purposes. This system was
applied not only to the double-battalion regiments,
but also to those with but one battalion, by linking
the latter in pairs. Palmerston had, in 1825,
attempted to reintroduce something of the kind, but
it broke down because the number of regiments
abroad was always in excess of those at home.
Cardwell adjusted this by reducing or withdrawing a
number of Colonial garrisons, and it was in pursuance
of this policy that the regular garrison of Canada, and
Wolseley with it, had been brought home. The reorganisation was only completed some years later by
amalgamating the linked battalions into one regiment, and by substituting territorial for numerical
designations. The principle of the plan was that the
country should be divided into territorial districts,
each to contain two line battalions, two militia
battalions, and a certain proportion of the Volunteer
regiments of that date, formed into an administrative brigade; the whole based on the brigade
depot or centre. The depot itself consisted of two
companies from each of the two line battalions,
and the Army Reserve men residing in the district were attached thereto for payment, training,
and discipline. At the depot also were to be stored
the arms and clothing of the Militia and Army
Reserve.

The MacDougall Committee prepared sundry other reforms of scarcely less value to the Army. Among these were the power to discharge soldiers of bad character—a power for a long time too sparingly exercised—and the abolition of the anachronism under which officers in the Foot Guards enjoyed a higher rank in the Army than that which they held in their regiment. An ensign in the Brigade of Guards was entitled to the army rank of lieutenant; a lieutenant that of captain; and a captain that of lieutenant-colonel. Thus a senior subaltern, an officer of only perhaps seven or eight years' service, on promotion to the rank of regimental captain, would often supersede not only every captain but every major in the Line. Moreover, if employed on the staff, he became in four years' time a full colonel, and after another few years a major-general, with perhaps less than twenty years' service in peace and none at all in war. The broom was vigorously wielded to sweep away other old crusted institutions, and stirred up a good deal of dust. The reformers were bespattered with abuse, but undeterred they went on from strength to strength, supported by the sturdy though silent force of public opinion, and their first success was registered when, at the end of a clear twelve months of the new short service system, the number of recruits was 23,000, the double of those who had enlisted the last year of long service.

Reform was not restricted to matters of administration. In the year 1871 Army manœuvres for the first time in our history were instituted, and took place in Berkshire and some of the adjoining counties. The need of systematic training was painfully apparent. The troops of either side were duly brought to their respective camping grounds. They were given their tents, but hardly any one knew how to pitch them. They were handed their field cooking utensils, but few knew how to prepare food in them. To the general confusion there were, however, notable exceptions. The regiments of the old Light Division of the Peninsular War retained the traditions of Sir John Moore, and their field training was far ahead of the rest of the Army. A battalion of one of these regiments, the 4th Battalion of the 60th Rifles, commanded by Colonel Hawley, was conspicuous at the manœuvres for efficiency, and its pre-eminence was challenged by that of the 10th Hussars, commanded by Colonel Valentine Baker. Wolseley attended these manœuvres as Chief of the Staff to Sir Charles Staveley, and one evening when he was acting as an umpire he witnessed a collision between these rivals. The " Cease Fire " had been sounded, or anyhow Hawley had been so informed, and the 60th were marching quietly home to their camp, when from behind a coppice Valentine Baker and the 10th pounced down on the rear of the riflemen. Although taken at a disadvantage, Hawley was equal to the occasion. He turned his rear rank about, presenting a new front to repel the cavalry attack. Sir Garnet galloped up and said to Hawley, " Your battalion is attacked in the rear, you are out of action ". " Go back to your General ", thundered the infantry colonel, " and tell him that the Rifles have no rear." Hawley angrily resented what he regarded as an insult to his darling battalion, but Wolseley did not forget either the incident or the man, and applied, though unsuccessfully, for his battalion when, two years later, he was appointed to the command of the Ashanti Expedition. Manœuvres were again held in 1872, Wolseley being this time on the staff of Sir John Michel, but battalions at home so evidently required more training before they could act in large bodies, that they were not repeated on so large a scale until Wolseley ordered them as Commander-in-Chief.

In 1873 Wolseley was again called to active

service. For close on three-quarters of a century the British settlers in West Africa had had difficulties with the Ashantees, who inhabited a large tract of country on the Gold Coast. In 1824 an expedition under the leadership of the British Commissioner, Sir Charles Macarthy, had been disastrously defeated, and Macarthy's skull adorned the walls of Kumasi, the capital of the Ashanti king. In 1825 another expedition, under Major-General Turner, achieved nothing, and though in the following year a native force with a few British troops under Lieutenant-Colonel Purdon crushed an invasion of the Ashantees, the effect of this soon disappeared.

The British and Dutch had settlements on the coast, which had been so intricately intermingled that in 1868 a friendly partition was effected with a view to a clear definition of the frontier between them. The natives thus transferred from British to Dutch rule objected to the arrangement ; and in 1871, by the terms of a new covenant, duly submitted to and ratified by the king of Ashanti, the Dutch abandoned to the British the whole of their rights on the coast. Notwithstanding his consent, King Koffee Kalcali despatched from Kumasi an army to invade the British Protectorate. This army defeated the Fantees, a tribe of friendlies, and attacked the seaport town of Elmina, but was repulsed by a force made up of seamen, marines, and soldiers of the West India Regiment under the command of Lieutenant-Colonel Festing, R.M.A., who, however, could do no more than hold his ground, while the Ashanti army overran the Protectorate and played havoc with the trade of the settlements. The Government could not sit down under this, and it was clear that nothing less than a British occupation of Kumasi would impress the Ashantees with the reality of British power.

As soon as difficulties arose on the Gold Coast,

ASHANTI

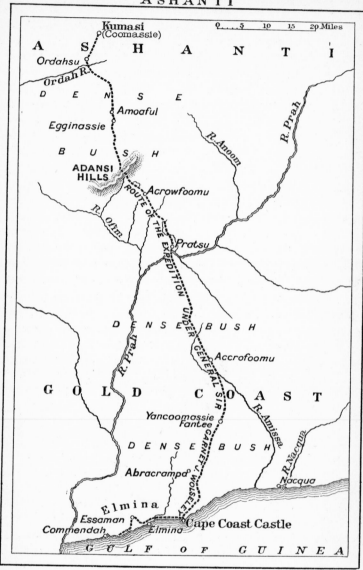

Sir Garnet prepared for Mr. Cardwell a memorandum on the situation. This, in August 1873, Cardwell sent to Lord Kimberley, then Secretary for the Colonies, with a note saying, " Sir Garnet Wolseley, who successfully went to the Red River, is now ready to capture Kumasi. Pray read his paper." The paper was read, the Cabinet approved the plan, and Sir Garnet was told to execute it. He suggested that he should be allowed to assume the civil as well as the military government of the Gold Coast Settlements ; and in view of the obvious insufficiency of the West Indian and native forces, already assembled, to deal with the Ashantees, that two British battalions should be placed at his disposal. Climatic conditions of the Gold Coast limited active operations by Europeans to the months of December, January, and February, and as September was too early in the year to despatch British troops, Wolseley proposed that he himself, with a party of specially selected officers, should embark for Cape Coast Castle, and there prepare for the December campaign. The Government gave a general approval of that plan, but added the cautious rider that " nothing but a conviction of necessity would induce Her Majesty's Government to sanction the employment of European troops ".

Accordingly, Wolseley left England on September 11th, 1873, endowed with the local rank of Major-General, and accompanied only by thirty - five specially selected officers. This band was scornfully labelled by people not devoid of jealousy as the " Ashanti Ring ", and later as the " Wolseley Ring ". The majority of its members followed their chief through all his campaigns and enterprises, and few failed to justify his choice, though when first selected they were all young and many untried men. In the party which sailed with Wolseley on the *Ambrig*, or joined him soon after, were Major Colley,[1] intellectually perhaps the most brilliant of them all, whose doom was Majuba Hill ; Lieutenant-Colonel Evelyn Wood, V.C. [2] ; Captain Redvers Buller [3] ; Lieutenant-Colonel McNeill, V.C.[4] ; Major George Greaves [5] ; Major B. C. Russell [6] ; Major T. D. Baker [7] ; Major Home, R.E., whom Lord Beaconsfield described as the ablest officer he had ever met, and who met an untimely death five years later ; Lieutenant F. Maurice [8] ; Captain Butler [9] ; Captain Brackenbury [10] ; and Captain Bromhead of the 24th Regiment who, a few years later, was to receive from his chief's hands the V.C. for his part in the defence of Rorke's Drift. Most of them we shall meet again in the course of Wolseley's life. None of them was chosen through any personal influence. McNeill, Buller, and Butler, Sir Garnet had learnt to know and appreciate on the Red River ; Evelyn Wood he had heard of in the Crimea and Indian Mutiny ; Brackenbury and Home commended themselves to him by their military writings ; Maurice's only passport to his favour was that he had beaten him in the competition for the Wellington prize. If many of the party could use the pen, none was an amateur with the sword ; four were actual or prospective wearers of the V.C., and of the remainder one of the V.C.'s said that two were the bravest men he had seen in action. This selection from a crowd of eager volunteers is evidence that Wolseley possessed in high degree that most important qualification for command, judgement of men.

[1] Afterwards Major-General Sir George Colley.
[2] Afterwards Field-Marshal Sir Evelyn Wood, V.C.
[3] Afterwards General the Right Hon. Sir Redvers Buller, V.C.
[4] Afterwards General Sir John McNeill, V.C.
[5] Afterwards General Sir George Greaves.
[6] Afterwards General Sir Baker Russell.
[7] Afterwards General Sir Thomas Baker.
[8] Afterwards Major-General Sir Frederick Maurice.
[9] Afterwards Lieutenant-General Sir William Butler.
[10] Afterwards General Sir H. Brackenbury.

On arrival at the Gold Coast on October 3rd, the General found that the situation required careful handling. Captain Fremantle, R.N.,[1] with a handful of marines, had gallantly kept the Ashantees from the coast, but they were well established in our territory, and of the 800 regular troops available 150 were on the sick list. Moreover, the men of the West India Regiment were natives, and of the 130 British soldiers on shore, only 22 were fit for duty. Excepting for three months in the year the climate was quite unsuited to Europeans, and the Gold Coast had well earned the name of " The White Man's Grave ".[2]

Wolseley, remembering his experience in Burma, set the War Office agog by designing a special uniform for himself and his officers, consisting of a loose tunic of thin material, well provided with large pockets, and a pith helmet with a pugaree of blue and buff colour. He also desired his medical officer to supply to every one a short table of advice as to health, which led off with a recommendation to shun spirits.

The organisation of a force had to be started from the very beginning, and the special service officers set eagerly to work. Evelyn Wood, Baker Russell, and Butler raised regiments of local levies; Colley organised the transport, Buller an intelligence service, Home an engineer and labour corps, and in an astonishingly short time a body of troops was made ready to take the field. The Ashantees were not far from the coast towns, and had made their name a terror by ruthless plunder and still more ruthless slaughter. It was very important to score an early success so as to hearten the friendly natives, more especially as most of

---

[1] Afterwards Admiral the Hon. Sir E. Fremantle.
[2] One traveller, who knew the coast, and was asked by Wolseley for advice as to equipment, replied cheerfully, " I recommend every man to take a coffin with him ".

65   F

the chiefs in our zone were either afraid to side with us, or had such faith in King Koffee as to be openly defiant. One of the latter class, the chief of Essaman, when invited by Evelyn Wood to come into his station, replied by a counter-invitation to Wood to come and fetch him. Sir Garnet decided to bring this gentleman to reason immediately.

Forgetful of the very real services rendered to the Army and the country in the Crimea by " Billy Russell ",[1] the correspondent of the *Times*, Wolseley, like most British commanders, resented as a nuisance the presence of representatives of the Press. In the first edition of the *Soldiers' Pocket Book* he described newspaper correspondents as " those newly invented curses to armies, who eat the rations of fighting men and do no work at all ". " These gentlemen," he went on, " pandering to the public taste for news, render concealment most difficult, but this very ardour for information a General can turn to account by spreading fake news among the gentlemen of the Press, and thus use them as a medium by which to deceive the enemy." The handling of the Press in war is an ever-recurring difficulty. The Press can prove itself the finest instrument for preserving national *moral*, or it can, by untimely divulgence of information, help to bring armies to disaster.[2] The question requires far closer study than it has ever received.

On this occasion Wolseley followed his own advice. He let it be known that a detachment on the Volta, away to the east, was in trouble, and that he was going to its relief ; he then promptly marched due west to Essaman with a small force, of which the European troops were only 149 marines and 29 seamen ; he occupied the place on October

---

[1] Afterwards Sir W. Russell.
[2] The classical example occurred in 1870, when von Moltke learnt through English newspapers of MacMahon's march to Sedan.

MAJOR-GENERAL SIR GARNET WOLSELEY, K.C.M.G., C.B., 1873.
From a Photograph by Messrs. Maul.

To face page 66.

14th, after a sharp skirmish in which Colonel McNeill, the chief of the staff, was severely wounded. This little success immediately made easier the task of raising levies, and the force grew. On November 4th the Ashantees made a determined attack on Baker Russell at Abracampa, but Wolseley, arriving promptly with reinforcements, drove them off, and thereafter the Ashantees left our territory and retired across the Prah.

The first stage of the little campaign was then over. An advance on Kumasi was not possible without the aid of British troops, and the question was whether the Government would agree to this. The Cabinet was, as a matter of fact, impressed with the speed with which our zone had been cleared, and sanctioned the despatch of a brigade, consisting of the 2nd Battalion Rifle Brigade, 2nd Battalion 23rd Regiment, and the 42nd Highlanders, under Brigadier Sir Archibald Alison, the son of the historian, with a battery of field artillery and a company of engineers. While they were on their way the deadly climate was taking a heavy toll of the British officers. By November 15th, out of a total of 64, 29 had been in hospital, 7 had been invalided home, and one had died. On November 9th the chief succumbed to a severe attack of fever and dysentery, and was for a time in danger, but his wonderful constitution and the devoted nursing of Lieutenant Maurice — the foundation of a friendship which lasted till Wolseley's death—pulled him through, and he was ready for work again before the arrival of the British troops. The last of these reached the Gold Coast on December 17th, and by then the arrangements for the advance—which included the organisation of a number of columns of carriers, for no other transport was possible through the bush—were practically complete.

A start was made on January 5th, the British

troops crossing the Prah between the 21st and 24th. Wolseley's plan for the movement on Kumasi was to advance through the bush in four columns. Of these by far the strongest, and indeed the only one intended to do any serious fighting, was the centre column, which marched by the shortest route across the Prah direct on the Ashanti capital. This body comprised all the British troops, the bulk of the native troops, the best of the levies, and with it went Wolseley himself. A second column of native levies was on the left flank, a third also of native levies on the right flank, while a fourth under Captain Glover, R.N., far away on the right, was far stronger than the other detached forces, and was stiffened by a number of regular native troops.

The plan of campaign was afterwards criticised by amateur strategists, who condemned the general for dividing his forces, and maintained that his success was due more to good luck than good guidance ; but these critics entirely failed to understand Wolseley's dispositions. The centre column was made strong enough to overcome any resistance which the Ashantees might offer. The others had for their mission to mislead and confuse the enemy without exposing themselves to danger, to cause him to divide his forces and so make the task of the central column easier ; they fulfilled these purposes admirably. The left column never actually penetrated into the territory of the Ashantees, but it succeeded in attracting to that side a considerable body of Ashanti warriors ; so did the troops immediately on the right of the central force, though when the enemy appeared to be menacing they retired without fighting. Glover's column had a more serious mission, and it eventually reached Kumasi after that place had been occupied by the main body ; but its movements were throughout carefully regulated by Wolseley in such a way as to remove the risk of its being attacked by a force large enough to put it in peril.

The principal difficulty presented itself in the organisation and provision of transport. A large number of carriers had to be found : a British battalion 650 strong required 650 carriers, and in all 3500 of these native porters were needed. But just as the advance began, the terror of entering Ashanti territory proved too much for the nerves of a large number of the carriers, who bolted in a panic. This was serious, as the time during which the British troops could be kept on the Coast was strictly limited. The crisis was overcome by reducing the number of British troops with the main column, and by enlisting the services of the West India Regiment and some of the native levies as carriers. In spite of this check the Ashanti army was brought to battle and heavily defeated on January 29th at Amoaful in an action in which Lord Gifford, who led, in the most literal sense of that word, a body of native scouts, won the V.C. After another engagement at Ordahsu, when a slug penetrated Wolseley's helmet — but, luckily checked by his thick pugaree, did no more than knock him down and bruise his forehead,— Kumasi was entered on February 4th.

The goal of the expedition was certainly not then a pleasant spot. There is a grim entry in Wolseley's journal : " The whole locality stank with the human blood with which it may be said the ground was saturated. I have been in many barbarous lands, where man's life is held cheap, but here alone was the spot where man made in the image of his Maker was butchered daily in cold blood in hundreds to appease the manes of some cruel ancestor, or to obey the mandate of some bloodthirsty fetish priest. There was a grove of trees hard by into which the murdered bodies were always thrown, the stench from which poisoned the surrounding atmosphere. Hating all horrors, I did not venture into it, but others with stronger stomachs did so, and their descriptions of it made me sick. Without doubt the most loathsome object my eyes ever rested on was a sacred stool saturated with human blood, which stood near the place of execution, and which was always kept

Sketch by Lieut.-General Sir Robert Baden-Powell, Bart., G.C.V.O., K.C.B., illustrating the manner in which this drum was sounded in order to raise the tribes to the king's banner. The drum is in the R.U.S.I. Museum.

wet with the blood of victims. Great fresh clots on it showed how recently some poor creature had been sacrificed. Then near it stood the huge 'Death Drum', some four or five feet in diameter, and decorated round its outer rim with human skulls and thigh bones.'' But if Kumasi was a city of horror, it proved to be no vain rumour

70

that it was also a city of gold. The terms of peace required the payment of 50,000 ounces of gold, the renunciation of all rights in the British zone, a guarantee of freedom of trade between the British zone and Kumasi, and a promise to check the practice of human sacrifice. Besides the indemnity in gold, the king's treasure was seized, placed in the hands of prize agents, and sold by public auction at Cape Coast Castle, where some of the objects fetched fancy prices. " I had set my heart ", wrote Wolseley to his wife, " upon a bronze group of about fifty little figures representing the King of Ashanti being carried in state, and had asked one of my staff to bid £6 for it. It went for £100." The "showy" treasures included the king's state umbrella, given by Wolseley to Queen Victoria, and now in the museum of the Royal United Service Institution, and a number of masks of beaten gold, the largest of which had decked the sacred ram on state occasions. This was acquired by the artillery officers of the expedition, and now adorns the Mess of the Royal Artillery at Woolwich. There were also quantities of heavy gold neck ornaments and two gold pipes, of which one was purchased by Lieutenant Maurice, and is in the possession of one of the authors of this biography. A sword which had been presented by Queen Victoria to the king was bought by the officers of the headquarters staff and given to their Chief. A more curious find was a silver George II. coffee-pot, which Wolseley bought. "I thought ", he wrote to Lady Wolseley, " it would be a subject for conversation at breakfast whenever we might have very stupid people staying with us."[1] He also bought the king's crown and orb, the latter to become his infant daughter's[2] rattle, and these two

---

[1] This and other European silver articles had been exchanged by traders for gold dust.
[2] Frances Garnet succeeded to her father's peerage.

are now also to be seen in the museum of the Royal United Service Institution.

The terms of peace arranged, the British troops were hurried away, and the last of them had left

KING KOFFEE'S CROWN.

before the end of February ; not a man had been kept as much as ten weeks in the country. The bill was £900,000. The Commander had done all he had said he would do, well within his self-imposed limits of time, and with rigid economy of means. He

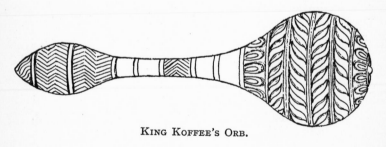

KING KOFFEE'S ORB.

landed at Portsmouth on March 20th, 1874, to receive a rare welcome from the nation. The Queen reviewed his troops in Windsor Park. Wolseley received from her hands the Grand Cross of the

Order of St. Michael and St. George, and the K.C.B.,
both Houses of Parliament voted their thanks to
him and his troops, and the House of Commons
passed unanimously a generous grant of £25,000,
Disraeli and Gladstone outvying each other in their
encomiums. The Lord Mayor entertained him at
the Guildhall, and the Corporation presented him
with an address and a sword of honour. The
Universities of Oxford and Cambridge conferred
upon him honorary degrees, and the Prince of Wales
proposed his health at the Royal Academy banquet.
But of all the honours that he received that which he
regarded as the most serviceable was promotion to
Major-General, " for distinguished service in the
field ", at a time when his substantive rank in the
Army was " major, half-pay, late 90th Regiment ".[1]

This shower of honours seems somewhat ludicrous,
when one compares the little enterprise for which
they were awarded with the struggle in which the
British casualties were a thousand times greater
than the number of British troops who penetrated
the Ashanti bush. But the public at home had been
seriously perturbed by the controversies which had
raged round the Cardwell reforms, and by repeated
statements as to our unpreparedness for war; while
the leaders of both political parties were loth to
spend more money upon the Army than the driving
force of public opinion made necessary. They were
therefore quite willing to deceive both themselves and

---

[1] Wolseley refused a G.C.B., being unwilling to go over the heads
of older and—as he said—more distinguished soldiers : he declined a
Baronetcy, telling his friends he did not care to share an honour with
the Duke of Devonshire's gardener, but he wrote to the new Prime
Minister :
" DEAR MR. DISRAELI—Upon my return home yesterday evening,
I read for the first time your speech in the House of Commons, proposing the large grant so liberally bestowed upon me by the country.
I thank you very much for the flattering manner in which you then
alluded to my military services and for the substantial manner in
which they have been rewarded.　　　　　　　　　G. W."

the public—always ready to forget the unpleasant—into the opinion that the success of a little expedition in which 2500 British troops had taken part, proved that we had an Army and that it was efficient.

It is strange, but it is a fact, that there were many politicians who really believed that this was the case. Even Cardwell wrote exultantly to Lord Northbrook, who had been his under-secretary at the War Office, and was then Viceroy of India : " You and I had great reason to congratulate ourselves on the success of the Ashanti Expedition. We were told that we had disorganised the War Office and reduced the Army to a force ' that could not march '. For the first time in history the selected General sat down at the table in the War Office with the heads of the various departments, the Secretary for the Colonies, the First Lord of the Admiralty being present, and made the arrangements, every one of which resulted in complete success."[1] It reflects oddly on the attitude of British Governments towards preparation for war, on the state of the War Office, and on the efficiency of the Army at this time that a method, born of plain common sense, should have been adopted " for the first time in history ", and be a matter of congratulation.

Wolseley's foresight, judgement, and leadership obtained very ample reward, and the country was in due time to get an even more ample return for its generosity. At the age of forty he was a Major-General, he had become a public character, he was known not only to the chiefs of his own profession, but to the actual and prospective heads of the State, and last but not least, his financial position was secure. He was soon to put those advantages which he had won to the service of his country. In June 1874 he was again accredited to the War Office as Inspector-General

[1] *Lord Cardwell at the War Office*, Biddulph, p. 224.

of the Auxiliary Forces. The choice was appropriate, for on the MacDougall Commission he had been a strenuous advocate for bringing the militia and volunteers directly under the Crown and so into the Army. He had only time to prepare plans and to produce for the auxiliary forces a special edition of his *Soldiers' Pocket Book*, for in February 1875 he was called upon by the Government to proceed to Natal.

CHAPTER V

NATAL, 1875 · CYPRUS, 1878

WOLSELEY was, for the first time, to fill a post of a quasi-political character. He was to proceed to Natal and deal with a difficult situation due to an outbreak in 1873 on the part of a Zulu tribe perched on the border of the colony. A law in Natal prescribed that no Bantu should own unregistered guns. A chief of one of the Hlubi clans —Langalibalele [1] (in English, "a sun is burning")— had refused to register the arms he had acquired as payment for labour in the diamond mines, to render any account of them, or, in response to repeated messages, to report himself at Maritzburg. This worthy was also generally suspected of being in treasonable correspondence with other chiefs, and he had openly boasted of being able to deal with any European encroach on his independence. An armed party was sent to enforce the demands of the Natal Government, and in Bushman Pass a detachment of volunteers came up with the rearguard of the rebels. The volunteers had been told not to fire first ; their opponents, unembarrassed by any such restriction, while pretending to send for the chief, hustled them, surrounded them, drove them back, and shot down five of their number. The colonists

---

[1] "I call him 'Long-Belly'," Wolseley admitted, "for I never can spell his infernal barbarian cognomen."

were roused to a sense of danger ; if all the natives
of the Hlubi tribe were allowed to unite with the
rebellious clan, there might ensue a general racial
rising. Cape Colony and the Orange River and
Transvaal Republics offered help—if help were
needed—to Natal, but the rising was quickly quelled,
the misbehaving clan broken up, and its territory
occupied by the Government. Langalibalele crossed
the Drakensberg to Basutoland, and eventually ran
into the arms of the Cape Mounted Police ; he was
tried and sentenced to banishment, and—as Natal
had no outlying dependency for his accommodation—
an Act was passed by the Cape Parliament authorising
his detention on Robben Island. The story evoked
some hubbub at home. The Natal Government was
said to have set afoot repressive measures, opposed
to English law, which were loudly denounced by the
Aborigines' Protection Society and by Bishop Colenso,
the thick-and-thin champion of the native, who,
however, found himself ranged against the clergy and
missionaries of different denominations in Natal.[1]
The trial, it was murmured, had not been according
to the rules of an English court of justice ; the
prisoners, according to Bantu law, could not have
counsel ; the President of the Court was the Governor who had previously outlawed and set a price on
the head of the principal prisoner. Langalibalele's
crime, however, was so notorious, and he had so
nearly brought about a general war, that under
no conditions could he have escaped the penalty
imposed.

Popular sentiment at home prevailed. The
Governor of Natal, Sir Benjamin Pine, was recalled,

[1] "The Bishop", Wolseley wrote in May, "by the line he takes
widens the breach already existing between him and the white
colonists, and seems to endeavour to establish himself as the supreme
chief of the natives, sending emissaries about the country, through
whom erroneous views as to your intentions are spread among the
Kaffirs."—Private Letter.

though for some time he declined to return home. Compensation from the Colonial Treasury was given to a clan which had suffered loss when in sympathy with the rebels ; various convicted Hlubis were released from prison. Langalibalele was promised removal to a farm on the mainland, where he might enjoy the society of his wives, and it was decided that a Constitution under which breaches of legal form had occurred needed amendment.

Theoretically, of course, the Sovereign could annul or alter a charter ; but the prerogatives had languished from lack of exercise, and for the gentler course of altering legislature by legislature Lord Carnarvon, the Colonial Minister, was sure that no better man than Sir Garnet Wolseley could be found. The colonists whom he was to persuade would be flattered by so important a person being sent to them ; Natal would figure in English periodicals and form the theme of conversation at home ; and a prudent soldier would be sure to insist, as he did, on the future provision of a sufficient garrison, which was a crying need.

Wolseley was to examine and settle matters connected with native law and the defence of the colony ; he was to deal with questions as to the police and the supply of firearms to the natives ; he was—and here, of course, lay the most difficult duty—to induce the Colonial Legislature to surrender for the time part of its control of the affairs, or at all events of the finance, of the colony. The office was not altogether to his liking. He always professed himself ready to undertake any military duty in any climate or circumstances, but he had little appetite either for politics or diplomacy, especially that form of the latter which he described as "popularity-hunting", and politics and diplomacy he foresaw would figure largely in his new adventure ; the draught offered to him, however, was sweetened by the assurance that his mission need not last more than six months,[1] and would in no wise interfere with his military career. His pay from the Colonial Office was fixed at the rate of £5000 a year ; he was to be placed on the staff of the Army serving in South Africa, with the rank of Major-General ; he was to receive his unattached pay and £200[2] for his outfit; and he was to enjoy the services of four officers whom he selected : Colonel Colley,[3] Major Butler, Major Brackenbury, and Lord Gifford. Wolseley and his staff sailed for South Africa on the 23rd February.[4] From Madeira[5] he telegraphed and wrote stipulating that his military command in Natal during his stay there as Governor was to be separate from, and in no way subordinate to, the G.O.C. at Cape Town, Sir Arthur Cunynghame.[6] He also asked if he might promise the people in Natal an Imperial guarantee of the loan required to

[1] The War Office minuted the Colonial Office on 27th February '75 " that there is no objection to the appointment of Major-General Sir Garnet Wolseley to be Administrator of the Government of Natal during the period which may elapse until the successor of Sir B. Pine arrives to assume the Government ".

[2] To be reclaimed from the Colonial Office.

[3] Colley, by arrangement, was to act as Colonial Secretary.

[4] Wolseley to Duke of Cambridge, 26th February '75. " I did not, in the hurry of departure, read over my written orders very carefully, but I knew it had been arranged that my military command in Natal was to be an independent one. But Sir Alfred Horsford's letter to Sir A. Cunningham [Cunynghame] may lead him to think I am to be under his command, as there is no indication that Natal is to be an independent command."

[5] The telegraph did not go then beyond Madeira.

[6] In his instructions he is, however, told : " Sir Arthur Cunynghame will be informed that, looking to your high standing in the Army and to the expediency of relieving you from correspondence with him on local military matters, the troops in Natal will, while you remain there, be placed under your separate command ".

Wolseley asked for a further 800 troops to be sent to Natal, " as there is a sparse white population living among twenty times their number of Kaffirs " ; also to safeguard his N.W. frontier against the Zulus, and, in the event of trouble, to safeguard the prestige of H.M. Army. He urged also that Natal should be an independent command under an able and well-selected Colonel on the Staff. The direction of military affairs in such an outlying Province as Natal should not be left to the chance ability of the senior regimental officer serving with the troops.

construct the projected railway line. This guarantee, he urged, would be a great lever for him to handle in his endeavours to bring about the required change in the Legislative Council, and would, as a matter of £ s. d., effect a saving of £10,000 a year to the colony without costing the mother country a shilling. The military demand was at once accorded ; the financial suggestion, although favourably considered by Carnarvon, was still, four months later, a matter of debate.

On his way out Sir Garnet, who had little personal knowledge of South African politics, absorbed himself in the study of what lay before him, and especially congratulated himself on the temporary absence from Natal of two politicians, Mr. Barter and Mr. Foss. Barter, the leader of the party which had begun to clamour for responsible government, had gone to England in the fond belief that the incoming Governor would require two or three months to look about him before doing anything. "He does not know me," Wolseley observed, " and has exactly played my game. I would have willingly paid all his travelling expenses during his tour out of my own pocket as an inducement for him to have done what he has now carried out without its costing me a penny." Mr. Foss, another opponent to Imperial rule, was also taking a long holiday, expecting to return in ample time for the opening of the Council. "If I can carry my measures through the Council [1] before they return I shall be fortunate."

Wolseley arrived in Cape Town on March 20th, 1875, and at once showed his instructions, "both the recent ones and those I mean to publish as soon as I get to Natal ", to the Governor, Sir Henry Barkly, who professed little knowledge of Natal politics and

[1] The original Legislative Council in Natal consisted entirely of nominees, but in 1856 a charter was granted, when it became chiefly elective.

conveyed the impression of some annoyance at Wolseley's special mission. He heard that Mr. Molteno (the Prime Minister) had difficulty in carrying out Carnarvon's wishes as to placing " Langa " on the mainland : if he attempted to escape and was recaptured, was he to be tried ?   If he was a pardoned man, as described in the Queen's proclamation, how was he to be kept in durance vile ?   Wolseley himself was extremely anxious that so long as " Langa " remained in South Africa he should stay on his island, and, anyhow, protested against the weakness of allowing the chief to be joined by his 10,000 followers as well as by his wives and immediate family.

After more than one interview with Molteno while the guest of the Governor at his villa at Rondebosch, Wolseley left on March 25th on board the cruiser *Raleigh* for Durban. Here his first duty was to dispose of his predecessor, whose continued presence was highly irksome, and who pleaded in justification of it that the Colonial Office, for some unknown reason, continued to address despatches to him personally. Wolseley politely told him that his prolonged stay, after his recall, had been prejudicial to the true interests of the colony, and then gave him positive instructions to take the steamer due to sail in three days. " I feel certain ", he added, " that you will not only comply with my request, but that, duly appreciating the motives that have induced me to make it, you will pardon me for having urged it."

On the 2nd April, Wolseley, who had arrived the previous day and been duly sworn in at Pietermaritzburg, held his first Executive Council, when his instructions were read and discussed, though their publication was postponed until Pine was off the premises. He told the Council then and there that a change must be made in the Constitution of the colony so as to increase the powers of the Crown. It was for them to decide how this change should be wrought in a constitutional manner, but if it were found impossible to effect it constitutionally, the home Government would step in to do what was necessary. The members of the Council, with the solitary exception of Mr. (afterwards Sir) T. Shepstone, seemed men of undecided and uninformed opinion. They made it evident to Sir Garnet that he had judged rightly as to the importance of the railway guarantee, and of securing Carnarvon's approval for a £50,000 immigration loan, which would probably win over the coast members.

Wolseley fixed the 5th May for the assembly of the Legislative Council, when the momentous bill was to be put forward. Roughly, the main purport of the bill was to add 8 nominated members to the Legislative Council. Previously there had been 5 official and 13 elected members, the former being paid and constituting the Governor's Council. Under the new law there would be 15 nominated members, of whom 8, though chosen by the Governor, would receive no emoluments. The net result of the bill would be that the Executive could rely on thirteen votes, and would be certain of a majority of voices in all matters of legislation. To assuage any latent fears of the colonists, it was to be enacted that no new tax could be imposed on them without the consent of two-thirds of the members present at the time of its being voted upon, and that no person could be nominated for the Legislative Council unless he could claim a fixed property of at least £1000 and residence in Natal for at least two years.

The new Governor realised that hospitality would form an important item in his programme. The salary accorded to him was liberal, and although his personal fortune was slender he had no thought of economising at the expense of his mission. He presented cups and prizes at every athletic or race meeting, and during the five months he spent in Natal scarcely an evening passed without his entertaining a party at dinner ; on his tours, although he complained of being shamelessly robbed by every innkeeper, he cheerfully defrayed all the charges imposed on him for his staff as well as himself. He notes his first entertainment of the 13th April : " Gave a very good ball ; about 180 or 200 people present ; they were all away about 2.30 A.M., mostly sober ; one old young woman squeezed my hand to nearly breaking point in the hall as she was leaving and addressed me in a very incoherent manner ". His difficulties with and dislike of the Bishops of Natal and Maritzburg were similarly dealt with. " I will ask both of them to dinner and go to neither of their churches ", he said, and restricted his religious exercises to attendance at military services.

Interested as Wolseley was in the work he found to his hand, the fighting instinct was always dominant. " I see by the newspapers ", he wrote to Lord Carnarvon, " that a war in Burma[1] is quite on the cards. Nothing can be done there in the way of military operations until the end of November, and as I shall be disposable long before that month, I am writing home to request that my services may be accepted in the event of a General officer being required. I began my military career by a war in Burma, so I know something of the country and its people.

" I am writing to the W.O. requesting the services of two subalterns of engineers and some

---

[1] On the 12th June he wrote to Carnarvon : " If the difficulty with Burma should expand into a war, your Lordship would confer a great favour upon me by bringing my name before Lord Salisbury with a view to obtaining employment. If selected, I could be sent direct with my staff from Natal to Galle."

Carnarvon replied on June 15th that in the event of war generals would be selected from India.

staff-sergeants at once, for I can do nothing in the Public Works Department without extra assistance, which is not to be had in the colony. I hope your lordship, to whom I am sending officially a copy of my application, will back it up, for the P.W. Department, as it exists, is of little service to the colony."

And writing on the 5th May to announce to Sir Henry Barkly the opening of the Legislative Council, he told him : " Cetewayo (the Zulu king) is preparing for war. I am told that he will most probably turn his arms against the native tribes on his borders, but it is possible he may try a round with the Dutch. I wish, if he is to make war, he would try the latter, for a war just now with the Transvaal would help to postpone all railway construction in that country, and would also tend to make the Dutch more disposed to listen to negotiations for the transfer to Natal of the disputed strip of territory between them and the Zulus, a strip of land that we badly want. I expect to hear from the Zulu king very soon, and will let you know the tenor of his message to me."

Three days earlier Carnarvon had written to Barkly desiring him to arrange for a conference of delegates from the various states and provinces of South Africa, to discuss questions of general interest, with the main purpose of ascertaining whether it would be possible to bring about a scheme of federation between all the different South African governments.[1] Wolseley was duly informed on this subject, and was reminded that reforms in the Natal Constitution must be such as to lend themselves eventually to federation. Carnarvon, curiously enough, chose

[1] Carnarvon to Wolseley, 30th April '75. " In my proposals for a conference there is nothing which I think can possibly interfere with your work in Natal ; on the contrary, it may give you fresh materials and a fresh escape from local opposition if this should prove unusually strong."

for the exponent and advocate of his scheme, not the Governor of the Cape, but the eminent historian, Mr. Froude. Froude landed at Cape Town in the middle of June, to find that the Colonial Office despatch, which had preceded him by a few days, had given considerable umbrage, and that already a motion had been carried in the House of Assembly which practically shelved the conference by asserting that any movement towards federation should originate in South Africa and not in England.[1] " The Cape Parliament ", Froude wrote to Wolseley on 5th July, " is no better than a collection of pert schoolboys."

Meanwhile, on the 20th May, the Natal Bill had passed its second reading with slight amendment, after three days' debate. It was carried by eleven votes to seven ; one of its intelligent opponents having voted, by mistake, in its favour. Wolseley, who did not tread political ground with confidence, wrote, however, to Carnarvon that he was by no means certain what would happen to the measure in Committee. " There are so many elements of un-certainty about everything debated in this Council that no one, short of being a prophet, can possibly predict the result of any proposal made therein. In opposition there are by far the ablest of the elective members, and they work together, whereas my majority last night was composed of men who differ from one another on most points, and whom it is most difficult to induce to work cordially as one team." But eight days later the bill, almost as much to Wolseley's surprise as to his delight, emerged safe and sound from the Committee ; the only compromise, which he thought well to accept, being the reduction of 15 nominees to 13. " My in-

[1] Froude should, of course, have immediately returned to England instead of carrying out, as he did, a political campaign which did infinite harm to the cause of Federation.

structions ", he told Carnarvon, " to the Attorney-General were to get the bill passed in some form or other without any pledge from me that it would or would not be accepted by the home Government."

The bill through, Wolseley breathed again; anyhow, there would be no need to go to the Imperial Parliament for compulsory legislation. The progress which he would make through the country was far more to his taste than urban vote catching, and he was much relieved to find that even if the proposed conference on federation should take place, he would not be required to sit at it. " I shall now very soon have the departments here on a better footing, and I do not care how soon my successor arrives ", he wrote to Barkly on the 14th June. " I am starting on a tour round the province that will occupy me during the remainder of my stay. I hope to settle many vexed questions by the information I shall be enabled to obtain personally."

In mid-June Sir Garnet set out for the Drakensberg, saddle - horses and mule - wagons being his means of locomotion. He took with him Butler, Brackenbury, and Gifford, having sent Colley to Pretoria to feel the pulse of the Boers as to relations with England and confederation with Natal. His own trek extended as far as Newcastle, whence he followed the Tugela Valley, sending off Butler through the Orange Free State to Kimberley. The roads were bad, the mules were unreliable, the accommodation of the inns was filthy but exorbitantly dear, the speeches were numerous, the war-dances were boring, the missionaries were often a little irritating, but the weather was perfect, sunrises and sunsets of equal beauty, and the relief from political intricacies intensely refreshing.

If the copious journal which the tourist kept be a true test of his feelings, a fly settled in his ointment with the mail to hand just after leaving Newcastle.

" No news [1] except three Field-Marshals have been named, and a number of men with no claim upon the score of war service have been made members of the Order of the Bath. I am not surprised at the list, but I am, and I am sure the whole Army will be, disgusted at it."

At Durban, on his return journey, he hoped to hear definitely that his successor, Sir Henry Bulwer, was on his way. But Froude arrived from Cape Town with a story, happily unfounded, which made Sir Garnet shake in his shoes. It was reported that Barkly was to be recalled and Wolseley to hold the office of High Commissioner for a year. " I am now in bodily terror ", he wrote, " that Froude's letter to Carnarvon giving an account of the position may be the cause of my being asked to stay on] here." [2] One of his final difficulties was that of filling up satisfactorily his nominated members, and he was finally obliged to recommend some divergence from the qualifications clause. At last, on the 27th August, the signal-gun announced the arrival of the steamer at Durban with Sir Henry Bulwer on board. " I feel like a schoolboy ", Wolseley wrote to his wife, " just told that I may go home for the holidays." At Maritzburg, where he had gone to recover from an attack of fever, there was a farewell dinner with the 13th Light Infantry, whose host and guest he had frequently been, and the next day, in an open drag with four horses, changed every eight miles, he dashed at full gallop to Durban, where he at once called upon the incoming Governor, whose staff, Wolseley observed, " consisted of a leggy-looking

---

[1] " I had been looking forward to this Gazette," he wrote to Lord Airey, " expecting that the names of the officers employed in Ashanti, whose claims to promotion H.R.H. had recognised, would have been inserted therein."

[2] As a matter of fact, Wolseley was asked to visit the Diamond Fields before he returned home, but the request was not pressed.

youth, not long, I should say, from school, who seems the picture of weakness and dullness. He little knows what is before him if he thinks he can get on in Natal with such help alone." A dinner of welcome to the incoming and farewell to the outgoing Commissioners was given by the Mayor of Durban. "My speech was tolerable," Wolseley wrote, " Bulwer's badly delivered in a very halting manner, but what he said was good. Froude's lasted at least an hour. Occasionally he was eloquent, but, strange to say, it was then upon topics that are unpopular here. How I hate speaking, especially when I have nothing important or particular to say."

At Cape Town Sir Garnet was treated to a banquet and reception at the Castle, a guard-mounting parade and a trooping of the colours, and a grand ball given by the citizens of Cape Town. There were long interviews with Molteno, who remained obdurate as to federation, and some conversation with Saul Salamon, the dwarf editor of the *Argus*, who, although equally bitter about the conference, had turned his pen against Molteno. On September 10th Wolseley sailed for England on the *Windsor Castle*, having sent a cypher telegram to Froude that, under the existing administration in Cape Colony, confederation was out of the question.

Sir Garnet landed at Plymouth on October 4th, and, after a few weeks' holiday, resumed his duties as Inspector-General of the Auxiliary Forces; but he was not destined to impress himself specially on the organisation of the Volunteers. Time is always requisite to propel proposals through War Office machinery, and time was lacking. In November 1876 Lord Salisbury, as Secretary of State for India, called Wolseley to the Council of India, which was then concerned alike with the effect upon India of the Cardwell army reforms and with the defensive policy to be adopted there. Lord Lytton had just arrived as Viceroy to find that Russia's steady advance towards the northern frontier of Afghanistan was the problem overshadowing all others. Russia had occupied Khiva in 1873, and made little attempt to conceal her negotiations with the Ameer, Shere Ali, at Kabul. The Viceroy found on the headquarters staff of the army in India, Major-General Frederick Roberts, V.C., who was then Quartermaster-General; Roberts he determined to use much as Cardwell had used, and Salisbury was using, Wolseley. Then was revived a controversy which had begun in the consulate of Lord Lawrence and the echoes of which may still be heard. There were those who desired to go into the Himalayas and secure the passes leading into India ; there were other experts who held that the Indus should be the defensive frontier of India, with a direct message to Russia that any encroachment, territorial or political, into Afghanistan would mean war with England. Roberts was a keen advocate of the former or " forward " policy. Wolseley took up the opposite ground; he argued that if we moved into the Himalayas we must become involved in the most difficult mountainous country in the world, and deal with a wild and manly race of mountaineers, before coming into contact with the " grey-coated swarms ", so dreaded in India ; the battle-ground would be chosen by our enemy, and be ill suited to us; on the other hand, if our sea - power were properly used, it would enable us to tackle Russia where she was weakest and where we would be most happily placed. Such were the main lines of the Lawrence policy, which, modified by changing conditions, has had the support of Lord Curzon and of many of the ablest Governors of India. Roberts and the forward school protested that Afghanistan, unless propped up, would surely succumb to Russia, and that no pressure in other parts of the world would make India safe if Russia had control of the passes. In 1874 a Conservative Government had come into power with a strong anti-Russian policy as an important part of its programme.[1] Lytton, with a mission from Disraeli, and Roberts with the reinforcement of the prestige gained in 1879–80 from his brilliant conduct of the second Afghan War, and from his dramatic march to Kandahar, won the day for the "forward policy", but in a second bout with Wolseley were not so successful.

Short service was regarded with even less favour by soldiers in India than at home. Indian expeditions incurred small casualty lists and the need for a reserve to replace losses or expand the Army—the prime purpose of short service—was not so evident to military students in Calcutta as to the military reformers at home.

The Indian official would also plead expense, which the shipping to and fro would multiply largely, while the young soldier would receive his early training in a country none too healthy and entirely strange to him. Roberts declared that short service would destroy the efficiency of the British troops in India, with only a "paper reserve" as a set-off; but later on he became a most valuable witness against his own original tenet.

The Defence of India was the subject of first-rate importance, but Sir Garnet saw much else to claim the notice of the India Office. He had attributed the Mutiny to the over-indulgence of the Bengal Sepoy, and to the inability of many British officers in India to talk the language of the country, which kept them out of touch with the native soldiers. Of his experience on Sir Hope Grant's staff he wrote : " What struck me as very odd was

[1] " We don't want to fight, but by Jingo if we do " dates from this Administration of Disraeli.

that, though Sir Hope and his Adjutant-General had been for many years in India, neither of them could speak Hindustani. Indeed, neither could say more than a few words in it. But in those days the officers in the Queen's army had practically no inducement to study the native languages. The Indian staff was at that time by no means what it should have been. It had in it some extremely able soldiers, men like Sir Henry Norman, Sir Peter Lumsden, and others who would have risen to eminence in any army. But, as a rule, the staff I came to know in the Bengal Presidency were too old and too old-fashioned in their ideas. They were overweighted with out - of - date regulations which smacked more of the counting-house than of camps and garrisons, and which tended to dwarf the initiative and smother the natural intelligence of the officers for whose guidance they were intended." To re-write the many volumes of Indian Army Regulations was beyond even his energies, but Wolseley set afoot a movement which thirty years later reached, under Lord Kitchener's guidance, its logical conclusion. From the India Office he was called away in the summer of 1878 to a fresh emprise.

On July 8th, 1878, the Duke of Richmond, in reply to a " put-up " question by Lord Granville, ponderously announced in the House of Lords that the Sultan of Turkey had consented " to assign the island of Cyprus to be occupied and administered by England ; Her Majesty ", he added, " has been pleased to appoint Sir Garnet Wolseley[1] to administer the government of the island ".

Wolseley notes in his diary how, having snatched a half-holiday for a river trip with his wife, he was

[1] It was generally understood that Wolseley was to succeed General Staveley in the Bombay Command that autumn.

" swallowing quantities of *salade* " when he received a telegram to say that a letter of urgent importance was awaiting him. He hurried home and found directions to call at once on the War Secretary, but in such a manner as not to attract attention. At the War Office he ascertained that Stanley[1] had gone down to the House of Commons and that the Duke of Cambridge, just returned from Malta, was in a specially unhappy mood, partly because the secret of Cyprus had not been confided to him, partly because Wolseley's appointment as High Commissioner had been made without his knowledge, advice, or consent. The Duke was further ruffled because officers had been already warned for Cyprus in whose selection he recognised Wolseley's hand, although the War Secretary had tactfully destroyed the paper in Wolseley's handwriting on which their names appeared. " Stanley ", Wolseley wrote, " was so nice in every way — so anxious to get me all I wanted without embroiling me more than is absolutely necessary with H.R.H." Stanley pressed for an early departure, and Wolseley only pleaded for two days for preparations which he had not allowed himself to make for fear of betraying the Cyprus secret.

On the 11th Wolseley dined with his mother at Wimbledon, but told her that he would not leave until the 20th, in order to save himself the good-bye. " I have always avoided doing so when possible," he told his wife; " and now she is a very old woman, and to think that I may never see her again is the bitterness in my cup of life. Although I see her seldom, still as long as I am near her I seem always to expect the arrival of the time when I can settle down near her and see her every day."

The question of the garrison for Cyprus—to be

[1] Col. the Hon. F. Stanley, Secretary of State for War, 1878–1880, succeeded his brother as 16th Earl Derby.

derived for the moment from Malta—was smoothly adjusted ; Sir Adrian Dingle, the Crown Advocate at Malta, a Maltese well versed in international and Levantine law, was to assist Wolseley in framing his instructions, which practically left him *carte blanche*. The public men on whom Sir Garnet called during the few hours at his disposal were mostly reticent as to the benefits likely to accrue from the possession of Cyprus, Lord Northbrook alone being outspoken as to his " hatred of the whole arrangement ". Sir Garnet himself was more anxious to perform his duty than to form any definite opinion as to its genesis, but he estimated the acquisition of Cyprus— grandiloquently described to him by Beaconsfield [1] as obtaining a counterpoise in the East for Russia's new territory in Armenia—as a rather poor half-measure. His military dream was the occupation of Egypt, whence a steady flow of soldiers could have been secured for service in India. " The fellah," he shrewdly prophesied, " well disciplined under English officers, would enable us to economise the use of the British soldier in the East."

Three crowded days, of which it was complained the Duke took up an undue and unnecessary proportion, and Wolseley travelled overland to Brindisi, crossed to Malta, where he spent one day pleasantly with the Governor, Sir A. Barton, and sailed on the 18th July in the *Himalaya*, reaching Larnica four days later.

His first telegram bade him communicate direct with the Foreign Office. " I need hardly dwell on the pleasure I experienced ", he told Lord Salisbury,

[1] Beaconsfield left the impression on Wolseley's mind that he had no desire for Egypt; and the latter suggested, on one occasion, that the dreamy Judaism apparent in Dizzy's books attracted him to Palestine rather than to Egypt. He said later, " I had always heard that the Turk was a clever diplomatist, but of all the good bargains he had ever made, this one about Cyprus is much the best—he takes all the plums out of the Island and throws upon us the responsibility of governing it well ".

" in once more having the privilege of serving directly under my late master at the Indian Council."[1] His first request was for a judge, and he proposed one Mr. Phillips, whom he had known in Natal, " a first-rate lawyer of a rough-and-ready type, with great experience in dealing with natives through interpreters and without the assistance of clerks, etc., whom English judges seemed to regard as indispensable ". " An Indian official's ideas are so grand and extravagant ", he was constrained to say, " that the revenues of Cyprus would not support the expense if their wishes were complied with." [2]

He admitted himself disillusioned with his new scene of activity. " Until I arrived here I had pictured Cyprus to myself as an island abounding in old Venetian palaces easily convertible into public buildings. I find that none exist, and that for years to come the Governor and all his officers will have to content themselves with huts and bell-tents, and rough it in a manner unknown to Indians, and that in a climate which for at least two months of the year is nearly tropical."

Something more than the usual crop of difficulties which besets an incoming Governor demanded Wolseley's anxious consideration. Cyprus under protracted Turkish rule had subsided into utter stagnation, and a strong hand was needed to stir her energies and set forward her welfare ; in his general purview there must have arisen a bewildering succession of such subjects as currency, constructions, customs, cadis, cantonments, consuls, religious properties, harvests, and finance. It was thought undesirable, for the time at any rate, to dislocate the

[1] Lord Salisbury was transferred from the India Office to the Foreign Office in April 1878.

[2] " Every one who comes here has extravagant ideas of the position they should occupy, and Cookson at once began about having a private secretary. He does not want to be a judge, but my legal adviser. I want workers, not advisers."

prevailing machinery; and Wolseley, when stepping
into the shoes of the Turkish Governor, simply
nominated six British officers—of whom the first was
Colonel Biddulph (eventually his successor)—to take
the places of the Turkish Kaimakans, who had
administered the six districts into which the island
had been divided. True to tradition, these functionaries were rapid and effective in remedying the chaos
to which neglect and apathy, rather than misrule
and tyranny, had brought the towns and villages.[1]

Before all things it was necessary to face the land
question, of which the salient difficulty was to be
found in the Turkish Government's preposterous
claims and the Sultan's irregular purchases. " As
regards the property said to have been purchased by
the Sultan ", Wolseley at once told Lord Salisbury,
" the purchase is clearly illegal, as it was never
registered here. If for political reasons it be deemed
advisable to wink at this job, I do earnestly trust
that it be clearly explained to the Sultan that the
only position he can be recognised in here is that of a
private landowner, and that he will not be permitted
to exercise any sovereign rights whatever in the
district we allow him to reserve." [2]

A mixed Commission, including two Mussulmans,
was appointed forthwith to define the extent and
terms of the lands alleged to be the property of the
Turkish Government or of the Sultan, and to report
as to what property was available for colonisation
by the Maltese, whom it was hoped to induce as
immigrants, with the further mandate to exhibit
the church properties respectively of Christians and
Moslems. Notice was given to our Ambassador
at Constantinople, that no land could be sold
until this Commission had furnished a report which
was not necessarily binding, but would at least

---

[1] Cf. Baker's testimony, Orr's *Cyprus*, p. 67.
[2] W. to Ld. Salisbury, 2.12.78.

prevent any future or further Turkish claims. Wolseley arrived from Larnica the last day of July at Nicosia, which he described as " a great cesspit into which the filth of centuries has been poured ". He wished to make his headquarters at a monastery a mile away, but was obliged to remain in camp pending the erection of any sort of Government building—" owners of houses being so avaricious they cannot even make up their minds to what extent they will be satisfied to rob us ".

His first visitor here was an official from Constantinople with a startling statement, conveyed in a very lame story, that the Porte expected that all waste land would be sold or leased for the benefit of the Constantinople Government, a contention which Wolseley represented would inevitably and perpetually prevent Cyprus from paying her way, and would preclude the construction of necessary buildings which civilisation demanded. Wolseley was not over sanguine in saying that when the Constantinople claims were committed to paper and referred home they would be reduced to their true proportions. Within a month he heard that our Ambassador, Sir Henry Layard, had been warned that the Queen's Government could not allow an article of the Convention to be so interpreted as to include in the Sultan's property the waste lands in Cyprus. He could then ask that the prohibition of the sale of Crown lands might be withdrawn, the only argument against it being that the Sultan might " try on " a sale of property to which his title was disputable. On the other hand, the impecunious peasant proprietors were in the hands of moneylenders—largely owing to the double tax imposed for the war with Russia—and the withdrawal of prohibition, by causing foreclosures, would rid the land of wholly insolvent farmers, and introduce capital of investors who were at present unable to buy real estate. Under his own legislative powers he would be able to ward off speculating companies by imposing conditions which would only allow land to be owned by individuals who would improve it.[1]

Sir Garnet had truly taken the measure of the Sultan's past, but he had in no way infringed decorum or even etiquette. He was therefore equally surprised and annoyed to hear that the Ambassador had asked the Foreign Office to urge him to prevent any violent proceedings regarding the lands claimed by the Sultan, Palace gossip having hinted that documents affecting the Sultan's titles had been seized. Wolseley telegraphed curtly that Layard's information was baseless ; that no papers had been seized ; that every facility had been given for survey ; that the alleged purchases of the Sultan were irregular ; of violent proceedings he knew nothing. He took the opportunity of stoutly deny-ing the notion that he was anti-Turkish ; on the contrary, he infinitely preferred the Turk to the Greek Cypriote, and would welcome an influx of healthy Moslem refugees into the island.

Impartial justice, he asserted, was his motto, and in illustration he mentioned that he had—with general approval and within three months—im-prisoned one tax-collector for robbery, one Greek dignitary of the Church for refusing to pay the tithes, and one Maltese antiquity-hunter for breaking the law.[2] Crime among the inhabitants and unhealthy

---

[1] " I look forward to making Cyprus a model province to which all men in Asiatic Turkey shall point as what a Turkish province may be converted into when removed from the influence of Constantinople intrigue."—W. to Ld. S., 25.10.78.

[2] This person had been discovered employing a gang of labourers in excavation contrary to Wolseley's express orders. " I wish the British Museum could be induced to send out some scientific man to explore the antiquities here. I am very anxious to preserve the ground for English research."—W. to Ld. S.

The earliest petition presented to the new Governor met with an unhesitating and uncompromising negative. A deputation of sanguine Greeks, remembering that, of a population of 186,000, over

H

conditions for the troops were troubles which reared their heads, and Wolseley insisted on the immediate deportation of a large number of convicts whose presence on the island was as undesirable as it was dangerous. He deprecated the gloomy reports which were appearing in the newspapers as to the climatic unhealthiness of Cyprus, and did not think that the troops would suffer more than those at Malta if—but this was a large if—there were proper arrangements and proper accommodation. " The doctors ", he wrote to the Duke of Cambridge, " seem to take gloomy pleasure in painting the health of the men in the blackest colours. Living in a bell-tent at this season is simply diabolical. In a hospital marquee yesterday the thermometer was 110° F., and such a marquee is luxuriously cool when compared with our wretched bell-tents. I presume that had it been known what the heat was like here, no British troops would have been sent here until due preparation had been made for housing them."

When huts were sent out they were of an American pattern ; Sir Garnet protested these would not last beyond a year, would be extremely uncomfortable, and would afford very poor protection from heat or cold. " I am all for economy," he remarked, " but I don't call any course economical when it leads to subsequent large outlay."

Two stations would be required for British troops, and within a month of his arrival Wolseley had selected sites for winter quarters and for the summer a hill-station at an altitude of nearly 6000 feet.[1]

---

two-thirds were Greek-speaking, urged that theirs should be the official language, to be firmly told that the English tongue would prevail. The mere suggestion that Cyprus should be a mirror of Malta in the matter of insular language made Wolseley shudder.

[1] " Next year I hope to have every British soldier in the Island in the mountains during the summer and autumn on a lovely spot that I have had examined and that is well suited to be converted into a hill-station."—W. to D. of C., 4th Sept. '78.

He realised that this double establishment would largely increase military expenses, and therefore proposed that a British battalion should be replaced by a Turkish battalion, for which no hill-station would be necessary.[1] It was stipulated that the Turkish battalion should not be composed of Cypriotes, and it was suggested that Colonel Valentine Baker (who had taken a distinguished part with the Turks in the Russo-Turkish War and was then commanding a large force of Turks near the Bosphorus) could easily raise this unit with volunteers.

The pursuit of justice led Wolseley into thorn-strewn paths. " Of one thing I am quite certain," he wrote, " that the sooner we get rid of Turkish cadis as judges the better ;[2] my idea is to retain them as expounders of the existing law, but to give them no voice in the verdict, and that the sentence should invariably be delivered by an English judge or commissioner. As long as the cadi is retained in his present functions, the Greeks—the mass of the population—will never feel satisfied that justice is being done them, and I confess that I myself have no confidence in the cadi's honesty." [3]

Admittedly the pay of the cadis was poor, and one of them pleaded naïvely he was unable to make two ends meet, being prevented by the presence of the English Commission from taking bribes. Another

[1] " I am very glad to find that you contemplate raising an English-Turkish regiment for service here. I hope it may be raised by British and not by Indian officers. It should, I think, be raised in Asia Minor. Sir Arnold Kemball would know best the localities and the tribes where we could obtain the best men. In order to obtain the services of good English officers, I think you would have to double their pay, as no man would leave his regiment, who was worth having, to serve with Turks, especially in such a very uninviting quarter as Cyprus."—W. to Ld. S., 20th Aug. 1878.

[2] " Scarcely a day passes without my finding out some fresh pieces of rascality on the part of the Turk officials here."—Private Letter.

[3] A year later Colonel Biddulph was writing : " The people have lost all faith in native judges ".

of these functionaries had to be dismissed, as his pleasant habit was to accept *douceurs* from both litigants. Wolseley, quoting Warren Hastings' reforms, urged that officials should receive sufficient emoluments to render them independent of bribery ; that dismissal from office should be a punishment in itself, and imprisonment should attend on corrupt practices.

If the cadi was to act fairly he must have fair play, and on behalf of one of them Wolseley must even withstand Lord Salisbury, who had acquiesced in a wish expressed at Constantinople, and furthered by Layard,[1] that the chief cadi should be replaced by an individual who could only claim that he was a favourite of the Grand Vizier. " I am very anxious to carry out your wishes," the High Commissioner wrote to the Foreign Minister, " but I can fancy nothing worse than the impression that would go abroad here if I dismissed the present cadi, against whom there are no charges whatever, merely at what would be considered a whim of the Grand Vizier, who wanted to provide for a favourite. I cannot even transfer him to any other place here, because his present pay is between three and four times as much as that given to any other cadi in Cyprus. His post is far the best-paid here. The only way I can see out of this difficulty is for the Porte to name the cadi they wished to send here to be the Mussulman Resident in Cyprus . . . fixing his pay at what they like, upon the understanding it was not to be paid out of the ordinary revenue of Cyprus. . . . I shall telegraph this to Layard, telling him also that as another alternative I can promise the cadi in whom he is so deeply interested the first vacant judgeship

---

[1] " A long letter from Layard, who writes of Turkish Pashas as if they were immaculate. His remarks about the Cadi whom the Porte wishes to send here are most curious ; so much so that if he were not an English official I should, not knowing him personally, have written him down as thoroughly dishonest."—W. to Lady W.

here, and as we have seven, all men more or less
advanced in years, he may not have long to wait."

Sir Garnet was adamant against even the com-
bination of the Foreign Secretary and the Ambassador.
" Layard ", he wrote to Lady Wolseley, " has been
impertinent enough to warn me against abusing
Turks, and Lord Salisbury is evidently much put
out because I would not give way about the cadi ;
he tells me that Layard's position will be so much
the worse. I say, so much the worse for him. Why
should I be asked to be unjust and dishonourable to
get him out of a scrape ? " The cadi was even made
to militate against a military requirement. Sir Garnet
asked for a hundred good Turkish soldiers to act
as military police in Cyprus ; the request could not
be complied with, because of the alleged unpleasant
condition of British relations with the Sultan owing
to the cadi. Wolseley could only suggest that the
Ambassador was adding a further misrepresentation,
and was puzzled to think how Lord Salisbury could
be taken in by him.

" The influence of England depending upon the
nomination of a cadi ! Good heavens, how low we
must have fallen and how very badly we must have
been served diplomatically at Constantinople if such
were true." [1]

An Order in Council of 14th September 1878
established a Legislative Council consisting of the
High Commissioner and not less than four or more
than eight other public officers and persons in the
island, to be nominated under His Majesty's sign-
manual, one-half being officials and the remainder
non-officials. An Executive Council was also named,
whose advice, however, the High Commissioner was
not obliged to take.

Wolseley had proposed to himself, and also to
the Foreign Office, the introduction of drastic reforms

[1] W. to Lady W.

in all the institutions of the island, so as to bring these into something like British shape. He was pulled up a little short by something more than a hint that the home Government required, at any rate for the time, purification rather than a conversion of Turkish institutions, and he bent himself at once in this direction.

Then a British annexation of Cyprus rendered urgent a revision of the jurisdiction of Consular Courts. It was possible by carrying out all custom-house work for the island on the Turkish system to avoid disputes with foreign vessels, but complications could not fail to arise in respect of the Consular Courts authorised by " capitulations ", or by treaty, for trial of disputes. In strict law a right acquired by treaty could not be abrogated by convention entered into by one of the contracting nations with a third power. Meanwhile, if a Frenchman were to accuse a German of an attempt to murder him, was the German Consular Court to be a vehicle of justice ? Or if an Englishman had suffered injury at the hands of an Austrian, must the Austrian Consul's Court deliver judgement ? The High Commissioner was legally advised that privileges conferred on foreigners, under stipulations made by foreign powers with Turkey, would be upheld by the convention still in force, but he determined that any foreigner should be dealt with as if he were an Englishman or a Cypriot, and the foreigner might freely appeal to his own Government. Even if legal niceties were affected, common sense dictated that, as there were now no British Consuls, the machinery for trying aliens under the capitulations had lapsed, as if they were to be re-garded strictly, an alien might snap his fingers at authority, there being no power to try or punish him.

Wolseley was somewhat startled to find that the foreign Consuls and Vice-Consuls, who habitually imported goods, nominally for personal consumption but really for trade purposes, claimed all the privileges usually accorded to Ambassadors and Ministers. Bound up with this subject was the whole question of exempting foreigners from certain taxes, such as that on trades and professions. The Greek Church was a special offender as regards non-payment of taxes, and large arrears were due from wealthy monasteries. The Caimokov of a district would apply to a monastery for a due, and would receive, in lieu of cash, a fat sheep. If he put the law in motion to recover the official tax, he would be represented at Constantinople as an oppressor of the Greek Church, and his dismissal from office might well ensue ; it was obviously better for him, there-fore, to swallow the rebuff and the sheep, and allow the tax to remain in abeyance. Wolseley, who disliked monks and monasteries, was not long in forcing clerics to keep pace with laymen in the matter of official payments, though he failed to extract their former liabilities.

The bishops and their methods were also very trying, more especially in the matter of their visitations to villages ; one visitation from a bishop was said to be more ruinous than two from a Pasha. Apparently the Turkish Government had assisted the bishops in collecting their dimes from the people, the income being the amount which the bishop thought he could screw out of the villagers. Shortly after Wolseley's arrival, the Archbishop blandly asked him for some police as an escort during a forthcoming visitation ; this request was refused point blank, and the bishops had to fall back on the less drastic method of closing churches and threaten-ing excommunication. Nor was the private life of these ecclesiastics beyond suspicion, and Wolseley reported one as having the reputation of " a very sad dog ", while another had been suspended for a grave moral offence.

The High Commissioner's depreciation of religious ceremonial did not prevent his using the first day of the Feast of Bairam as an opportunity to announce his appointment of the Legislative Council.

The festival was fixed for a Sunday, and Sir Garnet pleaded at first a difficulty in that Sunday was the English holy day. This, however, he told Lady Wolseley, not because he was himself a strict Sabbatarian, but because he wished to remind the Moslem that Christians also set certain days apart. "The Bairam came off last night unexpectedly; the beginning of it depends on when some particular priest sees the new moon, *i.e.* a clear sky. What a bore it would be to be a Moslem in a climate like England, where during the early phases of the moon one might not see it for several days."[1]

By Michaelmas Wolseley could report to the Foreign Office that he could estimate his revenue at £170,000, and his expenditure, including some new roads, at £64,000. After paying the Turk £103,000 there would remain a net balance of £3000. The accounts for the five years preceding the British occupation showed that the surplus of revenue over expenditure had been less than £100,000 per annum, and the Turks had astutely taken half that sum from the revenues of the island before the British took it over. The sum of £103,000 had been quoted in the annex to the Convention, but Layard had since proffered a preposterous suggestion of the Porte that this sum should be raised to £150,000. Wolseley told Lord Salisbury that with an annual outgoing of £100,000 Cyprus would get on without difficulty, so long as no charge was made for military expenses; but he naïvely reminded him that a Liberal party in power would try and make the island pay for everything.

By the annex to the Convention, England had

agreed to pay to the Porte whatever was the present excess of revenue over expenditure in the island ; this excess to be calculated upon and determined by the average of the previous five years.

After considerable correspondence the payment was eventually fixed at £92,000 in round figures, to which a large addition was made when Cyprus took over the control of the lighthouses in the island, and this sum was made a charge on the revenue of the island. It was shrewdly said at the time that we occupied Cyprus as tenants, paying £92,000 per annum for the ruined house and leaving ourselves no balance from revenue for necessary repairs. Moreover, the revenue was, later on, found to have been over-estimated, and the expenditure set out too low,[1] so Parliament had to vote each year a sum of about £30,000 to meet the deficit which occurred after the tribute had been paid. Various complications and much Cypriot heartburning ensued, the more so as the so-called tribute was utilised to pay the shareholders of the Ottoman Loan of 1855. Eventually in 1907 the Imperial Government asked Parliament to vote a fixed sum of £50,000 as a grant-in-aid of Cyprus revenues, until, on the outbreak of war with Turkey, the so-called " tribute " appeared in the annual Budget as " Share of Cyprus of the Turkish Debt Charge ".

Late in October Wolseley went down to the coast to meet the War Minister and the First Lord of the Admiralty,[2] who in the course of a Mediterranean tour called to take stock of England's last acquisition. Wolseley wished them to visit every place of interest and point of importance on the island, but he noticed that " riding is evidently not a strong point with the Ministers, so I feel that they will

---

[1] The expenditure for the following year, 1879–80, was estimated at over £110,000.

[2] Col. the Hon. F. Stanley and Mr. W. H. Smith.

not do long distances at a fast pace ".[1] Not only could the Ministers " not be screwed into a gallop ", but a tense political situation at home compelled them to cut short their visit of inspection ;—not, however, before they had confided to Wolseley that the Cabinet had been much misled by the Intelligence Department as to Cyprus and its condition, and that the island by no means answered the purpose for which it was taken over, namely, to be a place where a considerable force could rendezvous and be employed either in Asia Minor or in Egypt.

The two military proposals which Stanley made were that the 42nd Regiment,[2] which contained a

---

[1] " Mr. Smith doing the First Lord is sometimes as good as any play ; he is such a good-natured good fellow that one hates oneself for laughing at him, but one cannot help it. He has learnt some simple nautical terms which he occasionally brings out, and talks of the relative advantages of going alongside the ship on the starboard or port side owing to the state of the weather and the condition of the sea."—W. to Lady W.

[2] The embarkation of the 42nd Regiment, while Wolseley was absent on a tour, was the cause of his reading a homily both on the Q.M.G.'s department at the War Office and the Admiralty. He wrote to the Duke of Cambridge :

" *20th Nov.* 1878.

" I am sending the Q.M.G. a report of the embarkation of the 42nd Highlanders. The arrangements made in England were most unsatisfactory. I was on a tour when the telegram ordered the regiment to be collected at Larnika.

" The largest ships in the fleet have many times gone round the Island calling at all the ports, and there was no good reason whatever why the *Jumna* should not have done so also ; the delay would not have been 24 hours if so much, and the troops would have been spared the inconveniences and danger to health that they have incurred in carrying out the order received from home. Of course, I presume, those arrangements were made by the Admiralty, to whom the comfort, health and convenience of the troops are of little concern. Those at home have not got a sufficiently good knowledge of Cyprus and of its peculiar geography and the appliances existing for embarking and disembarking troops with reference to sanitary considerations to enable them—I humbly submit—to make the best arrangements for the movements of soldiers here. The *Humber* is simply a detestable ship for soldiers : there is no deck room and the space below available for troops is not fit even for healthy men, much less for those suffering from debility like the 42nd Reg. I told the Lords of the Admiralty, when here, that nothing short of an emergency would ever make me fill her with soldiers. . . ."

very large proportion of sick men, should go home, to which Wolseley agreed if a hundred Turkish police were substituted, and that an officer of less rank than that of Major-General would suffice for purely military supervision in Cyprus. Sir Garnet wrote that he had been delighted to see Stanley, who, as a matter of fact, had vainly urged him to come home for a few days to talk to Lord Salisbury, and that he hoped great things from the ministerial visit to the island. At any rate, the First Lord and the War Secretary on their return urged the Foreign Minister that the capital for which Cyprus was crying aloud was being arrested largely by the uncertainty of land tenure; on November 22nd Layard was authorised to offer to commute the rights reserved for the Ottoman Government under Article IV. of the Annex at an annual payment of £5000, the first instalment of which the Sultan would touch on the first day of the ensuing financial year.

In Cyprus Wolseley first made the acquaintance of Herbert Kitchener, then a lieutenant in the Royal Engineers, who had been borrowed by the Foreign Office to make a survey of the island. Kitchener pleaded for a thorough geographical survey, based on triangulation, which Wolseley pronounced to be unnecessary, too costly, and a work of several years. The High Commissioner only required for Government purposes traversed surveys and sketches of all the main lines of communication on the military principle with which he was familiar.

" If ", he wrote to Lord Salisbury, " Cyprus is to pay the expenses of Mr. Kitchener's survey, under these circumstances I would strongly recommend that he should devote all his time and the time of his party to a Revenue Survey. The scientific work he is employed upon may safely be postponed; it is of no immediate practical value to us, whereas every day I feel more and more that until the cultivated lands have been measured and their extent computed, holding by holding, our revenue from land can never be satisfactory. To measure a field or a farm and compute its acreage is a most simple process, but still it requires a man instructed in the art to do so. My proposition would therefore be to place Mr. Kitchener at the head of the revenue survey work, and hand him over as many intelligent natives as I could find to be taught this simple art of land measurement. In employing natives who spoke some European language besides their own I should save the expense of interpreters. In making the revenue survey—say of a village and its lands—it is necessary to examine the titles of every landholder in it. These title-papers are all written in Turkish and describe the holding in the very vaguest manner, and not one man in fifty understands what is written in his title-papers. The surveying party must therefore have with it some one capable of reading Turkish, by no means a common talent here. I am asking you officially by this post for the ' tools ' required to start this revenue work." [1]

Wolseley's trump card in his argument was economy, and it won ; but under his successor the map of the island was drawn by Kitchener, and 3500 square miles accurately delineated between 1879 and 1882.

From the day that he received his commission to Cyprus, Sir Garnet determined that sooner or later, and the sooner the better, Lady Wolseley should join him there. He was equally determined that he would deprive himself of this pleasure until adequate accommodation could be found for her and his little daughter. At the time of applying for some pro-

[1] W. to Ld. S., 5.2.79.

vision for himself, as well as for officers, married families, sergeants' messes, and so forth, he had written to Lady Wolseley : " This is against my grain, as I hate to think that the authorities at home should put me down as one anxious about my own vile body, and disinclined in any way to rough it. A Governor, even of the poorest place, should have a house where his wife can live, and it is not fair to ask me to be an exception."

By Christmas the modest building which was to do duty as Government House was ready, and Wolseley could resume the family life which he preferred to everything. If the position of Nicosia had been badly chosen, as lying in a flat and exposed to plunging fire from an enemy perched on the heights, the site of Government House was an admirable selection. The wooden building, forming three sides of a quadrangle with detached wooden huts for the military staff,[1] stood on a flat-topped hill a little more than a mile from Nicosia, which, as well as the surrounding country, it entirely commanded. The panorama, for a distance of nearly thirty miles, was superb, and Wolseley's interest in afforestation, which his daughter was to inherit and give expression to in horticulture, was agreeably exercised in planting acres of eucalyptus, in ordering every sort of seed and root from England, and in transferring fully grown date-palms to the natural terrace which fronted and flanked the house he was to occupy only for a few short months.

The correspondence from the island with the Duke of Cambridge was strictly limited to purely military concerns, and there was little chance for disagreement. The Duke evidently and entirely appreciated Wolseley's moderation as to military

[1] " It would be a bore ", he wrote to Lady W., " to have a staff living with us ; I would sooner allow them £200 a year towards their mess expenses than have them always to share our meals."

requirements and his concern that the comfort and health of the troops should be looked after; the Queen herself telegraphed to ask if sick men could be sent on a cruise.

But although the High Commissioner spared no effort in his work of administration, his heart remained in his own profession; whenever and wherever the military trumpet sounded the desire to respond to it was irresistible. He reminded Lord Salisbury that as an apostle of military reforms he was *mal vu* at the Horse Guards, and that, if the post of Commander-in-Chief in India should become vacant, his appointment under the Foreign Office might debar him from securing a position which seemed the only outlet for his military ambition. When he heard that the Ameer had refused a passage through the Khyber to the British Mission he said he would like six months more in Cyprus to set the Government machine in motion on its new English wheels, and then start off for a war in the Kandahar or Kabul valleys. But he let the Viceroy of India know that if an expedition were sent beyond the Indian frontier he could—if selected—start for Bombay at once;[1] at the same time he pleaded with the Duke of Cambridge that his Governorship should not obviate his being chosen for command.[2]

---

[1] " A cypher telegram from Colley in answer to mine about the military command in Afghanistan. ' Commands already detailed ', etc. All is for the best. I have always found that everything in the end turns out for the best. I have done what I could to get to Afghanistan if there is to be a war and I must rest content, sorrowing in my heart as much as I like. If I am not to have the command I hope it may be given to some young man capable of carrying it out. When we invaded Afghanistan before, we sent out a dying old gentleman to command who was about as useful as any old apple-woman the Home Government might have picked up on the Parade Ground outside their windows."—W. to Lady W.

[2] " . . . I hope and trust that Your Royal Highness will always regard me as available for military service in the event of active operations being undertaken by us anywhere, for although I like my

A month later he could not help telegraphing to Lord Salisbury begging him to further his wishes with regard to India. "No appointment contemplated by Cabinet", ran the reply. "Whole affair, which it is hoped will be small, left with Indian officers. As to your general wishes you may rely on my support if the occasion arises."

"It seems so foolish", Wolseley reflected, "for those who have to select a commander to leave one, who for a General Officer is young, here to carry out a civil administration, when a man of nearly sixty years of age is selected for command although he has never held any command in war before and is entirely unknown to fame or to his countrymen at home. When I am old and nerveless perhaps my turn will then come, but it will come when I shall no longer be able to do my country the service I could do it now."

In his whole correspondence there are constant references to his thirst for active service in the field, and on the last day of the year he wrote presciently : " I hope this day twelve months I shall not be here if these wars in Afghanistan and Zululand become serious. When I was in Natal I took notes in preparation for an invasion of Cetewayo's territory, thinking then I should have command when the war, which every one in South Africa knew and felt must come off sooner or later, did take place. With his 40,000 men armed with firearms he will be no mean enemy." Two short months later he was moved once more to appeal to his chief at the Foreign Office : "Telegram just received says that a new Commander is to be sent to Cape of Good Hope. Will you send me ? "

Cyprus was not favoured with any news tele-

---

civil work as Governor here very much, I would give up the first civil appointment there is for active work in my own profession in any part of the World."

III

grams, and it was not until the 18th of February that Wolseley heard of the disaster of Isandhl-wana,[1] which had occurred a month earlier. Sir Garnet's first thought was to send his Natal notes to the War Secretary; he gave his opinion that operations against Cetewayo should not begin before the month of May, nor be prolonged beyond the 10th September. "If the home authorities", he wrote to Lord Salisbury, "insist upon carrying on this Zulu War in accordance with Horse Guards practice the result may be failure, but it requires no philosophical powers to say that the expense will be enormous. To carry on a war as we did in Abyssinia [2] with an utterly reckless disregard to public expenditure is a simple process for the General employed, but it is an unwarrantable extravagance. Our former wars at the Cape were conducted chiefly by men ignorant of their trade who took their inspiration from books of regulations, and who seemed to think that everything was all right as long as they guided their conduct according ' to Act of Parliament '. Of course, when it is a question between failure and success, England can never pay too much to avoid the former, but she may, I think, pay too highly to secure the latter."

On the 27th April Wolseley, returning from a pleasant picnic, found a cypher telegram which pleased him even more; he was to return to London and report to the War Office. He nourished a hope, though he did not admit it even to himself, that Cyprus would see him no more, and packed his trunks to be sent after him. He telegraphed that

---

[1] On the very date of the disaster Wolseley, regretting that he was hidden away in the Levant, said to one of his staff, " I put my hand to the Cypriot plough and must hold it until the furrow is finished ". As he was speaking, the wrecked camps in Zululand were being evacuated, and the demand for Wolseley in South Africa would be voiced with the arrival of the news in England.

[2] The cost of Lord Napier's march to Magdala was £9,500,000.

he would leave in a fortnight's time, and asked that a war vessel might pick him up at Marseilles. The Admiralty said he must embark at Syracuse. Sir Garnet then suggested Venice, and finally compromised with Brindisi. "This I thought very ungenerous," he told a friend, "for I knew the *Salamis* had been sent from Malta to Venice for Layard, and I vainly thought that I was deserving of as much consideration as he was." Two days were spent in Paris, and, arriving in London on the 21st May, Wolseley, in a long interview with Lord Salisbury, recorded his stewardship at Cyprus, and resumed his military career.

CHAPTER VI

SOUTH AFRICA, 1879–1880

SIR GARNET had been summoned from Cyprus, ostensibly to join a committee to report on "Short Service" with relation to small wars, such as that in Zululand. The real reason was that he had been chosen to command in South Africa, a choice which the Cabinet thought it prudent to conceal for the time from the Horse Guards, where Wolseley, on reporting himself, met with little favour. The Duke of Cambridge took the opportunity of reading him a stern lecture on "Short Service", overjoyed to find that for once he had something of a case. Short service was calculated to create a reserve for major emergencies, but no Government could call out the reserve to fight Zulus, and the training given to the young soldiers who filled the ranks of the home battalions scarcely fitted them to tackle Zulu warriors. The Duke told Wolseley that "his damned new-fangled methods" had ruined the regiments with which H.R.H. had fought in the Crimea and were the prime cause of all our troubles in Zululand. But the controversy over short service had to be hung up, for the troubles in Zululand were serious, and the Cabinet had made up its mind how to deal with them. The disaster of Isandhlwana (January 22nd, 1879) had shocked the public mind, and given Beaconsfield's Administration a severe jolt. The usual scapegoats had to be found, and as Lord

Chelmsford, the Commander-in-Chief, was thought an insufficient sacrifice, the High Commissioner, Sir Bartle Frere — who was held responsible for military mismanagement — must be offered up. Wolseley, therefore, was not only to supersede Chelmsford, but to take over Frere's authority in Natal, the Transvaal, and Zululand. Therefore, if Sir Garnet was frowned upon by the Commander-in-Chief, he was caressed by the Cabinet. Beaconsfield, though a little cross at being kept waiting while Wolseley changed after a Levée, was the pink of politeness,[1] while Colonel Stanley was impressive in compliments and explicit in confidence.

The Cabinet was prompt to publish Sir Garnet's dual appointment as Commander-in-Chief and High Commissioner in Natal and the Transvaal ; the Press and public were loud in approval, but the War Office was coldly critical, and began a policy of pin-pricks. Wolseley received sharp reprimand for having selected a group from his now famous and obnoxious " ring " to accompany him without first consulting the Commander-in-Chief. The authorities had to be coerced into giving Colley the status of Brigadier, and the four A.D.C.'s, to whom Wolseley was entitled, were made a bone of contention. Nor was the atmosphere at Court any warmer. The Queen naturally formed her opinion of Wolseley from conversations with the Duke, and was disposed to regard him at this time as a pushing adventurer who should be kept in his place. Her Majesty had to be pressed to give him even the local rank of full General, necessary to make his position *vis-à-vis* Chelmsford quite clear, and Beaconsfield had more than once to exercise all his tact to smooth over her dislike of his nominee. Once Wolseley was in South Africa the Prime Minister could write : " With

[1] He asked how soon Sir Garnet could start. " By the 4 o'clock train this afternoon if you wish it ", was the reply.

regard to Sir G. Wolseley, Lord Beaconsfield will write to Your Majesty with that complete and unlimited confidence which has always, he trusts, distinguished the remarks he has had the honour of submitting to his Sovereign. It is quite true that Wolseley is an egoist and a braggart. So was Nelson "[1]—a delicate hint that her woman's judgement of the man might be right and her opinion of the soldier wrong. And to Lady Bradford : "I have confidence in Wolseley, but I believe Chelmsford committed at the last as many mistakes as are consistent with what is called success ".[2] Beaconsfield's "complete and unlimited confidence " was directed more towards getting what he wanted than to giving Her Majesty his real opinion of the soldier he had chosen to get him out of a difficulty.

Wolseley reached Cape Town on June 23rd. " Is the war over ? " was the enquiry from those on board ; " No ", was the welcome answer—precisely the same question and answer which were put day in and day out for thirty months twenty years later. He sat up most of that night with Frere, who insisted that history would justify him and exhibit how weak-kneed was the Cabinet. He told Wolseley that he was tired of writing private letters to Hicks-Beach[3] and receiving no reply, and that he missed the cordial relations that had existed between him and Lord Carnarvon.

Chelmsford's movements filled Wolseley with anxiety, and he left Cape Town the next day fully expecting when he reached Durban to hear of a severe check, if not of another disaster. " Nothing could be more unpromising ", he wrote on his way out, " or more fraught with danger than the existing condition. Of course a happy stroke of fortune

---

[1] August 24, 1878. *Life of Disraeli* (Buckle), vol. vi. p. 435.
[2] *Ibid.* p. 449.
[3] Sir Michael Hicks-Beach, Secretary of State for the Colonies.

might end the war at any moment, but I confess I
see no probability of it under present circumstances,
with a demoralised army, the men of which, in all
ranks, are thoroughly sick of the war, and have lost
all confidence apparently in their leaders. It is very
probable that I shall find myself forced to postpone
all operations till January, which would create a bad
impression at home politically speaking, and would
be a fearful disappointment to the Ministry ; however, they have only themselves to blame for not
having sent me here three months ago.''

Reaching Durban on June 28th, Sir Garnet
hurried at once to Maritzburg. He had left the train
before reaching railhead and he drove at top speed the
last part of the way, his carriage arriving at the door
of Government House before the guard of honour had
formed up, or the Commissioner, Sir Henry Bulwer,
had buttoned himself into his uniform. No cheerful
news from Chelmsford was to hand, but Wolseley
to his satisfaction had learnt on the way that the
Amatongas had plucked up courage to tell the Zulus
that they would give them no support. He summoned
the Natal native chiefs to Maritzburg, and with some
pomp and circumstance told them that he intended
to put a term to the war ; with fine disregard for
the military conditions at home he grandiloquently
stated that the Great White Queen would send one
army after another until Cetewayo was defeated,
and added that the savage king and not the Zulu
people was the enemy. He honeyed his remarks
with some compliments, and elicited from his hearers
promises to do all that he asked. Returning to
Durban he embarked to go up the coast towards
Zululand, and anchored off Port Durnford on July
2nd. On the following morning the weather was
stormy, and a futile attempt, fraught with considerable danger, was made to land. Eventually the ship
had to be put about and go back to Durban. The

short cut by sea having proved to be the longest way round, on July 5th Sir Garnet hastened by rail and wagon to Fort Pearson on the Tugela River, where in his camp he found among many telegrams one from Mr. Archibald Forbes of the *Daily News* from Landman's Drift announcing Chelmsford's success. He "had moved down without tents into the Umvolosi Valley on the 3rd instant, and had been attacked on the 4th instant, whilst advancing in a hollow square towards Ulundi. The enemy were beaten off and the cavalry went in at them, cutting them into mincemeat. Loss ten killed, sixty wounded." [1]

Wolseley was but human, and the news could only have given him qualified pleasure. He would get rid of Chelmsford, who, as he said, could return home with a " halo of success ", and he could set afoot at once his plan for pacifying Zululand ; but after strenuous efforts to be in time he had just missed the chance of administering the *coup de main* which he had hoped to deliver, and he knew that this would cause exultation, quite incommensurate with the actual military achievement, at home. This surmise was fully justified ; the telegrams which flashed between the Queen and the Duke of Cambridge and all who supported the Commander-in-Chief sounded the same note of satisfaction, that Cetewayo should have been put to flight before Sir Garnet Wolseley came on the field ; Wolseley himself at once telegraphed congratulations to Chelmsford and his thanks to Forbes for the prompt information.

The relations between the two soldiers were not made easier by busybodies both among Wolseley's enemies at home and in Chelmsford's entourage

[1] Wolseley had intended to move with the Coast column at once towards the king's kraal at Ulundi. It was therefore due to the raging of the sea that he took no part in the action with which Chelmsford put a term to the Zulu War.

on the spot. The latter made the mistake of retiring after Ulundi, which might have had serious consequences, and did in fact encourage some of the bolder spirits among the Zulus to renew their raids into Natal. Sir Garnet learned that some of Chelmsford's staff had declared that this withdrawal from Ulundi had been ordered by him, and to scotch this snake he at once posted copies of his correspondence with Chelmsford to the Secretary of State. " If Chelmsford ", he wrote on the 28th July, " had remained at Ulundi and pursued with cavalry and native troops, he might easily have turned the occasion into a final victory. His policy of having made raids into Zululand has been very unfortunate, and has given rise to these reprisals, as the people near the Middle Drift are giving us a great deal of annoyance." The misrepresentation had, however, gone far, and Beaconsfield must write to the Queen : " Had he not been furtively apprised by telegraph that he was to be superseded, Lord Chelmsford would probably never have advanced to Ulundi. His retreat from that post was his last and crowning mistake, and the allegation that he was instructed to do so by Sir Garnet Wolseley has been investigated by Lord Beaconsfield and found to be without foundation." [1]

Wolseley was a little perturbed to receive at Maritz-burg an invitation to a public dinner in honour of the outgoing General. The banquet, however, passed off well : the Mayor spoke tactfully ; Wood sparkled with epigram ; and Chelmsford gracefully alluded to the splendid services of both Buller and Wood.[2] " He is a gentleman and a very nice fellow," Wolseley was moved to observe, " but the Lord forbid that he should ever command troops in the field." The

[1] *Life of Disraeli*, vol. vi. p. 459.
[2] Wood and Buller, who had served under him, had saved the situation after Isandlhwana by defeating the Zulus at Kambula Mountain.

next day Sir Garnet called to wish Chelmsford good-bye, but finding him out wrote him a pleasant note, wishing " to build a golden bridge for Chelmsford to retire by ". He then had to pacify Wood and Buller, who were reluctant to be bound up with Chelmsford in any way, but for whom he had no place. " I am sending away several regiments to England, and getting rid of all superfluous staff and special officers. Indeed, I am overloaded with officers."

The capture of Cetewayo, the Zulu king, was a necessary preliminary to any permanent pacification of the country. A cordon of troops was drawn round the area within which the king had been located, and on receipt of more definite intelligence a party of the 19th Hussars, under Major Barrow, with Lord Gifford in his usual rôle of leader of native scouts, and Captain Maurice, now intelligence officer on Wolseley's staff, were sent to catch him. The hunt was a long one, the cavalry horses were soon done up, and Gifford and Maurice went on with the natives. They had just located the king when he was snapped from under their noses by a patrol of the King's Dragoon Guards, under Major Marter, who was lucky enough to get a Zulu to tell him where Cetewayo lay. On August 29th Wolseley was able to write : " My heart is full of joy and satisfaction. Cetewayo is a prisoner at last ". The sable monarch, after a stay at Cape Town, was sent home to London, and for some time lived in a house in Melbury Road, where he delighted the nursemaids of Kensington by appearing daily on his balcony, and bowing in response to their greeting.

The king in safe custody, Wolseley turned to the uncongenial task of the political settlement of Zulu-land. Here he was not happy : he seemed out of touch with his subject and out of sympathy with his surroundings. His instructions from home made

a satisfactory settlement scarcely possible, and
his scheme had to be remedied not long after he
left the country. His demeanour was largely due
to an unfortunate misconception of Frere and of
Frere's policy which deprived him of the advice of
the man best fitted to help him. Wolseley's mind
had been prejudiced from the start by a Government
which had given him powers deliberately intended
to convey a snub to Sir Bartle, and Bulwer at
Maritzburg had inflamed his mind by a misrepresentation, perhaps unintentional, of Frere's ambitions.[1]
Frere's policy was the policy of confederation which
he had been sent out to enact, and so long as there
was any chance of setting it afoot, no slap in the
face from the Government would move him from
his post. Bulwer tried to persuade Sir Garnet that
Frere's policy was one of conquest, and that nothing
could be done towards confederation until his own
authority in Natal was restored. To Bulwer's unhappy words may be traced the lack of sympathy
between Frere and Wolseley which hampered progress
at the time and vitiated Wolseley's Zulu settlement.

As regards the terms of that settlement,[2] Wolseley
declined to give Frere any preliminary information,
and by an unfortunate blunder a copy of the despatch
containing the terms did not reach Sir Bartle until
it had been to England and back in the portmanteau
of the officer charged to deliver it at Cape Town.

His plans for Zululand in shape, Wolseley left

[1] " Of course, as General Commanding the troops in South Africa,
you will not allow them to be employed in expeditions planned by
Frere. Don't allow him to persuade you to move troops into Pondoland or Basutoland. If he could only get some troops there he could
at once embark on another war; and if you allow the nation to be let
in for another South African campaign no one at home will ever forgive you. Bellairs is too much a creature of Frere's to be entrusted
with power, hence my desire to have you here as soon as possible as I feel sure you will not go in for Frere's ' blood and iron '
policy. . . ."—W. to General Clifford, 20.4.80.

[2] Wolseley proposed to divide the government of Zululand amongst
a number of small chiefs.

on September 4th for Utrecht, where he had the pleasure of giving the Victoria Cross to his old comrade of Ashanti, Major Bromhead, and to Private Jones of the 24th Regiment, for Rorke's Drift. Here also he inspected the troops, whose turn-out pleased him better than their appearance at Aldershot, "saturated with pipeclay to please the Commander-in-Chief, who knows nothing of war and is bigoted in his own antiquated German views". The British General invited Joubert to visit him at Wakerstroom and to pay his overdue taxes ; both suggestions were for the moment declined, though the latter was eventually pressed home. At Wakerstroom as at Standerton the Transvaal patriots were evidently marking time until a reply was received to President Kruger's petition for independence. They curled their lips to Wolseley's rhetoric that the British flag would fly over the Transvaal as long as the sun shone ; they heard in scornful silence the metaphor that the Vaal would flow backwards before the British should be withdrawn.

The Boers were in no complaisant mood. They had been long fighting for existence against natives and knew the fighting methods of every tribe ; they had been close observers of our conduct of the Zulu War, and had not been impressed. They had indeed offered advice to our commanders, who, with the signal exception of Wood, had treated it with scant respect. Wolseley was quick to see that something more than the words put into his mouth by Hicks-Beach was needed to secure acquiescence in the policy of annexation upon which the British Government was determined. Nothing would be better than to show the Boers that in wars with the natives we could play their game as well or better than themselves, and the opportunity was at hand. In the north of the Transvaal a native chief named Sekukuni had established a robber fastness in the country between

Oliphant and Steelpoort Rivers. Sekukuni had in
1876 formed an alliance with Cetewayo;[1] the Boers
therefore had tried hard but wholly failed to crush
him, and he had become a terror to the farmers
who lived within reach of his stronghold. There
was much to be gained by removing a pest and at
the same time impressing the Boers, and Wolseley
made up his mind to strike quickly. He sent
Baker Russell to Lydenberg to keep an eye on
Sekukuni, and moved himself to Pretoria to prepare
the little expedition. Just before arriving at Pretoria
on September 27th he was horrified to hear of the
murder of Sir Louis Cavagnari and his escort at
Kabul. Lord Lytton, much distraught, had telegraphed three weeks earlier to beg Colley to return
to him at once, as he had no personal military
adviser. " Apart from my own selfish considerations ", Wolseley wrote home, " of losing Colley,
this news has dumbfounded me." But unhesitatingly, as well as unselfishly, Wolseley deprived
himself of assistance on which he greatly relied, and
issued a General Order, eulogising Colley's services,
and authorising him to proceed at once to India.
He would gladly have had his trusted lieutenant's
advice regarding a long letter to hand a few days
later from the Colonial Minister, enclosing Sir Theo-
philus Shepstone's minute which sharply criticised
the proposed settlement of Zululand.[2] Hicks-Beach's
own note hinted that H.M. Government would not
dislike an annexation of Zululand, which was quite
contrary to their original mandate. Wolseley at

---

[1] He was dubbed by the natives " Cetewayo's dog ".

[2] Rider Haggard was even more biting in his strictures. " Of the
chiefs appointed some were so carelessly chosen that they have no
authority whatsoever over the districts to which they were appointed,
their nominal subjects preferring to remain under the leadership of
their hereditary chief. Several of Sir Garnet's little kings cannot
turn out a hundred men, while the hereditary chief, who has no official
authority, can bring up three or four thousand " (*Cetewayo and his
White Neighbours*, p. 31).

123

once wrote to Hicks-Beach to say that there were only two courses to follow : (i.) annexation, (ii.) restoration of the country to its chiefs. He had followed the second course, believing it to be the most statesmanlike and therefore the most agreeable to the Government.

On October 19th, having received no news for a fortnight from Baker Russell, Wolseley left Pretoria for Middleberg, to direct the operations against Sekukuni. He decided to do as he had done in Ashanti, and rely mainly upon native levies led by British officers, and this for several reasons. The Boers, regarding as fools any white men who exposed themselves to risks which natives could be induced to run, adopted this procedure, and Wolseley would show them that we could do the same ; then there was the ever-present question of cost, and he was about to reduce the British garrison in Africa to a minimum ; and, lastly, British troops would require pony transport, and the country round Lydenberg was ravaged by horse-sickness. The force was therefore composed of a small body of mounted troops chosen from Boer and British volunteers, some 2000 Swazi, and 3000 other native auxiliaries, with some British artillery. The levies were assembled at Lydenberg on November 1st, and a week later the advance began. Sekukuni's "town" was in character not unlike the settlement of a robber baron of the middle ages : a congeries of native huts perched on the sides of low rocky hills formed a lower and an upper town which surrounded the "fighting kopje," the place of refuge for the people, and the castle of the chief. This kopje was a large conical hill, honeycombed with caves and defended with numerous stone breastworks, the approaches to which were barred by thick thorn fences ; at first sight this keep seemed to forbid direct attack, but a personal reconnaissance convinced

Wolseley that the very steepness of the hill and the roughness of the approaches to it would give ample cover to bold men, and he ordered Baker Russell, with Herbert Stewart as his staff officer, to make an assault. This took place at dawn on November 28th. The right attack was led by Ferreira, the leader of the Colonial Horse, who took the chieftain's kraal from the heights to the south; the central attack, led by Colonel Murray, was directed on the "fighting kopje"; while, on the left, Major Carrington[1] captured the lower town and cleared the hills above, sweeping round to join Ferreira at the big kraal. The Swazis hung back for a moment to see how their leaders would behave, having on more than one occasion been encouraged from behind by the cautious Boer, but finding that there was no doubt of the determination of the British officers, they followed gallantly, and Sekukuni's stronghold was quickly in our hands. Some of the natives, more eager for loot than for glory, went raiding cattle up the valley, but, meeting the exasperated Swazis on their way back, were relieved of the larger part of their booty.

Sekukuni's stronghold had been taken with a loss of two British officers and four men killed, and with about thirty other British and native casualties. It only remained to account for the chief himself, who had fled to a cavern a mile short of the great cave of Konako, having shed all his followers and retained only three of his ladies. At 9 A.M. on December 2nd Major McCalmont[2] galloped into Wolseley's camp to say that Sekukuni had surrendered three hours earlier; he was reported as very hungry as well as very ill, and had seized ravenously the first morsel of food obtainable. "Thank God", Wolseley ejaculated; "I shall now be off for Pretoria, and if God

---

[1] Later, General Sir Frederick Carrington.
[2] Later, General Sir Hugh McCalmont.

will only bless my dealing with the Boers as He has blessed my dealing with Zululand I may be able soon to get out of South Africa."

The Government at home was delighted, and had visions of success for their increasingly unpopular South African policy. Beaconsfield wrote to Lady Bradford: "Sir Garnet Wolseley has not disappointed me. He is one of those men who not only succeed but succeed quickly. Nothing can give you an idea of the jealousy, hatred, and all uncharitableness of the Horse Guards against our only soldier." But the British Government was never a good judge of the Boer temper. The Transvaalers were no more reconciled to annexation than before. Wolseley reached Pretoria on December 9th to hear that a Boer meeting some 2000 strong was being held outside the town. The convention was threatening in speech and demeanour, but at the end of a week dispersed harmlessly, in time for Erasmus to be arrested for having dealings with Sekukuni. The same evening, at a dinner given to him by the townsfolk of Pretoria, Wolseley made an emphatic statement, which within two years was falsified, that no Government, Whig or Tory, Liberal, Conservative or Radical, would dare, in any circumstances, to give back their country. The pronouncement was fortified by a letter from the Colonial Minister, which covered the Order in Council for a Legislative Assembly in the Transvaal,[1] but conveyed an unwelcome request that Wolseley should repair to Natal to extract from the Council there as large a contribution as possible towards the expenses of the Zulu War. He telegraphed that such a mission was doomed to failure, as he was about the most unpopular person in Natal, being regarded as the

[1] Yet early in March Wolseley had to telegraph, on the eve of the meeting of the new Legislative Assembly, to the Secretary of State for an explicit assurance that the Queen's sovereignty would be maintained—an assurance which was given.

official who had deprived them of their legislative
privileges, and " drowned their liberties in sherry
and champagne ".

Sir Garnet, never really happy unless every moment
of the day was occupied, found time hang heavy on
his hands. He read a good deal, though the books
he liked were rarely obtainable in Pretoria. His
private correspondence was large. His diary was
copious. He drafted an article on the system of
promotion in the British Army, but considered it too
plain-spoken for publication ; it might widen the
breach between him and the Duke of Cambridge, so
as to render future co-operation difficult. " I am
too good a loyalist ", he told a friend, " to wish to
do anything, even although it might have a beneficial
effect upon the Army, that would bring royalty, even
in the stout form of the Royal George, into contempt.
I don't blame him so much as I do the men about him."

Under further pressure from home to proceed to
Natal, Sir Garnet set out from Maritzburg on
January 22nd. He arranged to return, and among
other matters deal with a dispute with Pretorius,
who was furious at having been confined in a common
prison, but he cherished the hope that Pretoria would
see him no more. He clung to an idea that he might
be sent to India, and resented being retained for
what he termed " dirty work " in South Africa by
Hicks-Beach, in order, as he believed, to tide over
a difficulty with Frere. Travelling in a four-wheeled
buggy, he was at Maritzburg on the 26th, and
discussed with Bulwer the financial liabilities and
capabilities of Natal. The one man, according to
Wolseley, who could "make things 'smoke' in
Natal " was Colley, and the fact that Brackenbury,
who had taken Colley's place as chief of the staff, had
just been invited to become private secretary to the
Viceroy, indicated Colley's return to South Africa.

The sojourn in Maritzburg was far from enjoyable. Wolseley was not easy either in his relations with the Natal Council or in his arguments with the two bishops[1] on such subjects as mission-stations and polygamy, and he persuaded himself that Frere was misrepresenting him to the Colonial Office. He was fearful that he would be put in charge of the Empress Eugénie, who was about to visit the spot where the Prince Imperial fell, and he lashed himself with the thought that his absence from England would be highly detrimental to his military prospects. His cup was further embittered by information to hand that the clasp for Zululand would be restricted to men engaged in operations up to the battle of Ulundi. In a letter to Hicks-Beach he protested vigorously against a decision which would rule out military operations which led up to the capture of Cetewayo and the real end of the war. " I was careful," he wrote, " in my despatch at the beginning of September announcing the end of the Zulu War, to accord to Lord Chelmsford all the credit of having personally commanded at the battle of Ulundi; but that he ended the Zulu War I most emphatically deny. I am well aware of the jealous hostility with which I am regarded by some of the military authorities at home, but I cannot imagine that H.M. Government will permit me, when absent from home, to suffer in military reputation from the ill-will of those who would wish to see me deprived of whatever small amount of credit there may be due for having brought the Zulu War to an end."

Sore in spirit, he was also just then sick in health. He had recurring attacks of fever; he complained constantly of heartburn, the result of impaired digestion; he attributed his increasing baldness to premature old age; he was worried by the

---

[1] It was currently said of the two bishops of Natal that " one was a schismatic and the other a heretic ". Wolseley believed " Colenso to be a bitter enemy of mine ".

reflection that, had he known he would be kept so long in South Africa, his adored wife could have wintered abroad agreeably instead of being condemned to London cold and fog. The pith of his grievance was that he had been deputed to end the Zulu War and settle native disturbances, and that, his mission being completed, the Government had no right to tie him up, for political purposes, to a civilian appointment. Late in February he was back in Pretoria, where he was told to stay until the Boer meeting—called for early in April, but eminently liable to postponement—was peaceably terminated. His position in Pretoria was rendered the more trying by the persistent rumours that the surrender of the Transvaal to the Boers was imminent, and in mid-March he was again obliged to ask the Colonial Office for a final and positive assurance that British sovereignty was to be inflexibly maintained. " All the stories ", he wrote, " are based on speeches or published letters of men within the Liberal ranks, and unless the home Government makes an authoritative statement, my policy will be rendered nugatory and it will be difficult to govern the country." [1]

Just then, however, two welcome telegrams were received. His succession had been offered to and accepted by Colley. Colley was obliged to pay a flying visit to England, and could not therefore reach Natal before the end of May, but the nomina-

---

[1] 17th March 1880, Wolseley to Hicks-Beach : " The object of everything I have done since I entered the Transvaal has been with a view to make the people believe in the permanency of our position, and that, come what may, we should never leave the province we had annexed with the approval of Parliament. If I may presume to criticise my own acts and their results, I should say that until these disquieting rumours from England reached the Transvaal this last week everything had gone on here most satisfactorily, but the receipt of the news that Lord Hartington said in the debate on the Queen's Speech that we ought to retire from the Transvaal, had wellnigh ruined whatever good I had effected. . . . I earnestly hope that when this subject is debated in Parliament, Her Majesty's Ministers may speak in no uncertain tone upon it."

K

tion spelt finality to Wolseley's ennuis. Still better was the tender of the post of Quartermaster-General at the War Office. Wolseley strongly suspected that underlying the offer was a tacit understanding that his acceptance carried the relinquishment of his claim to succeed Sir Frederick Haines in India. He was careful, therefore, when accepting the appointment in conventionally grateful terms, to reaffirm his hope that the reversion to supreme command in India might fall to him. He came to Maritzburg on April 9th, in time for a farewell banquet to Bulwer, when he was able, in returning thanks for the Army, to "let drive" at a popular journalist's untruthful charges against the Army.[1] He fretted over each day's delay to embark for home. A rather sharp touch of the fever, which he felt was increasing its hold on him after years of trying climates, exaggerated such small annoyances as the Queen having consulted Sir Bartle instead of himself as to the cross to mark the spot where the Prince Imperial fell.

At last, on April 19th, just after an interview with Aylward the Fenian, whom Wolseley described as " a most amusing ruffian, full of Irish stories, which he tells inimitably ", he received permission to leave at once, if he himself thought he could do so without prejudice to the interests of the State. There only remained the visit of ceremony to the Empress Eugénie,[2] which he paid on board s.s. *German* at Durban before embarking for Cape Town. At Cape Town a few days were spent at Government House, where from Wolseley's later correspondence it is evident that many of his misconceptions regarding Frere were cleared away, much of the soreness which curiously

[1] Sir William Russell.
[2] The Empress had reached South Africa with Evelyn Wood as escort.

enough had lodged with the man who had no
grievance was allayed, and a fine character which
Wolseley at the time had been unable to appreciate
had revealed itself to him.[1]

On May 5th Sir Garnet shook the South African
dust off his feet and stepped on board the *Conway
Castle*. Twice had he landed at Cape Town to meet
with difficulties and disappointments wholly dis-
proportionate to any success he had achieved. His
attempt at a Natal Constitution in 1875 met eventually with nearly as much disfavour as his settlement

---

[1] June 1902, Lord Wolseley to Sir G. Arthur :

" MY DEAR SIR GEORGE ARTHUR—Many thanks for your interesting letter about Sir Bartle Frere's work in South Africa.

" Your uncle was a man of great ideas, but, as is too often the case
with those of lofty aspirations, he was misunderstood by his con-
temporaries.

" As I recall the history of that time, I feel that he and Lord
Carnarvon were about the only statesmen who then clearly foresaw
the great future of South Africa, and who then realised what the
Dutch in South Africa were then aiming at. The leaders in public
life at home are usually so wrapped in the immediate interests of
party politics that, in time of profound peace, few pay much attention
to Colonial affairs.

" But Sir Bartle Frere was an exception. At all periods a close
observer of events, as these occurred throughout our Empire beyond
the seas, he quickly saw through the aims of the Dutch in South
Africa, and realised what, if unchecked, these aims must lead to.

" Few to whom he preached, however, heeded his warnings.
Many pooh-poohed his advice as that of an autocratic Anglo-Indian
with visions entirely outside the scope of ' practical politics '. In
other words, too wide for the narrow limits of party considerations
and of party exigencies.

" All this is changed now. The South African Empire of which
Sir Bartle dreamt and hoped for and sought to build up has been made
a reality by our home and colonial soldiers and by the persevering
energy and statesmanship of Mr. Chamberlain.

" If ever the history of recent events be fully and honestly written,
the names of your uncle and of the present Colonial Minister will be
therein recorded as the founders of our South African Dominions.

" Holding these views, as one who was there somewhat behind the
scenes, it is only natural I should wish that some recognition should
be made, even at this late hour, of the great services rendered by your
uncle when he ruled over the Cape Colony.

" He was then neglected, but in such a case it can never be too
late to remedy the fault we then committed. The only question is,
in what shape or fashion such a national reparation could best be
made ? Believe me to be—Sincerely yours,   WOLSELEY."

of Zululand four years later. His military genius had little opportunity to display itself, and he manifested undue impatience with the conditions of a country whose strategical importance for his own he was the loudest to proclaim.

But if he had not been able to blaze a trail through the jungle of South African politics, he saw clearly enough the course the trail should follow, and he treated the expiring Conservative Administration to a forecast, which, if it had been heeded by either party, might have prevented a peck of troubles. In December 1879 he wrote to Hicks-Beach : " The Transvaal is rich in minerals ; gold has already been found in quantities, and there is no doubt that larger and still more valuable goldfields will sooner or later be discovered. Any such discovery would soon bring a large British population here. The time must eventually arrive when the Boers will be in a small minority, as the country is very sparsely populated, and would it not therefore be very short-sighted policy to recede now from the position we have taken up simply because for some years to come the retention of 2000 or 3000 troops may be necessary to consolidate our power ? "

Wolseley landed in England on May 24th, and the last entry in his South African diary runs : " This is the Queen's birthday. God bless her and preserve her from the dangers in which Mr. Gladstone's policy is certain sooner or later to involve the country.[1] She has been taught by those who dislike me to regard me as a Radical. I think she would change her opinion if she read my journal."

[1] In the General Election in the spring of 1880 the Liberals gained a large majority.

CHAPTER VII

QUARTERMASTER-GENERAL · EGYPT, 1882

ON his return from South Africa Wolseley found
his popularity at its height. For seven years
he had been the odd-job man of his country.
In administration he had not been so happy as in
the field, but his employers were not going to expose
the defects of policies when he had been their agent,
and the public only knew of a prompt, thorough, successful, and withal economical, soldier. The man in the
street was also vaguely conscious that reform of the
Army was very necessary, and was prepared to back
its champion, the more so because he was believed to
be leading a gallant assault upon strongly entrenched
vested interests. So Beaconsfield's sobriquet was
affectionately attached to his name, and the popular
Press, greatly to the Duke's annoyance, hailed him
as "our only general". "All Sir Garnet" became
the fashionable cockney synonym for "all correct".
Gilbert, in the *Pirates of Penzance*, poked fun at
his attainments, and any doubt as to the amiable
satirist's target was removed on the first night,
when Mr. George Grossmith appeared as the
"modern major-general" in a make-up instantly
recognised both by stalls and gallery. The "envy,
hatred, and all uncharitableness" was for a while
confined to the Horse Guards, other objectors to
reform directing their wrath mainly against Cardwell.
Both parties in the State claimed Wolseley as an

asset ; the Liberals knew him as a devoted supporter of Cardwell and an opponent of the more conservative elements in the Army ; Beaconsfield had enlisted him to exploit the acquisition of Cyprus and to remove some of the tarnish from his South African policy.

If Wolseley was disposed to class Mr. Gladstone as a "Little Englander", the Prime Minister [1] was determined to make the utmost use of a soldier whom he rated very high. Many of the Cardwell reforms were still in the mould, and those in being were certain to be attacked in Parliament, the Opposition benches holding many members with just sufficient military experience to give a savour of authority to their criticism. Gladstone remembered the fierce storm which had raged round the abolition of purchase, and Cardwell's difficulties. In November 1870 Cardwell had written to him : " I am painfully conscious of the impossible situation in which I am placed, as regards military knowledge, and consequent power of dealing with military subjects. I have spared no pains to learn all I could, and the more I know, the more conscious I am how small a proportion it bears to what must be known if the Department is to be properly represented in Parliamentary discussion. If there is no soldier in the House of Commons who can speak with that sort of knowledge which springs from a life spent in the service, the Government will come to grief. With such a soldier I should be very ready to undertake what a lawyer ought to answer for. If the Surveyor - General were in Parliament he would answer all Ordnance questions." [2]

The harassed War Minister, Mr. Childers, found himself, like Cardwell, in sore need of help in the House. To round off the scheme of localisation of

---

[1] Mr. Gladstone took office in April 1880.
[2] *Lord Cardwell at the War Office*, Biddulph, p. 102.

the Army, the territorial connection must be made more definite ; a closer link must be forged between the parts of the same regiment than had existed by grouping together battalions with different numbers. The line regiments were therefore to assume titles derived from the counties whence their men mostly came, titles they were to share with the militia and volunteer battalions of that county. This meant that the numbers of the line battalions which had historical associations very dear to their officers were to be abolished, and—a still more deadly blow—to simplify the clothing of the reservists on mobilisation, the cherished facings were removed. The outcry was long and loud. The battalion was to the regimental officer his military home ; he had then no sentiment about the regiment — a War Office innovation—and he knew little and cared less about mobilisation. He had been brought up to think his battalion the best in the Army, and the idea of bearing the same name and wearing the same dress as the officers of another battalion was repugnant to him. Some of the links made were a little clumsy, and between many battalions of regiments there existed a sense of dislike and jealousy to last many years, and not wholly to disappear until the Great War adduced fresh associations and larger ideas.

The new Quartermaster-General strongly backed the War Minister in effecting these changes, and contumely and reproach were soon turned against him. He was told that he had little regimental service, and that he did not understand or value the importance of regimental tradition ; Cardwell, now a sick man, ceased to be the chief target for the abuse of the military clubs, and Sir Garnet was to be shot at in his stead. As a matter of fact Wolseley set a very high value on regimental *esprit de corps*, but he put the efficiency of the Army even higher. He had himself penned the opening sentences of the report of the Localisation Committee of 1872 :

" The sole object of any military system is to provide for a state of war, and the test of any peace organisation must be its power :

" *1st.* To place in the field immediately on the outbreak of war, in the best possible state of efficiency, as large a force as is possible compatibly with the peace military expenditure.

" *2nd.* To maintain that force throughout the continuance of hostilities undiminished in numbers and efficiency."

That test he would apply to every part of our military system, and where regimental tradition could not pass it he sought to make the smaller interest give way to the larger. As Quartermaster-General he did his best to adapt the dress of the Army for work in the field ; the times were not ripe even to whisper of anything except scarlet for the soldier's service dress, but Wolseley was able to limit the activities of the military tailors and to convince a few people that there were considerations of greater importance than the fascination of nursemaids. He agreed to do away with the facings because it was impossible to provide stores of clothing for mobilisation if every battalion were dressed differently, not because he had any wish to remove prized distinctions.

Mr. Gladstone, thirsting to help Childers, and finding but scanty military support, hit upon the expedient of conferring a peerage on the one prominent soldier advocate of the changes he wanted to carry through, so that he might have some one to reply to critics in the House of Lords. Early in 1881 he asked Sir H. Ponsonby, the Queen's private secretary, to sound Her Majesty on the subject. The answer was prompt and peremptory. From Windsor came a telegram : " Such a thing has never been forced upon me, and cannot and must not be. Under any circumstances it must not and cannot be now." Gladstone tried again and again to alter the Queen's decision, but found her adamant, and in the end he had to give way, because he was wrong and the Queen right. It is astonishing that a statesman of Mr. Gladstone's experience should have thought it possible that an officer serving in the War Office, or indeed any officer in employment, could be used to answer for the policy of the Government of the day while retaining his military position. The Queen was willing to give Sir Garnet a peerage, but was determined that he should not, while he was Quartermaster-General, go to the House of Lords to serve Gladstone's particular purpose. Wolseley had but a vague knowledge of what was afoot. He heard from the Premier that it was proposed to make him a peer, and he would not refuse a well-earned reward, but he knew nothing of the political service he was to render in return, except that he was to take part in military debates in the House of Lords which, within well-defined limits, he was prepared to do. In August 1881 he wrote somewhat naïvely to Mr. Childers : " I had a note from Mr. Gladstone yesterday evening, in which he tells me that he finds it necessary to postpone making me a peer for the present, but that his promise on the subject still holds good. When Sir H. Ponsonby, by order of the Queen, spoke to me on the subject, he said that H.M.'s only objection to my being made a peer was my holding the position of Q.M.G. If I were not Q.M.G. she would have no objection whatever. I hope that you will pardon me for suggesting that I should be given some other military employment. The post I now hold is a sinecure. When the functions allotted to the Q.M.G. were taken away from him in 1871-2 the post itself was retained merely as a concession to the wishes of the Duke, a point upon which I think

Lord Northbrook can give you the fullest information. I have long felt that I occupy an anomalous position at Army Headquarters, and I know that were my post abolished things would go much more smoothly than at present, for I am certainly a fifth wheel to the military coach. Holding the Liberal views that I do, I can do very little good under an Adjutant-General of the Duke's selection, and if my office were abolished, a considerable saving would be effected. Lord Napier's turn at Gibraltar will very shortly be up, and if you thought me worthy to succeed him, I should be very glad indeed under present circumstances to exchange my position as Q.M.G. for that of Governor of Gibraltar. In that position, from what Sir H. Ponsonby told me, I am sure that the Queen would withdraw all her opposition to my being made a peer, and I could take part in any Army discussion in the House of Lords as Lord Napier has been in the habit of doing. Indeed I feel that I should be a much freer man and better able to help you than I should ever be as a peer occupying my present position as Q.M.G."

But this was not in the least what the Government wanted ; they had no intention of allowing so staunch an ally to stray from the War Office. The Army programme of 1881 passed through Parliament, the numbers gave place to territorial titles, flogging was abolished, and the Army Act of that year completed the work begun two years previously, and inaugurated a new era in military discipline. So the Government's need of assistance in Parliament ceased to be pressing, and the matter of the peerage lapsed.

Meanwhile, as his letter to Childers indicated, Wolseley's position within the War Office was not comfortable. He was pressing for reforms which his superiors were determined to burke; he was impotent to force through what he knew to be imperatively necessary. None the less his experiences in South

Africa had not made him in the least anxious to exchange a military for a political career, and at this time he rejected a proposal that he should become a candidate for a division of Edinburgh. " I am so convinced of the necessity of great reforms in our Army ", he wrote, " that my inability to act upon the suggestion causes me all the deeper regret." For the moment he had his work cut out to prevent the stifling of such reforms as had been adopted. The Duke could not stomach the Reserve. He told Wolseley in 1881 : " I hear from the Adjutant-General that some men of the Army must be allowed to go to the Reserve, as we are so much above establishment. I deplore this from my heart, for the Army is in such a transition stage that the less we muddle about with it the better ; moreover, drafts will soon largely be required for India. But at all events there cannot be a doubt *that not a man* should be allowed to go to the Reserve that we are able to utilise. . . . Do not let us sacrifice the Army, our *first line*, to the Reserve, which we are never allowed to see nor will except during a great European war, which we are not likely to take part in. Our object, whatever our views may be, must be the *good of the public service*, not the carrying out of theories." Within fourteen months of writing this letter the Duke was both to see the Reserve and to acknowledge handsomely the fine part it played.

This constant struggle within the War Office could not escape sharp eyes outside, and in the Press there began an agitation that Wolseley should be named Adjutant-General and given power to speed up the work of reform. Some of the remarks made about the Duke were not flattering, and he was not unnaturally hurt by them, while mischief-makers were quick to hint to him that Wolseley had been inspiring the papers. Major FitzGeorge, the Duke's eldest son, wisely informed Wolseley, who promptly sought an interview with the Commander-in-Chief. He told FitzGeorge :

" I had a satisfactory interview with His Royal Highness, and was very glad I acted upon your advice. I tried to impress upon him how impossible it would have been for me in the position which I occupied to have seen him earlier on the subject of the newspaper articles that had given him pain. In the first instance it was some time before I knew that I had been put down as the author or inspirer of the articles, and when I was told it by Mr. Childers I said to him frankly that I felt it insulting to me to imagine I had anything to do with them.

" I think it is rather hard that I should be set down as the author or inspirer of everything that appears in the Press against the administration of the Army. But let that pass ; I urged as strongly as I could that in my opinion it would have been most indelicate of me to have seen the Duke about articles discussing me as Adjutant-General: it would have looked as if I wished to ask for the berth, or to force myself upon His Royal Highness. I had never asked any one for it : if I had asked any one for it I should have gone straight to the Duke, although I should have felt, of course, that he would not have given it to me. It would be false modesty on my part were I to conceal the fact that I think that I should have been very hardly used had any one else been given the place and so put over my head, for I do not know any one who has seen the service I have seen, but still as Lord Ripon's application to have me made C.-in-C. in India had been refused, I thought it likely that my claims to be A.G. would have similarly been put on one side. I should not be human if I did not remember this fact about the India command, and *that* also, about my peerage, and the way I was dealt with upon my return last year from South Africa.

" Like other men I laugh when I am tickled, I bleed when I am pricked, and I am prone to hit back at the man who hit or pricked me. I have served under many general officers to whom I have been frank and as loyal as one man can be to another : but then they trusted me, and I think you will agree with me when I say no loyalty can be expected where no confidence is extended.

" I have freely stated to you some of what I feel are *my* grievances ; I am not ungrateful for kindness shown to me : on the contrary, I think that my worst enemy—and I have some powerful ones— must admit that I have always stood by those who have ever shown me kindness in my eventful career. His Royal Highness has showered good things upon others round me : every appointment *I* get, every honour *I* receive, I am made to feel comes to me from other quarters than from the Commander-in-Chief, to whom I would fain look for some recognition of my services, but I have hitherto looked in vain.

" I am very grateful to you for having interested yourself in my affairs. I feel I can be very useful to the Duke, and I am confident that it rests with His Royal Highness to say whether or not he will use me for the work he wishes to have done.

" I have written about myself, but I have only the interests of the Army at heart, and I think it to be of great consequence that there should be the closest trust and confidence between the Commander-in-Chief and his Adjt.-Generals."

At the end of 1881 General Ellice was due to vacate the office of Adjutant-General, and Mr. Childers had no doubt or hesitation as to who should fill his place. The Duke flatly declined to recommend Wolseley to the Queen : the strength of the Quarter-master-General's hand had been sufficiently manifest ; in the higher post that hand might prove irresistible. Childers had, however, steeled his mind against argument, and knew that the Queen—whatever her personal feelings—would never allow the Army to be deprived of the best man available. The Press was solid—and very vocal—behind the Minister. A rather childish compromise was eventually arranged. The Duke intimated that circumstances had rendered it "rather awkward" for him to recommend Sir Garnet except officially. Mr. Childers was therefore to submit the name to the Queen, who would refer it to the Duke, who would say that he had no objection to offer. The Minister accordingly suggested, the Queen's private secretary referred, the Commander-in-Chief did not object, and Sir Garnet, to general approval, became Adjutant-General. Clothed with his new authority he at once busied himself in examining the new-born system of mobilisation, and in the midst of his investigations there came the opportunity to test what good had been done and to discover what defects remained to be remedied.

On June 26th, 1879, the Sultan of Turkey had deposed Ismail Pasha, whose son Tewfik he made Khedive of Egypt in his place. Tewfik found himself ruler of a discontented people; his treasury was empty, and his army in ferment. Turkey's efforts to strengthen her hold on Egypt precipitated trouble, and in February 1882 a revolt of the army was headed by a Colonel Arabi, a man of peasant origin, who hated the Pashas and their ways. Great Britain and France despatched fleets to Alexandria to protect their numerous subjects, and a small body of British troops under Sir A. Alison was subsequently sent to Cyprus to be ready to intervene. From the beginning of the year, Wolseley, who had been kept informed by Brackenbury, then Military Attaché in Paris, of the political currents, had made up his mind that a campaign was inevitable. He was not in the least disturbed in his opinion by the Secretary for War informing the Commander-in-Chief early in May that no military action towards Egypt had been decided upon ; he was confirmed in that opinion when he heard a month later that the Cabinet had requested the War Secretary to make the most confidential enquiries in the prospect of sending British troops to Egypt. Facts and figures were quickly forthcoming from the Adjutant-General. He had carefully and constantly presided over a Mobilisation Committee charged to discuss, and decide, every detail of forming and equipping a force of prescribed strength to be landed in Egypt at short notice.

The Egyptian unrest came to a head in serious riots at Alexandria on June 11th under the guns of the Anglo-French fleet, but with the admirals impotent to interfere. In this *émeute* the British Consul was dragged out of his carriage and severely injured, the Greek Consul-General and the French Consular Dragoman were badly mauled, and nearly a hundred lives were lost. It was impossible for the Government to shut their eyes to this incident, or to hide from public knowledge that a mutiny was threatening a great highway of the world, and our own far-reaching interests in Egypt. Four weeks had been spent in leisurely Cabinet deliberations and ineffective parleys with France, Italy, and the Porte, when negotiations suddenly gave way on July 11th to a noisy naval operation against which Wolseley had emphatically protested. The bombardment of Alexandria was authorised on the ground that Arabi's work upon the defences of the place endangered the fleets; it was an act of useless violence, no less distasteful to the soldier than to the Quaker statesman, Mr. Bright, who promptly retired from the Cabinet. The French fleet, refusing to participate, sailed away. The town was badly

knocked about, and would have fared worse but for
the failure of many of the naval shells to explode,
blood ran freely in the streets, some ugly things were
done in the confusion, and no sound British purpose
was served.   Nevertheless the Lords of the Admiralty
were much elated : they cherished the belief that
the trouble was over, that Arabi had fled, and that
it only remained to land Alison's troops and let them
occupy positions on the Canal under the aegis of the
Navy.   Wolseley hotly protested against any body
of soldiers being under any other than military
command, and against minor enterprises which, he
asserted, would involve unwarrantable risks and
prejudice the issue.   A military campaign was now
a moral certainty, and he himself was fully prepared
with his own plan which designated Ismailia as his
springboard.[1] On July 20th Mr. Childers could state
that the Cabinet had approved of the expedition
of a force of all arms and of the strength prescribed
under military advice, that Sir Garnet Wolseley had
been recommended to the Queen for the chief command, with Sir John Adye as Chief of the Staff—
the latter having a dormant commission in his pocket
to succeed—in the event of casualty—the man who
was his junior by many years.   The Duke of Cambridge murmured against his Adjutant-General being
taken away, and fumed over the Government's
selection of Adye, but agreed with good grace to
the Divisional and Brigade Commanders whom
Wolseley proposed to him.   The Prince of Wales
at once sought an interview with the Commander-
in-Chief elect and begged to be allowed to accompany
the field force to Egypt.   Wolseley did not refuse

[1] On July 3rd Wolseley wrote a memorandum in which he fore-
casted the move to Ismailia, a decisive action in the neighbourhood
of Tel-el-Kebir, and a prompt pursuit to Cairo (*Military History of
the Campaign of 1882*, p. 5).   The day before he left England he put
the probable date of the battle of Tel-el-Kebir at September 15th.
It was fought on September 13th.

the request, although he thought—and wrote—that unattached Royal personages could scarcely pull their weight in the field. The Sovereign, however, after consultation with officials both within and without the Government, resolutely vetoed the idea, and it was only after much hesitation and many tears that a consent was wrung from her that her third son, the Duke of Connaught, should command the Brigade of Guards. Her cousin, the Duke of Teck, father of the future Queen Consort, an amiable Prince who had seen some service in Austria, was attached to the Headquarters Staff and detailed to look after the foreign attachés.

An Order in Council summoned to the colours nearly 12,000 men of the 1st class Army Reserve, whose prompt response testified to the success of the new system. The army corps to take the field was formed of two divisions, the 1st under Lieutenant-General Willis, with the Duke of Connaught and Major-General Graham as Brigadiers, and the 2nd under Lieutenant-General Sir Edward Hamley, his Brigadiers being Sir Archibald Alison with the Highlanders, and Sir Evelyn Wood, who, to his great indignation, was to be left in charge at Alexandria. Major-General Drury Lowe led a cavalry division composed of a British cavalry brigade under Sir Baker Russell and one of Indian cavalry under Brigadier-General C. M. Wilkinson. Colonel Goodenough was the Brigadier of Artillery, with two horse and six field batteries, and Colonel Nugent was the C.R.E. An Indian contingent was also formed under Sir H. Macpherson, composed of two British and three native infantry battalions. The number of troops embarked from England was 16,400, while 14,400 more came from India and the Mediterranean. The strength of Arabi's army was 60,000 Egyptian troops and some 6000 Bedouins.

The troops from England set out on August 1st

amid manifestations of their popularity, but the Commander-in-Chief's departure for the scene of action was somewhat inglorious. He caught cold in the train after bidding the Queen farewell at Osborne and developed erysipelas, an affliction which rendered him very unsightly in appearance and not a little anxious as to whether he would recover in time to assume his command. It was eventually decided by the doctors that although a rapid journey overland might prove most injurious, a sea trip with its inevitable rest for body and mind would probably act as a restorative, a prescription the more readily endorsed by Wolseley as it would obviate the "send-off" he always disliked. The Duke of Cambridge wrote a cordial note of God-speed; the Prince of Wales called to say good-bye but could not be admitted to the sickroom, and Wolseley would not brook the few hours' delay which would have enabled the Prince to come on board the transport at Cowes as he wished to do.

On the 2nd August Sir Garnet slipped quietly down to the docks and, accompanied by Colonel Herbert Stewart, destined to be Chief of the Staff of the Cavalry Division, embarked on board the *Calabria* with half the Household Cavalry Regiment. He was about to play the leading part in what was sure to be a rather "showy" campaign, and he remembered that precisely thirty years ago he had embarked from the same docks for India on a sailing vessel. " I was then an ensign," he noted in his diary, " having only just joined the depot of the 80th Regiment, and I had myself taught the manual and platoon exercise on board. I often hear men say they would like to live their lives over again. I say emphatically ' No ! ' I would like to live again such a day as when I was wounded in Burma, *e.g.* March 1853, but I shudder at the thought of having to go through my whole experiences."

146

At Gibraltar the veteran Governor, Lord Napier, climbed with some difficulty on board the transport, bringing the news that the French had definitely refused co-operation, that the Turks were unlikely to lend an active hand, and that Alison had frittered away a few lives in a reconnaissance of Arabi's position,—items which increased Sir Garnet's impatience with the slow passage his ship was making. From Malta, where he heard that his difficulties would be increased by Arabi having occupied Nefiche junction near Ismailia, he sent a peremptory telegram to Adye—who had proceeded by short sea to Alexandria—that no sort of action was to be taken until the Commander-in-Chief should arrive on the spot. Arabi must be met and mastered with one swinging blow, and to deliver that blow the main force would be required—with the cavalry to follow it up. He had little doubt as to the result of a pitched battle, but he did not believe his opponent to be an ignorant coward, as some wiseacres sought to represent; Arabi had, indeed, shown no little moral and political courage in plotting his rebellion, and no little skill in carrying it into effect and in his subsequent movements.

Wolseley's plan of campaign was as simple as it was sound; the only complication he really feared was interference with his water supply, and for this reason he regretted that the Navy should have drawn attention to the Canal. He had made no stipulation with the Government, but he understood that in carrying out its policy he would have a free hand, and the Queen, through her private secretary, encouraged him in this idea.

On the 17th August, the day after his arrival at Alexandria, his proposals were unfolded to, and entirely approved by, the Admiral in command of the Mediterranean Fleet in a conference which was practically a *tête-à-tête*. The attention of the enemy was to be diverted by a feigned attack on Aboukir and by activities on the part of the troops to be left at Alexandria under Evelyn Wood, whom Wolseley was certain would not let the grass grow under his feet. Meanwhile the main force would be

Troops to leave all baggage and the mens valise bags &c at Ismaillia

Officers to have tents & regulation cooking things carried for them — nothing else.

70 203 in pouches.

30 203 per man, 1st reserve on camels. (six boxes on 3 mules).

43 S·A·A· Carts to carry 2d reserve (with 2 horses each

1000 boxes to be on a R.R train — say 36 tons weight on 7 trucks

men to carry one day rations

? — Their great coats to be carried in carts

·· 2 days ration to be carried in carts & if possible

2 Hospital per man.
5 days rations, to be in R.R. train

FACSIMILE OF PART OF WOLSELEY'S NOTES FOR THE MOVEMENT
TO ISMAILIA.

transported to the Canal and disembarked at Ismailia, which would be the point of departure for the attack on Arabi's stronghold at Tel-el-Kebir, and the march to Cairo. The success of the move would lie largely in secrecy, and it was decided that neither to Sir E. Malet, who had just been appointed High Commissioner with precedence over the heads of both fighting services, nor, till the last moment, to his own generals, should the decision be disclosed. Alexandria was full of spies, who reported every rumour to the rebel leader, and Wolseley, taking the same measures to deceive the Press correspondents which he had employed in Ashanti, ostentatiously announced that his destination was Aboukir, where he would land as soon as he had silenced the forts.[1] When the concentration at Ismailia was complete, Childers was loud in his congratulations on the well-kept secret, though he had been a little nettled that he had heard nothing of the conference itself of which Seymour had told the First Lord. The Duke of Cambridge, equally forward in felicitations, was also sore at having been kept in the dark. " I think you were very wise and right ", he wrote, " in giving out that you were going to attack Aboukir while your real point was Port Said and the Canal, but I don't know if it was judicious of the Staff Officer to assemble the correspondents and tell them by authority you were doing so. I would not have told them anything, but if they proposed to telegraph anything you did not wish known, I would have desired them to omit it from the telegram. . . . I only name this to you as it strikes me, and it has been taken up by the Press."

On the afternoon of the 19th the ironclads and transports made sail for Aboukir, the former clearing

[1] " I have been dining again with the ' swell of the ocean', Sir Beauchamp Seymour. He is a *bon vivant* with a large stomach. The Government at home are very anxious for me to push on and do something : they seem to think that the moment troops have been despatched from England, we ought to do something, forgetting that ships take 14 to 15 days in coming here.
" It is very amusing that General Hamley who commanded the 2nd Division, and Generals Alison and Wood who command the two Brigades of that Division, are under the firm conviction that we mean to attack here on Sunday and that they are to take part in the attack : I am leaving sealed orders to be opened by Hamley at daybreak on Sunday morning in which I tell him the whole thing is a humbug and that my real destination is the Canal."—W. to Lady W.

for the imaginary action ; [1] at nightfall the whole fleet turned sharply eastward, the transports led by H.M.S. *Salamis*, with the Commander-in-Chief on board, entering the Canal next morning. The disembarkation at Ismailia began forthwith, Wolseley taking up his headquarters at the Governor's house, that subtle Oriental assuring him that he had been appointed to his post *malgré lui*, and that his heart was with the Khedive.

A minor duty, quickly accomplished, was to smooth down and bring to his proper bearings M. de Lesseps, who had put every possible obstacle in the way of our entering the Canal, but had been treated somewhat cavalierly by the Navy.[2]

On the 24th came the first brush with the enemy on the new front. As Wolseley had feared, the water supply was being arrested by dams which it was necessary to destroy. A small advanced guard was therefore promptly sent forward along the Sweet Water Canal, and it found a strong force of Egyptians sitting in a well-chosen position near Tel-el-Mahuta. The advanced guard kept the enemy in play, but late in the afternoon Wolseley decided that as the Guards and other reinforcements ordered up could not arrive before sundown, he would postpone his attack till the morrow, although the morrow would be a Friday, a day which he disliked for taking action. Before morning, however, the enemy had slid out of Tel-el-Mahuta, and the cavalry pushing on found and occupied—with little opposition —a camp at Masama Station well furnished with food and ammunition. " I shall make for Kassasin

[1] Wolseley wanted the fleet to aid his deception by opening fire, if only with blank cartridges, upon the forts round Aboukir Bay. The Admiral refused on the ground that it was not the custom of the Navy to make demonstrations of this nature.

[2] M. de Lesseps' one preoccupation was for his canal, and if he hampered us in one way he helped us greatly in another by assuring Arabi that if he left the Canal alone neither France nor Italy would intervene.—*Official History*, p. 16.

Lock at once and get water ", Wolseley had written from Alexandria, and on the 26th Graham with two infantry regiments, some 50 sabres, 70 M.I., and two guns, took possession of the lock and the supply of water was there and then fully secured. Two evenings later the Commander-in-Chief was startled, but not dismayed, by a telegram from Willis that Graham was being hard pressed and threatened with defeat.[1] " Willis is a very plucky fellow personally but an alarmist ", Wolseley curtly but correctly remarked. He arranged to start at three o'clock the next morning for Kassasin, and while dressing at 2 A.M. heard the true story, which was one of complete success. Arabi had nerved himself to try conclusions with Graham and had disposed himself to turn the ridge behind which lay the British right wing. He brought two heavy guns on railway trucks to within 4000 yards of the British troops, and had these been well served he might have done considerable damage.

Drury Lowe at Masama had turned out in the morning, and returned to camp at noon to hear by helio, at four o'clock, that the enemy was advancing in force. Graham's galloper, an excitable young cavalry officer, had conveyed to Lowe the erroneous impression that his General was hard pressed and only just able to hold his own. When this unduly alarmist message was received, Drury Lowe was, as a matter of fact, about to take the cavalry round by the right and attack the Arab left flank. The Brigade made a wide circuit until within a few hundred yards of the enemy, when the gallop was sounded and the attack, known in story and very poor verse as " The Moon-

[1] From General Willis at Tel-el-Mahuta to Sir G. Wolseley, Ismailia : " Enemy advancing on Masama station. Fear Graham is defeated ; will do all I can and hold on but send up available reinforcements." The circumstances which led to the despatch of this message and deceived General Willis are described in the *Official History*, p. 62.

light Charge ", was launched. Graham himself was in ignorance of what was going on in this part of the field, but had thought it wise to order a general advance. The Egyptians did not await the infantry, but, thrown into disorder by the attentions of the mounted troops which seriously threatened their flank, broke and bolted, being pursued towards their lines in pitch darkness.

A pause of some days now occurred—Arabi was occupied in fortifying the position at Tel-el-Kebir, the spot indicated by his opponent before leaving England as the probable scene of the final struggle; Sir Garnet was engaged with questions of transport and supply, his tactics having been already settled, and his troops being disposed for the day of reckoning with Arabi.

Like many great artists about to play an important part, he was outwardly quite calm but inwardly fevered with anxiety. He knew that his military reforms were about to be tested in the field; for the first time battalions would march to battle seasoned with men of that Reserve of which he had been an uncompromising advocate. He fancied that his enemies would feel compensation for defeat in an exhibition of his own failure. His railway line served him badly, and although the stores were lying on the quay, the troops twenty miles off were short of food. " The next time I come on any expedition ", he wrote, " I shall insist upon having a full staff of engine - drivers, traffic - managers, etc.[1] The R.E. are most willing and anxious, but railway management is a trade in itself; it cannot be learnt in a day, and special knowledge will not serve as a substitute for it." His staff, and especially his Chief of Staff, did not, he thought, fully realise the always present

[1] Two months later the intention of converting some companies of R.E. into a Railway Corps was announced in the House of Commons, with permanent cadres which could be rapidly expanded when required for active service.

difficulties of transport and supplies ; if he refrained
from an " I told you so ", he remembered how often
he had pleaded the necessity of every unit embarking
complete with its equipment and regimental transport, only to be pooh-poohed by Adye among others,
and told that men could go out in one ship, the stores
in another, and transport be handed over after
landing.[1] " I have all along said", Wolseley wrote
to Lady Wolseley, " that picking up hundreds or
thousands of mules did not constitute a transport.
The drivers whom we obtain are the *canaille* of the
Levantine towns, and we really have no authority
over them. To buy a canvas and a paint-box is not
to have a picture."

On the 7th September Sir Garnet could, however,
write confidently to the Duke of Cambridge :

" . . . I have now seven locomotives at work,
and the army front is consequently well supplied,
and the foundations of a reserve depot have been
laid down. I am consequently about to bid farewell
to Ismailia and form my camp at Kassasin on
Saturday—the day after to-morrow. Every one
will be in motion for the front at the same time, and
by the time I have pushed my reconnaissances
sufficiently well home and made my first plans, all
will be concentrated and ready for an advance upon
the enemy on Tuesday or Wednesday week (the
12th or 13th inst.) as the date of our ' grand event ',
and I hope to keep my appointment if I do not
forestall it. Arabi has about 30,000 regular troops
at Tel-el-Kebir,[2] besides an unknown number of
Bedouins : but of these regular troops many are

[1] " I hope the English people will be pleased," he wrote when it
was all over; " they can never know the difficulties an English
commander has to struggle against, with an army hastily thrown
together, without cohesion between its component parts, and no
organised transport."

[2] Arabi afterwards gave his strength at Tel-el-Kebir as 20,000
men and 75 guns, but in these figures some 6000 Bedouins were not
included.

old men recalled to serve after many years passed in civil life, who know nothing about rifles or any sort of new drill. We have taken some of these poor old creatures prisoners, and they can be of no use to Arabi whatever. In guns, I am not yet certain of his strength : some weeks ago he had only 36, but I am inclined to think he will now have over 60, perhaps 72. If he has not any large guns in position I don't mind ; but if he has heavy guns in his works I shall rush them at night. I have not yet told any one here this, but I have made up my mind it is best to do this with my inferior numbers : to attack a battery of large guns entrenched, by daylight, would entail a very heavy loss. I calculate that I shall take into action between 11,000 and 11,500 infantry, 2500 sabres, and 60 guns. If he were only out in the open I should only laugh at his numbers ; but then he has been for months past entrenching this position of Tel-el-Kebir, and he knows every inch of the ground, as it used to be at one time the place where the annual manœuvres took place. My troops, man for man, are equal and quite equal to ten times their own number of Egyptians, so notwithstanding advantage in position, etc., etc., I have no doubt whatever of the result. An old billiard-master who taught me to play billiards used to impress upon me never to play for any stroke I was not prepared to bet 6 to 5 on being able to accomplish, and I should say the betting was much more than that now in our favour. I never saw troops in better spirits, or looking better or healthier. The percentage of sick to-day was 2.9, which is about one-half what it is in England, and the climate is daily improving. To please the Navy I am taking a Naval Brigade with me : Sir Beauchamp Seymour and all under him have been helping us so cordially that I thought Your Royal Highness would like me to ask for their services.

" Long before this can reach England the result of our attack will be known at home, so I feel like a sort of Rip Van Winkle in writing what I have.

" *P.S.*—The military representatives of foreign powers are now beginning to put in an appearance."

On September 9th, Arabi, with 8000 men and 24 guns, sallied out from behind his fortifications and made what he knew must be his last attempt to rush Kassasin before the arrival of the Indian contingent and Highland Brigade should complete the British rendezvous. The attack, amateurish in design, was pushed with no little vigour, and both combatants enjoyed an opportunity of trying their respective artillery. Wolseley arrived on the scene a little before noon to find Willis within 5000 yards of the enemy's works and our cavalry nearly round their left flank. The Divisional General was un-decided as to whether he should follow the enemy into their entrenchments, stay on his ground, or retire to his camp. Wolseley had no doubt what-ever. He ordered a strong outpost to be left on the hill from which the enemy had opened fire, and the rest of the force to return to camp. " If Willis had pushed on ", he wrote to Lady Wolseley, " our losses would have been enormous, we might have failed—probably should—and even if he had suc-ceeded, his success would have ruined all my plans of saving Cairo by a forced march on that place. I had little more than half the troops up with which I meant to fight Arabi, and to have attempted to strike him hard before I was fully ready to follow up my success—even assuming I could obtain one with half my force—would have been most stupid. I have impressed on Mr. Childers that I mean to make my next action final if I can. I mean to follow it up, and if possible to save Cairo from the fate of Alexandria. This I can only do by pushing forward my cavalry to that place, via Belbeis, and my infantry to Zagazig the instant I have taken the position at Tel-el-Kebir.''

The Headquarters were now transferred to Kassasin, and the next two mornings Wolseley was out at daybreak reconnoitring the enemy's position, which had been carefully chosen and skilfully fortified. The front, about four miles in length, was made up of soft earthworks with hurdle revetments ; at well-selected intervals along the line redoubts mounted with guns were so placed as to deliver front and flanking fire, and connected by trenches. In support of the front lines, redoubts crowned some natural elevations artificially strengthened, the flanks being similarly protected. At dawn on the 12th Wolseley took all the general officers to the front and handed to each of them a copy of the disposition of the troops as they were to form up that evening, together with his plan of attack. None of his juniors raised any verbal objection to his plan of night advance, though more than one appeared concerned at the idea. The battle of Tel-el-Kebir set a fashion, and after 1882 night operations were assiduously practised ; but before then little had been done to accustom British soldiers to move in the dark, and some of Wolseley's Generals had doubted the wisdom of trying an experiment so bold. But the Commander-in-Chief had no doubts at all. He had satisfied himself that the open sandy ground in front of Arabi's earthworks offered no obstacle which could disturb the progress of his army, he was pretty sure that the enemy kept a bad look-out at night, and he counted on the full value of a surprise. '' I know '', he had told Herbert Stewart, '' what the best troops feel and do when suddenly surprised at night ; a surprise means a panic, and a panic under such circumstances means a general stampede, and the side which is sufficiently well drilled, disciplined, and handled to enable it to make an attack at night will generally succeed, whether the enemy be surprised or not."

Camp was struck that evening as soon as the light failed, and all baggage was piled along the railway so as to be easily loaded into carriages and sent off to the troops. The order of battle was thus : On the extreme right two batteries of Horse Artillery, and the Cavalry Division ; then Graham's Brigade, supported by the Guards ; in the centre the Field Artillery under Goodenough ; between the guns and the railway was the Highland Brigade under Alison, supported by the King's Royal Rifles and the Duke of Cornwall's ; behind these two battalions came the Marine Artillery and the 19th Husssars ; on the railway was the ironclad train manned by 250 blue-jackets, and on the south side of the canal was drawn up the Indian contingent. The Indian troops under Macpherson were so placed in the valley of the Sweet Water Canal as to prevent a hostile enfilading fire in case the British advance should be held up ; they were ordered to start an hour later than the rest of the line, lest any hurtling through cultivated land should take the edge off the hoped-for surprise. Wolseley wished the assault to be made in two distinct attacks, so that any failure on the part of one should not infect the other. The battery of 42 guns planted in the centre of the second line would, if necessary, be available to repair any mischief on either wing. Great precautions were taken that the troops should keep the right direction in the darkness. Guide-posts were set up to mark their positions for assembly and line of advance, and observations of the stars over the enemy's works had been taken in previous reconnaissances, the guiding of the Highland Brigade being in the hands of Wolseley's naval aide-de-camp, Lieutenant Rawson, a man well accustomed to steer by the stars. Having given his last

157

instructions to Macpherson to push his way to Zagazig as soon as the works were carried, and to Drury Lowe to spare neither man nor horse if Cairo could be preserved from flame, he left camp at ten o'clock at night and joined the army as it was formed up. He rode round the troops, lay down, prayed earnestly for complete success, and slept for four hours. " Who except a man in my position ", he wrote to Lady Wolseley, " can understand my feelings and thoughts as I lay on the ground among the troops, anxiously striking my repeating watch from time to time. It is only those to whom the lives of considerable forces and the honour of one's country have been entrusted who can really know what tension there is on every nerve at such a moment. I fully realised the danger of the operations I had determined upon, and I knew that if I failed every wiseacre in England would have said what a fool I was to have attempted a night attack."

The main body north of the canal moved off from its bivouac at 1.30 A.M. on the 13th, the Commander-in-Chief and his staff marching with the Royal Marine Artillery, who maintained telegraphic communication with the Indian contingent. The night was very dark, there were no sort of landmarks to play the part of guides, and it had proved extremely difficult, even with the help of connecting files, to keep the desired formation ; thus there were checks and delays in the advance which, as it turned out, bore no ill result, but for which Wolseley was inclined to blame, rather sharply, the Divisional Generals. This and a singular chance gave Sir Garnet, standing with his repeater in his hand—it was too dark to see watches—some bad moments. About 4.50 A.M., nearly an hour before dawn was expected, a streak of light appeared in the eastern sky. If day was coming the attack was clearly too late ; the anxiety was poignant. But the light did not broaden, mistakes in formations were corrected, and the troops moved onwards. It was afterwards discovered in Cairo that on this very morning of September 13th a comet had made its first appearance an hour before dawn, choosing its moment in a manner well calculated to maintain the reputation of comets.

The story of the assault on Arabi's trenches has often been told, and the Commander-in-Chief had in it no part to play other than to await the issue with such patience as he could command. By 6 A.M. the battle was over ; Arabi, huddled up in a railway carriage, was trying to make his escape, and the cavalry had started on a sixty-five mile dash to Cairo ; an hour later, on the parapet of Tel-el-Kebir bridge, among a medley of jabbering natives and grunting camels, Sir Garnet wrote his despatch to the Secretary of State, one of the last important documents to which he would affix his Christian name.

Arabi's army had been routed at a cost of 9 officers and 48 men killed, 27 officers and 355 men wounded. After satisfying himself that the pursuit had begun with all vigour, Wolseley's next thought was for his wounded, among whom was gallant Rawson, who had fallen, mortally stricken, at the moment of the first assault. When Sir Garnet found him in a tent crowded with dead and wounded, the dying man said simply to his chief, " Well, sir, I took the Brigade where you told me to ".

Wolseley spent one night at Tel-el-Kebir, and one night in the railway station at Zagazig " devoured by mosquitoes ", and early on the 15th he reached Cairo (which had surrendered to the cavalry the previous evening), taking up his quarters in the Abdin Palace, where, just a year earlier, Arabi, with 4000 troops in the square, had enforced, at the point of the bayonet, his terms on Tewfik.

The positions were now precisely reversed : Arabi, a prisoner in the citadel, was ruefully contemplating the possibility of expiating his offences on the scaffold ; the Khedive was the recipient at Alexandria of a hurricane of cheers which he, perhaps correctly, appraised with the comment, " A month ago they would have cheered as heartily if I had been the prisoner ".

The brilliant little campaign had lasted for three short weeks, and in comparison with later wars sinks into insignificance, but it served to open a new era of prosperity for Egypt, and to set a seal to the system of short service. Wolseley himself had good reason to be satisfied. He had played a bold game, with his own reputation as part of the stakes, and he had won. He had been fully sensible to the impatience of the men who disbelieved in him, and he knew that his detractors were ready to ascribe to him blunders, even before he had had time to commit them. But all and more that he had promised to do he had done, with mathematical precision and with strict economy in both life and treasure.

The entrance into Cairo and the surrender of Arabi were hailed with joy by the Government, which had been in some trepidation before the battle and had offered Wolseley more troops, and drew from Mr. Gladstone not only a telegram announcing the Sovereign's pleasure to confer a peerage on a successful soldier, but a personal letter of almost hysterical congratulations. " I have not ", he wrote, "in the course of a long public life, discharged a more agreeable duty than to-day has fallen to my lot, in proposing to you by telegraph that you should receive a barony in acknowledgement of your splendid services. I will not, while the flush of the accumulated good news is still upon me, trust myself to describe either the interest or the confidence with which I have followed your movements, or the admiration which your masterly conduct awakens in my mind, or the joy with which I contemplate the brilliant success it has pleased Providence to award to you as the crown of your efforts.

" There are a multitude of points which I could mass together in illustration of what I have now said, but I will not waste your precious time with the eulogies of an individual man.

" Heartily wishing for every blessing upon your public career and your personal life . . . ."

Wolseley's reply was duly grateful and cordial in tone, but his pleasure was tempered by the news that an equivalent honour had been bestowed on Sir Beauchamp Seymour for a very minor rôle, and his spirits were chilled by the receipt of a rather frigid personal letter from the Queen.

On the 25th September Cairo held high festival to greet the Khedive. The streets were lined with troops, the bands played, the flags flew, the crowds chattered with excitement, the ladies of the Khedivial household were given a coign of vantage from which to witness the return of their rehabilitated lord, and a great ovation was given to Wolseley, although, by the Queen's desire, the Commander-in-Chief resigned the place of honour in the carriage to the Duke of Connaught, and sat modestly with his back to the horses, by the side of the British Agent. Wolseley wished to make the most of opportunities for ceremonial to impress the people of Cairo, and on September 30th a grand parade of all the troops took place before the Khedive; five days later the occasion of the beginning of the annual journey of the Sacred Carpet from Cairo to Mecca was used for a further military display, and the Mohammedans of the capital were much impressed at the sight of the victorious British troops respectfully saluting the emblems of their faith. Thereafter the force in Egypt was reduced to 10,000 men, and Sir Garnet sailed from Alexandria on October 21st, reaching England a week later.

APPENDIX

Lady Wolseley to Mrs. (afterwards Viscountess) Goschen.

6 HILL STREET, W.,
October 30th, 1882.

MY DEAR MRS. GOSCHEN—You will have been surfeited by the newspapers on the subject of the *reception*, and yet I must give you my dose, of my own mixing, into the bargain. I will let you off Dover, except that after the address and Garnet's cheers, I had three cheers for myself, which I thoroughly enjoyed, and so did Frances.

At Charing Cross the crowd was immense, and if Garnet's campaign is supposed to have set Mr. Gladstone on his legs politically, the return of the hero very nearly carried him off them practically, for the poor old gentleman was sadly pushed and pummelled in the crowd. I saw *him* quite gasping for breath ; I saw Mrs. Childers disappear in a whirlpool of people double her height ; I heard Lord Granville say to me, " This is *your* Tel-el-Kebir ", and I should have liked to say, " Dawdling won't do *here* " ; but in the struggle for life, I don't think I said much to any one. The Duke of Cambridge cleared the way manfully and beautifully for us ; indeed, without him we should never have got into the carriage at all.

We found a bigger crowd outside, and there was a moment when I thought the brougham would have been crushed like an almond shell by the pressure. Then hands thrust in on each side to be shaken, and their owners not to be got rid of without a shake. Luckily we had a policeman running on each side, who kept up manfully till we got half-way up St. James's Street, and the hill which pumped *them* had pumped the crowd also, so we were all right, and only found a pleasant compact little crowd outside our door. Amongst them was an old soldier whom Garnet had carried wounded out of action years ago somewhere.[1] Very pretty of him to come and welcome " my little General ". He is looking *so* well, quite plump and pink and white !

The Prince of Wales sent a minion, a very nice Colonel Clarke, to greet Garnet at Charing Cross, and to invite us to dine at Marlborough House yesterday ; but Balmoral knocked that on the head, and he never managed to get near enough to deliver his message at the station (which I was quite pleased at in my vanity !), and had to send it here instead.

Garnet went off last night to those rocky fastnesses, and will be back Wednesday morning.

[1] Pte. Andrews (see p. 23).

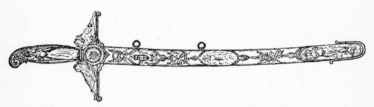

SWORD OF HONOUR PRESENTED BY THE CITY OF LONDON.

CHAPTER VIII

THE ATTEMPT TO SAVE GORDON, 1884-85

WOLSELEY was left in no doubt that the English people were pleased. The neatness and precision of his manœuvres delighted the public as much as they had pleased the Prime Minister, and the greeting he received from all sorts and conditions of men satisfied even his wife. The tribute was largely a personal one, for there was no enthusiasm for an occupation of Egypt. He was promoted full General, and for the second time he received the thanks of both Houses of Parliament, which voted him a grant of £30,000 to gild his coronet. He chose for his title Baron Wolseley of Cairo and Wolseley, a delicate hint to some of his detractors that he came of ancient stock. He received an ovation on walking up the Guildhall to shake hands with the Lord Mayor on November 9th, and the City gave him and his officers a special banquet. He professed to find his speeches a " more terrible thing than a general action ", but got through them with credit. As soon as the Guards were home the Queen held a special review in Hyde Park of the troops of the Expeditionary Force. It was hinted that Mr. Childers as Secretary of State for War should have a place at the review, a hint which caused a flutter among the masters of ceremonies. The troops were to defile past the Queen in column of route, the Generals would all be on horseback, the

Queen sitting in her carriage. A Privy Councillor's silk stockings and pumps would clearly be out of place in such a *milieu*, and the possibility of the appearance of an official top hat was not even considered. Within twenty years Ministers were not only to grace such functions in mufti, but a civilian War Secretary was to be seen complacently taking the salute, the very suggestion of which had been known to induce the Duke's horrified remonstrance.

Wolseley found himself under a cyclone of letters all on the same note. The Sovereigns of Germany and Belgium led a Continental chorus of approval, and at home congratulations rained down. No tribute, however, was more treasured than a blurred note from a pensioner, an old comrade of Burma : " Sir, you whipped Arabi proper. If you led 'em as you led us in Meatoon's, I bet you made the black beggars run ! " And under the glow of success there were inaugurated happier relations with the Sovereign and the Commander-in-Chief. The Queen had been much gratified by Wolseley's outspoken appreciation of the services of the Duke of Connaught, who in his turn had written in the warmest terms about his Commander. The Queen's rather cold letter to Egypt had been composed when she thought that her dear Guards were not being properly cared for. This was cleared up, and her reception of the victorious General was more than cordial. To the surprise of her Court, but not of her guest, whom she had graciously informed of her intention by letter, she proposed Sir Garnet's health at dinner. Wolseley forgot the text of her speech, and the Queen herself wrote it out for Lady Wolseley. In this first interview Wolseley impressed on the Queen, as he had done upon Ministers, that our troubles in Egypt were far from over, and he foretold early difficulties with the Soudan. He had scarcely left Balmoral when the Queen wrote him :

"GLASSART SHIEL, LOCH MUICH, *November 1st,* 1882.—The Queen looked back to the telegram which Sir G. Wolseley [1] sent her—one which caused her and the Duchess of Connaught and all of us such pleasure—and sends him a copy of it ; as he will see, he used the words ' we have suffered severely '. She is so much disturbed to-day by letters from Arthur and Sir J. McNeil speaking of the great sickness amongst the Guards. Arthur has mentioned it in several letters, and he fears that they have complained, and think it his fault they were kept there so long—which it certainly is *not*—and she fears she is as much to blame about that as any one. Only, of course, if we had known they were getting worse we could have altered this and let them come home earlier.

"Arthur says in a letter she got to-day dated 23rd : ' I went all over the hospitals here two days ago, and I regret to say there are a very large number of sick, especially among the Guards. Nearly all the cases are enteric fever, and I am sorry to say that many have ended fatally. Eight men had been buried the day before my visit to the hospital. I have great hopes that the healthier weather of the last few days may bring a change for the better.' Sir Garnet can imagine that the Queen is dreadfully disturbed about this, and she is sure Sir Garnet will be sad too, when comparatively so few were killed. Does he think they are well cared for now ? Could nothing more be done for their comfort ? Nurses sent out, beds obtained ?

"The Queen has telegraphed and written strongly to Mr. Gladstone and Lord Granville to see Sir Garnet without delay upon the failure of the medical arrangements, and on the very critical state of Egypt and the great mistake we are making about Arabi,[2]

[1] Wolseley's patent had not been made out at this date.
[2] A reference to proposals to deal leniently with the rebel commander.

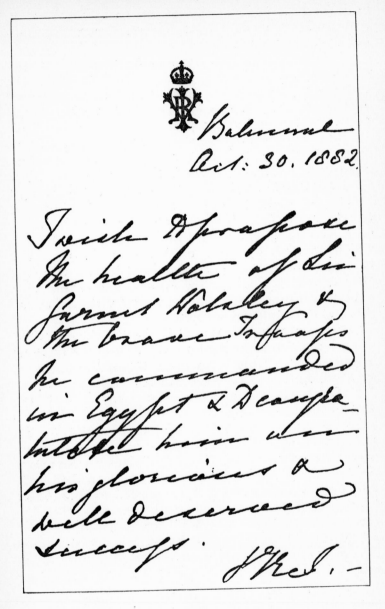

Balmoral
Oct: 30. 1882

I wish to propose
the health of Sir
Garnet Wolseley &
the brave Troops
he commanded
in Egypt & Congratu-
late him on
his glorious &
well deserved
success.

V.R.I. —

and she wishes Sir Garnet to speak as strongly *as he can* on the subject to both Ministers, warning them of the consequences.

" Perhaps Sir Garnet would mention to the Commander-in-Chief what she has written about the sickness of the poor Guards and others. He never anticipated it. The Queen hopes Sir Garnet is not the worse for his hurried journey."

From this time forward the Queen and the Duke of Cambridge found in Wolseley an ally in their opposition to Mr. Gladstone's Egyptian policy, while the Duke had been pleased and touched by Wolseley's action in making Major FitzGeorge his private secretary for the campaign and in sending him home with the despatches [1] — a proof that any ill-will which existed was not on Wolseley's side. The two men were never in the least likely to agree on the question of Army reform, but from 1882 onward mutual suspicion began to yield to something akin to mutual respect.

On re-entering the War Office one of the questions Wolseley found awaiting him was that of the Channel Tunnel. This project had been mooted as far back as 1838, and had received the general approval of Mr. Gladstone's Government in 1871. But the scheme hung fire mainly for business reasons until 1880, when it was taken up energetically by Sir Edward Watkin, Chairman of the London, Chatham, and Dover Railway. One of Wolseley's first acts on becoming Adjutant-General in December 1881 had been to write a strongly worded memorandum condemning the proposal, and this was the first reasoned statement of the military objections. " To assert ", he wrote, " that no such operation as a surprise can be effected without our obtaining ample warning of it, is to assume that the General charged

---

[1] It was then the custom that the officer bringing home the despatches of a successful commander should receive a brevet.

[*Portrait by Frank Holl, R.A.*

GENERAL LORD WOLSELEY, G.C.B., 1883.

To face page 168.

with its accomplishment is as entirely ignorant of the business of war as the man must be who made such an assumption." But Sir Edward Watkin was not a man to give way without fighting, and he continued to pull every string on either side of the Channel upon which he could lay his fingers. Lord Wolseley therefore, early in 1883, returned to the charge. Maurice was asked to draft " Hostilities without Declaration of War ", a long list of cases in which offensive military action had preceded any formal rupture of international relations. In July 1883 a joint Committee of both Houses of Parliament, of which the Marquis of Lansdowne was chairman, reported against the Tunnel, and Wolseley wrote to Maurice : " I send you Lansdowne's report. It is not nearly strong enough, but should suffice to kill Watkin's mad enterprise, if there is any common sense in England. The very fact that the backers of the Tunnel propose to have all sorts of elaborate defences is sufficient to condemn it. We know that there is no so-called ' impregnable ' fortress which has not been captured, and that all plans for destroying the Tunnel depend at the last upon the human element, which is apt to fail at the least convenient time. How many railway tunnels did the French forget to blow up in '70 ? I wish you would write something about this as soon as you can. It is sheer lunacy to link ourselves by railway to the Continent, while we have a small voluntary Army and the other fellows compulsory service." The Channel Tunnel question remained a hardy annual, but to the end of his life Wolseley never changed this opinion.

Though personal relations with the Duke were easier, there was renewed the old struggle to get the men and the means for the work to hand. The Government was not sure that it was necessary to keep a British garrison in Cairo, but on this point military opinion was unanimous. The Duke of Cambridge wrote shrewdly : " I wish you would see Lord Hartington [1] on this subject, for I feel satisfied that the Government contemplate shortly to give up Cairo, and keep a small garrison only at Alexandria. Now, to my mind, no greater mistake could be made. Cairo is virtually *Egypt*, Alexandria is not, and therefore at Cairo we ought to have our troops till the whole organisation of the country has been amended in the spirit and sense in which we went there originally. This does not mean *annexation*, to which I know there would be at present great objections. It simply means benevolent occupation for a long period. When Evelyn Baring [2] reaches his post he is certain for financial reasons and economical ends to press for our departure. This is an additional reason for you doing all you can to counteract this mischief. Alison took this view on your departure, and so does Stephenson [3] now, and you are all three *quite right.*"

Wolseley had not less difficulty in convincing the Government that the re-creation of the Egyptian Army, which had been virtually disbanded on the collapse of Arabi's revolt, should be placed in the hands of British officers ; that accepted, he had even greater difficulty in inducing the War Office to entrust the task to Evelyn Wood, who, as first British Sirdar of the Egyptian Army, set afoot the selection of the body of picked officers who eventually under Kitchener's leadership were to fight their way to Khartoum. A more protracted struggle began with the Commissariat, which, though shorn by Cardwell of some of its powers in 1870, still maintained

---

[1] In December 1882 Childers had become Chancellor of the Exchequer and Lord Hartington (who became 8th Duke of Devonshire in 1891) had succeeded him at the War Office.

[2] Just appointed British Agent and Consul-General.

[3] General F. Stephenson, in command of the British troops in Egypt.

a vigorous existence, and was endeavouring, on the plea that supply was a business, and that soldiers were not and never would be men of business, to recover what it had lost. Wolseley maintained that soldiers, if trusted and allowed training and experience, could be just as careful guardians of the public purse as any civilian administrator; he had proved that this was so in his own campaigns, and he asserted that as only soldiers could deal with the special problems involved in the supply of an army in war, they must surely be given the opportunity of learning their work in peace. The battle was not won till 1888, when by Order in Council the Commander-in-Chief was charged with " obtaining, holding, and issuing to all branches of the forces, food, forage, fuel, and light "; then began a steady improvement of the soldiers' menu in peace, and the system of victualling to be triumphantly vindicated during the Great War, in which the British Army was conspicuously the best fed of any that fought.

From all this laborious office work a trip to Russia in 1883 afforded a pleasant relief. The Duke and Duchess of Edinburgh were to attend the coronation of the Emperor Alexander, and invited Wolseley to accompany them, a journey from which dated a close friendship and frequent correspondence with the Duchess. On his return he found that his prediction of trouble in the Soudan had been verified more quickly even than he had feared. In August 1881 one Mohammed Ahmed rose in rebellion in the Soudan and proclaimed himself to be the expected Mahdi. When we occupied Cairo the Mahdi had already gained considerable following, and the Egyptian Government began to take serious measures against him. In April 1883 Hicks Pasha, a former officer of the Bombay Staff Corps, who held the rank of Major-General in the Egyptian Army, was sent to

Khartoum to organise an expedition to El Obeid, where the Mahdi had established his headquarters. In the following November Hicks with a force of some 7000 men was attacked by the Mahdi's men, his little army was annihilated, and he himself fell with all his staff in a gallant attempt to charge through the swarms of Soudanese. This victory not only raised the prestige of the Mahdi, but placed Khartoum, and indeed all the Egyptian garrisons in the Soudan, in peril. Public opinion at home was deeply stirred, and the Government was pressed to "do something" to help the local Egyptian troops. At this juncture men began to ask, "Where is Chinese Gordon ? " the man who after suppressing the Taiping rebellion had been in turn Governor-General of the equatorial provinces of Egypt, and of the Soudan, where he had put down slavery with a strong hand, and created some semblance of order and of just government. Gordon was on his way home from Palestine. He had accepted an offer of employment under King Leopold of the Belgians in the Congo, and on learning that the Government would not let him take this up while he was on the active list of the Army, had determined to resign his commission. On January 15th Wolseley received a letter from Gordon announcing his arrival at Southampton and his early departure for West Africa. He asked Wolseley to help him with the War Office in the matter of the pension of his rank, from which in the circumstances he was debarred by the Regulations. Wolseley at once wired to his old friend to come to London, and met him at the station. He persuaded him to give up the Congo plan, of which he had never approved,[1] told him that the Government wanted to evacuate the Soudan, and discussed at length with him the situation there. Gordon

[1] Wolseley to Hartington, October 16, 1884 (*Life of the Duke of Devonshire*, vol. i. p. 415).

told him that he thought it would be far better to evacuate the Soudan than to reconquer it, if reconquest meant handing it back to the Egyptian Pashas whose injustice and tyranny had, he said, been the real cause of the rebellion. He had no belief in the Mahdi's power, which should melt away as soon as the people knew that they were to be governed by British officers. The Government, he told Wolseley, would do well to send him to Suakin to study the situation and advise them on it. Evacuation might be the best—perhaps the only—course, or again it might be better to attempt to constitute some settled form of local government before coming to a final decision as to the future of the country. In the latter case he suggested his own reappointment as Governor-General.

Wolseley at once reported this conversation to Hartington, who asked him to warn Gordon that he would be wanted for the Soudan and to invite him to an early meeting with such Ministers as were in town. Wolseley brought Gordon to the War Office on January 18th. Lord Hartington, Lord Granville,[1] Lord Northbrook, and Sir Charles Dilke met them there. Gordon has left a racy account of the interview, the essential part of which is : " *They said,* ' Did Wolseley tell you your orders ? ' *I said,* ' Yes '. *I said,* ' You will not guarantee future government of the Soudan and you wish me to go up and evacuate now ? ' *They said,* ' Yes ', and it was over." [2] There is no doubt that evacuation was in everybody's mind, in Gordon's as much as in any other's ; there is no doubt that the Government wanted not only to evacuate the Soudan, but to come away from Egypt ; but there is equally no doubt that both Gordon and Wolseley were agreed that the proper course was that which any experienced

[1] Then Foreign Minister.
[2] Gordon's letter to Barnes, 1885.

soldier would have recommended, namely, that Gordon should go and see the situation in the Soudan before advising on any definite course of action. That is what Gordon told Wolseley and what Wolseley told Hartington, but most important of all it is what Gordon put into writing and gave to Hartington, who passed it on to Gladstone. Gordon told Hartington that he " might recommend absolute and immediate withdrawal. He could give no opinion without seeing the state of affairs on the spot."

The first paragraph of Gordon's own draft of his instructions runs : " I. To proceed to Suakin and report on military situation of Soudan and return. Under Baring for orders, and to send through him letters, etc., under flying seal." [1] Lord Morley in his *Life of Gladstone* unaccountably confuses this document, which he does not mention, with the formal instructions of the Government, which he says were drafted by Gordon himself. These formal instructions began : " Her Majesty's Government are desirous that you should proceed at once to Egypt, to report to them on the military situation in the Soudan, and on the measures it may be advisable to take for that country, and for the safety of the European population of Khartoum. You are also desired to consider and report on the best mode of effecting the evacuation of the interior of the Soudan." Lord Morley quotes this last sentence, by itself, as being Gordon's own draft, which it was not, and on it bases largely his defence of Gladstone.[2] It is obvious that the official instructions must be read in the light of Gordon's conversation with Wolseley as reported to Lord

[1] For Hartington's letter to Gladstone written immediately after the meeting of January 18th and containing a transcript of Gordon's own notes, see *Life of the Duke of Devonshire*, vol. i. p. 418.
[2] Morley's *Life of Gladstone*, vol. iii. p. 153. Lord Morley gives the text of the instructions in an Appendix, p. 554.

Hartington, of Hartington's conversation with Gordon as reported to Gladstone, and of Gordon's own written interpretation of his instructions. Yet Gladstone, wishing for the evacuation of the Soudan, to his death allowed himself to believe that Gordon had been sent out expressly to carry out the evacuation, and that the Government had made the mistake of choosing for a particularly delicate mission an eccentric genius and a visionary, who set his own will before the wishes of the Government. As Lord Morley puts it, Gladstone and many of his colleagues came to think that they had " improvidently let the genie forth from the jar ".[1] In fact, they had failed, with the notable exception of Lord Hartington, to understand the implications of a military situation and the instructions which they had given to a soldier. To this misunderstanding may be traced the hesitations and delays by which Wolseley was agonised and Gordon was sacrificed. The two intimate friends had, throughout these rapid negotiations, been in the closest touch, each acting in full agreement with the other, each with a clear understanding of the other's mind. Wolseley therefore felt that he was personally responsible for Gordon's mission, and he was never able to forgive Gladstone for the lethargic attitude which was to him incomprehensible. The British soldier entrusted with a mission in war has usually found that what Ministers require of him is a precise plan : " I will go out and do this and that ", a plan which can be checked and controlled in London. Such a plan the soldier, who knows that his actions must depend upon the actions of an enemy, the working of whose mind can only be vaguely foreseen, cannot in nine cases out of ten provide. Wolseley in 1882, in dealing with the precise conditions of Arabi's rebellion, had been able accurately to forecast his

[1] Morley's *Life of Gladstone*, vol. iii. p. 153.

actions, and Gladstone may have believed that what had been done once could be done again. But in the dark situation of the Soudan in 1884 no educated soldier would have promised evacuation, and it needed but a very slight knowledge of Gordon's character to be sure that he would in no circumstances come away leaving behind him those whom he had been sent to save.

At 8 P.M. on January 18th Gordon left by the boat train for Calais and Brindisi, Wolseley carrying to the carriage the small bag which contained his kit. Knowing his friend's ways, Wolseley asked him just as the train was leaving, "Have you any money?" Gordon, searching his pockets, produced a few shillings, his sole provision for the journey to the Soudan. Knowing that his own store of cash would not be enough, Wolseley pressed on him in addition his watch and chain, and with a final "God bless you", the old comrades of the trenches before Sebastopol, the two men who remembered each other nightly in their prayers,[1] separated.

At Sir Evelyn Baring's request Gordon came to Cairo instead of going to Suakin, and went thence up the Nile to Khartoum, where he was received with wild enthusiasm on February 18th. He had, with Baring's approval and Lord Granville's consent, accepted from the Khedive the appointment of Governor - General of the Soudan, which he had suggested to Ministers should be conferred upon him. This appointment, the implications of which Lord Granville appears to have overlooked, made official Gordon's responsibility to the loyal Egyptians

---

[1] Gordon told Wolseley that he prayed daily for two men. Wolseley was one. The other was Captain J. F. Brocklehurst, who afterwards commanded the Royal Horse Guards and became Lord Ranksborough. Gordon dined with Brocklehurst at the "Blues'" Mess on his last night in England before going with Wolseley to the train.

of the Soudan, which till then might have been considered only as a moral obligation.

Hardly had Gordon left England than the news from the Soudan became worse. A slave dealer named Osman Digna rose in the Eastern Soudan, declared himself an adherent of the Mahdi, and inflicted some ugly blows upon Egyptian troops in the province of Suakin. A force of some 4000 of these under Valentine Baker Pasha was assembled at Suakin to relieve Tokar, which was invested by the Soudanese, but on February 4th it was severely defeated at El Teb. The Government could not resist the popular demand that this disaster should be retrieved and Tokar saved from the rebels. A British force 4000 strong was therefore brought to Suakin, and on Wolseley's advice the command was given to Major-General Sir G. Graham, with Colonel Herbert Stewart to lead the cavalry and Colonel Sir Redvers Buller the infantry. Graham defeated the rebels at El Teb on February 29th, and at Tamai on March 13th, but despite this success it was evident that our authority did not extend beyond the range of our guns. The Mahdi continually gained fresh followers, the revolt spread northwards down the Nile, Berber was invested, and direct communication with Khartoum was cut. Wolseley no sooner knew this than he, on April 8th, addressed a memorandum to Hartington on the organisation of an expedition for the relief of Gordon up the valley of the Nile; in a further memorandum written on April 14th he gave November 15th as the latest date to which Gordon could be expected to hold out, and said that the expedition should be at Berber not later than October 20th,[1] which meant that it would have to start from Wady Halfa not later than the end of August. He was in fact able

---

[1] For the text of these memoranda see *History of the Soudan Campaign*, Part I. pp. 26 *et seq.*

N

to begin his enterprise from that place on October
7th. The Government found excuses for delaying
a measure to which they were averse, firstly, in
Gordon's confident tone, and, secondly, in a difference of opinion amongst the soldiers as to the route
to be taken. While Wolseley was in the act of
preparing the memorandum Gordon telegraphed :
" I wish I could convey to you my impression of the
truly temporary character of this revolt, which 500
determined men could put down. Be assured that
for the present and for two months hence we are
as safe here as at Cairo. If you would get by good
pay 3000 Turkish infantry and 1000 Turkish cavalry
the affair, including crushing the Mahdi, would be
accomplished in 4 months."

But the two months and more were allowed to
pass while the Cabinet squabbled, and Wolseley in
desperation tried every expedient to induce the
Government to act. He proposed to raise a small
expedition to secure Berber, as the forerunner later
of a larger undertaking, if such should be necessary ;
he offered to go out himself and take command at
Suakin : " As Suakin is not an agreeable summer
residence," he wrote to Hartington, " perhaps you
will believe that I make the proposal upon public
rather than upon personal grounds. Those public
grounds are—I state them as they strike me at the
risk of being thought self-conceited—the announcement that I was to start without delay would make
every one feel that you were thoroughly in earnest.
In Egypt this would do good, and might even tend
to relieve Gordon from some of the pressure he
now suffers at Khartoum." Nothing could wring a
decision from the Government.

What was at the time called " the battle of the
routes " was a difference of opinion between Stephenson in Cairo and Wolseley in London as to the best
line of advance. Stephenson did not believe that

boats could get through the cataracts, and wanted to move from Suakin on Berber. Wolseley was convinced by his experience on the Red River that boats could be used, and proved that he was right. His objections to the Suakin route were the difficulty of finding the number of camels necessary for transport and the possibility that a small check at the end of a long march across an almost waterless desert might bring disaster. When the news came that Berber had fallen he was more firmly convinced than ever that the Nile route was the right one ; for with the goal of the desert march in the hands of the Dervishes, a battle before reaching water would be inevitable. After his failure to reach Khartoum in time the critics said that he ought to have gone the other way, but Gordon was of his opinion that the Nile valley was the only practicable line of approach for a British expedition, and Kitchener, with the experience of the past to guide him and ample time for consideration, confirmed Wolseley's choice. At length, early in August the Government agreed to preparations being made for an advance up the Nile, but even then Hartington, expressing the views of the Government rather than his own, had to write : " Her Majesty's Government are not at present convinced that it will be impossible for General Gordon, acting on the instructions which he has received, to secure the withdrawal from Khartoum, either by the employment of force or of pacific means, of the Egyptian garrisons and of such of the inhabitants as may desire to leave ".[1] But the most qualified permission was enough for Wolseley, who pressed through his plans long prepared. He bade his Red River comrade, Colonel Butler, supervise the construction of special boats for the Nile, he sent for *voyageurs* from Canada and Kroomen from the West Coast of Africa to help in

[1] *History of the Soudan Campaign*, vol. i. p. 44.

their navigation, and he placed orders for the stores needed for the expedition. Then came the crux as to who should lead the troops. Stephenson was told that as the plan he opposed was to be adopted, it would be unfair to ask him to carry it out. Rather than thwart the Government, the fine old Guardsman bowed to a decision which was perhaps expedient rather than equitable. No other name than Wolseley's seemed to present itself for serious consideration, and Gladstone, who hummed, hawed, and hesitated, chiefly because any nomination meant a definite expedition, suddenly made up his mind on the 23rd August that Wolseley must go out. Hartington at once conveyed this decision—which he strongly backed—to the Queen, who in her turn hesitated and objected. She thought that if command were bestowed on Wolseley, the cheap cry of "our only General" would be renewed and partially justified, and against this her pride in her Army revolted. The Duke did not hesitate at all. He protested vigorously, taking up the rather loose ground that it was unfair to deprive him of the services of his Adjutant-General. There ensued a triangular telegraphic correspondence between the Queen at Balmoral, the Duke at Edinburgh, and the War Minister at Bolton Abbey, and it was not until the 26th August that Wolseley, when at dinner with Baroness Burdett-Coutts, received an intimation that the Sovereign had preferred the advice of her Ministers to the advocacy of her cousin, and had agreed to Wolseley's appointment being published forthwith. The next day he received the Government's orders to take up the command in Egypt, but even then he was without authority to relieve Gordon,[1] his instructions for this being only issued

[1] On September 13th, 1884, Gladstone wrote Hartington: "Wolseley's telegram of the 11th. We have reached a point at which I cannot dispute the propriety of putting Wolseley in a

in London on October 9th, two days after his forward movement from Wady Halfa had actually begun.

On August 30th Wolseley was barely able to take half a day from the preparations for his new adventure to obey the summons of the Sovereign to pay her his farewell visit in her island home ; the following evening he travelled with Lord Northbrook to Trieste, being detained one night at Vienna in consequence of a railway accident. He embarked on the 4th September on H.M.S. *Iris,* and from the deck of that very lively boat, in a less than usually legible hand [1] but in more than usually suave language, he invited Evelyn Wood to command his lines of communication, and unfolded to the War Secretary and the Commander-in-Chief his requirements, which he had carefully refrained from expressing to them *viva voce.*

Quality rather than quantity was what he coveted for his Expeditionary Force, and, besides the troops already in Egypt and two battalions from Malta, he asked for what was nothing less than a *corps d'élite.* This would comprise a Heavy Camel Corps composed of forty men with three officers from each of the Household Cavalry and Heavy Cavalry regiments ; a Light Camel Corps to be extracted in like numbers from the Light Cavalry regiments ; and a Guards Camel Corps, to which each battalion of the Brigade of Guards would furnish forty of their best. If the composite character of the corps dismayed the military authorities, the notion of camelry

---

condition to proceed if necessary, and this telegram I only consider as indicating the military means, of which you and he, aided too by Northbrook, are the proper judges. I therefore can make no difficulty and I rely fully on what you lately told me about Wolseley's desire to avoid if it be possible the advance for which nevertheless he requires to have the means at his hand."

[1] " It was impossible ", Wolseley said, " to write steadily anywhere but in the stoke-hold."

itself was in many quarters openly derided. The *Times* was moved to scornful periods : " Now, under conditions in which the element of the grotesque is not wholly wanting, both Household Brigades are called upon to send their representatives to take part in the expedition for the relief of General Gordon " ; the illustrated journals made play with cartoons representing the Life Guards drilling on zebras in the Zoological Gardens, and the Corporal of Horse of the future mounted on a hard-tyred tricycle. Wolseley surmised that the mere thought of skimming the cream off the cavalry regiments would take the Duke's breath away ; the Duke admitted this is precisely what happened when this startling, " outrageous " proposal was put in his hands, with a somewhat peremptory rider that the despatch of the Gordon Relief Force brooked no delay.[1] There was a little coating of sugar for the pill. " Upon thinking the whole subject over," Wolseley wrote, " I see the force of H.R.H.'s objection to the employment of the Brigade of Guards in Egypt at the present time,[2] and ", he tactfully added, " I have not asked for any more men of the line, as I feel there are none to be spared, but as the Rifle Brigade did not take any part in the 1882 Campaign, I think it would be well to give them a chance now. I am sure it would be very popular with them " ; and in order to please both Hartington and the Duke, he naïvely asked how it would do for Lord Rosebery's brother, Colonel Primrose—then Military Attaché at Vienna

---

[1] Hartington wrote Wolseley, September 19th : " H.R.H. did not like the composition of your Camel Corps, which he considered destructive of the *esprit de corps* of the regiments which are to furnish detachments. However, Herbert and Norman approved your proposal so energetically and showed his alternative proposal to be so impracticable that he gave way."

[2] Two months earlier the Duke had written to Wolseley : " If you are called upon to go into details with the Cabinet to-day, don't press for the Guards to be sent to Egypt. . . . Don't let us touch the *only available* reserve we have on the roster ".

LORD WOLSELEY GOING UP THE NILE.

Caricature by "Assus".

To face page 182.

—to command the Guards Camel Corps,[1] and suggested that Major FitzGeorge, the Duke's third son, who in 1882 had failed to pass a board of doctors, might take charge of the contingent of the 11th Hussars.

Wolseley reached Cairo on September 9th and took up his quarters in the Kasr-el-Noussa palace. Tewfik had brushed up his knowledge of English in constant conversation with British officers, and gracefully used that tongue in begging his deliverer of two years earlier to occupy, not only any of his palaces, but also his best yacht, which he had fitted out and sent up the river. The plan of operations was complete, and in uncovering it to Stephenson Wolseley put on record an intense admiration for the fine old Guardsman's demeanour. " He naturally feels most deeply the fact of being superseded. It is the heaviest blow a man can receive. Canrobert had to live through it in the Crimea, and very possibly the keenness of the pain may yet be in store for me. May Almighty God deliver me from it, however. In this present instance I can compare Stephenson's conduct with that of other men whom I have superseded on various occasions, and I am bound to admire it."

Wolseley had already applied for the services of the officers on whom he always could and did rely. " Some think I favour my friends," he wrote to the Duke of Cambridge, " but these are simply officers whom I pick out on active service as very good men. As soon as I find I have made a mistake, I drop them remorselessly." Buller was to be Chief of the Staff ; Wood, Grenfell,[2] Brackenbury, Butler, Ardagh,[3] Maurice, Harrison,[4] Grove,[5] and

[1] Primrose was eventually made Commandant of Wolseley's advanced headquarters, and died a few months later of fever.
[2] Afterwards Field-Marshal Lord Grenfell.
[3] Afterwards General Sir John Ardagh.
[4] Afterwards General Sir R. Harrison.
[5] Afterwards General Sir Coleridge Grove.

Herbert Stewart were to be fitted in their special
niches. Here was indeed a chosen band, yet such
was the strain and stress of the next three months
that before the final advance was ordered only two
of their number had escaped the severe criticism of
their Chief. A picturesque and practical addition
to his personal staff was Zohrab Bey, a highly
cultured and ardently Anglophile Egyptian ; and
at the earnest request of the Prince of Wales, Lord
Charles Beresford—who two years earlier had asked
in vain to share in the military operations—was
invited to take charge of the Naval contingent on
the Nile. Two stipulations were made: "I am
indeed glad to have you with me, but I must ask
you to undertake that while you are under my
orders you will not communicate to the Admiralty
except through me, and I have been told in several
quarters that you are very fond of newspaper
correspondents, and have acted for the *Morning
Post* in that capacity yourself. It is very necessary
to *manipulate* correspondents, and to be at all times
on the best of terms with them, but it must be done
upon a system and always with the knowledge of
the Genl. Officer Commdg.

"Now I trust you to give me an assurance that
you will not directly or indirectly correspond with
any newspaper, and that you will have no relations
with any of their correspondents except with my
knowledge and permission."

The conditions were smilingly accepted and
rigidly adhered to. Beresford's work earned his
leader's highest encomiums, and the two men remained thereafter constant correspondents and
mutually helpful friends.

For nearly three weeks every hour of the day
from 5.30 A.M. was occupied with military preparations, purchases of camels, and experiments on
the river. A most important contribution to the

184

Nile Expedition was the steel-bottomed Yarrow boats, which were completed and placed on the water with extraordinary rapidity. Wolseley wrote to a friend : "I begin to see some daylight through the job I have before me. I can afford to say to you privately that if I had not come out there would have been little chance of relieving Khartoum this winter." Even quasi-ceremonial visits he rigorously, if reluctantly, paid so as to leave no stone unturned to popularise the British troops in the forthcoming expedition.

It was, above all, important to get foodstuffs as far and as fast as possible up the river, as Wolseley had fully realised that eventually his main trouble would be to feed his force 1600 miles from its base in a country which produced nothing for daily rations. He made this very difficulty a peg on which to hang a renewed plea to the Duke as to the special merits of composite corps. The immense task of delivering and maintaining men at the front demanded that the rifle strength should approach as nearly as possible the ration strength, and two picked men, it was urged, were fully equal to three taken at random from any battalion.

"Every day makes me realise the difficulties I have before me if we must go in fighting condition to Khartoum by the Nile Valley. Those who constitute the troops think only of the excitement they may have in fighting with a brave enemy, but I have to think of and prepare for a greater difficulty than the fighting part of the affair, namely, the feeding of the men, horses, and camels to be employed. Our time is so short that we cannot easily collect all the grain and chopped straw we require at Dongola or Dabbeh."

Four months later he was writing : "It is really curious that men should be found capable of writing the nonsense that has been written about our doings here. It is not that non-military writers jumble up strategy and tactics, not having any conception of what these words mean. I am astonished to see letters and articles in which the movement of 5000 men here or there is referred to as if the Soudan had no deserts, and was as well provided with roads and railways as Belgium and as rich in produce as Yorkshire. Men discuss the march of a force from Suakin to Berber as they would of marching from Aldershot to Plymouth. Camels are referred to as if they were as plentiful as rabbits are in Richmond Park, as if they required no food and never required rest and never died."

At the end of September, Wolseley, with a firman in his pocket in case Gordon should refuse to obey orders, and having in vain sought to evade the detested ceremony of " seeing off ", left Cairo for Assouan and Wady Halfa. His journal on the boat contains an elaborate account of the Nile Valley through which he passes, and is replete with the military, political, and social reflections in which he would indulge in times of comparative leisure. The temples and other ruins were perfunctorily visited or frankly neglected. " They refer to a period of which I know nothing, and of which even the most learned in the subject know little. I become worn out in contemplating their hieroglyphics, one set being exactly a repetition of the other. To me York Minster or Lichfield Cathedral appeals more and more when I see the temples here. And when I am told such or such a monolith was erected by Rameses the 3rd of the 18th dynasty, it is gibberish to me ; it recalls nothing I take any interest in or care to investigate."

The river journey marked a break in Wolseley's habits. Hitherto he had been an inveterate smoker ; cigars of a choice brand being the only luxury he ever permitted himself on service. He determined to test himself by giving up tobacco for a month.[1] The privation was considerable, and on the appointed day he resumed his former use with even increased gusto. Yet two months later he took a vow to abjure smoking altogether, and kept his resolution to the end of his life.

At Halfa he found a telegram from Kitchener[2] with the grim story of the murder of Gordon's companion, Colonel James Stewart.[3] The tragedy and the treachery of the Sheikh of the Monasir,[4] who had lured Stewart and his party to their deaths, raised his anger to white heat. " If only ", he cried, " Stewart had died in battle in place of being murdered like an Irish landlord by a cowardly skulking reptile such as this country and Ireland produce in large numbers! May that murderer fall into my hands!" But after the first shock of the telegram Wolseley curiously allowed himself to surmise that Kitchener might have been misled by his very knowledge of the vernacular, and to doubt the accuracy of a report based though it was on positive proof; he courted every suggestion which seemed to traverse the statement of his intelligence officer; and it was not until a month later that he accepted the murder of Stewart as a fact.

As a slight set-off to this gloomy news, Wolseley heard from Assouan that the first lot of the specially designed boats—now officially termed " whalers "— had been rowed, tracked, and poled up the first cataract without damage. " This will be strange news ",

---

[1] " So also ", he wrote to a friend from Dongola, " I am looking forward to the day when our little stock of wine is exhausted and we shall drink nothing but tea."

[2] Major Herbert Kitchener was one of the Deputy Assistant Adjutant-Generals in the Intelligence Department of the Expedition.

[3] Three weeks earlier Gordon had telegraphed to Wolseley, " Sending Stewart to take Berber—hold it for a fortnight, and then burn it ". " This ", Wolseley noted, " will perhaps cause Mr. Gladstone to believe that an expedition is necessary."

[4] Monasir is the district about Abu-Ahmed.

Wolseley chuckled, "for the Admiral, who wound up his report on the proposal to use whalers by asserting that they could neither be rowed, tracked, or poled up the Nile." He also found complete justification for the proposal which he had made before leaving England, but had been turned down by Wood's staff, to run out a line of rail from Serah to the head of the second cataract. "Had I insisted", he wrote, "on some one being sent out to examine the ground accurately, this line might now have been in working order, and our difficulties about this troublesome cataract at an end."

The progress of the whalers was a matter of alternate hope and fear, and Butler's [1] fretful complaints about the naval management of them were an unfortunate irritant. Wolseley, remembering the Irishman's fine work on the Red River, was disposed to accept him as an oracle of truth on all such matters as portage, hauling, and tracking of the flotilla, and to compare unfavourably the efforts of the sister service. "Rode to the Bab-el-Keber,[2] where Butler is now encamped", is an entry in his journal of October 25th. "Found he had early in the morning got one of our whalers through the Bab with a small party of natives before the sailors appeared on the scene ; he was in the seventh heaven of delight. The sailors and swarms of natives employed all the morning in rigging up their very heavy gear for taking the whalers through according to their notions. They are right good fellows at sea, and could, I have no doubt, haul an ironclad up a hill, but they have as much idea of working boats in rapid water as my big boot has. Having worked for hours at these preparations, they began about 1 P.M. trying to get a boat up, and a pretty mess

---

[1] Colonel Butler was in charge of the whalers, and later accompanied Earle's column from Korti up river.
[2] The " great gate " of the second cataract.

they made of it. The boat, having shipped some water, was at last got up, but I thought she must have been wrecked, so badly was the affair conducted. I then interviewed Koko, the Sheikh of the cataract, who had taken up boats for Butler early in the morning, and made a contract with him to take up twenty boats per diem for 25 piastres each, and for 30 piastres for every boat over twenty taken up any one day. The Navy to bring the whalers up to the foot of Bab."

On the 28th October, Lord Wolseley with his personal staff started on a five-days' desert ride to Dongola. The last few miles of the journey were made by water, and the General stepped ashore to find a large crowd on the landing-place, the Mudir's army at the salute—but no Mudir. This was most annoying; for once Wolseley wished his arrival to be with full ceremonial, as he was determined to emphasise the fact that he was in plenary power. Zohrab was at once despatched to fetch the wily Circassian, who then arrived in hot haste, paid fulsome compliments to the British General, and accompanied him to the Mudirate.[1] Kitchener had been unfavourably impressed by the Mudir, but Wolseley, when so informed, was until much later loath to accept this measure of the Mudir's good faith. He had been elated by Mustafa Yarver's defeat of the Mahdi's adherents in September, and had then proposed to Baring that the victor should be made a ruling prince over Khartoum. He hastened to invest the Mudir with the insignia of St. Michael and St. George, an investiture which later events went to show might well have been postponed

---

[1] Mustafa Yarver was a Circassian who had been sent to the Soudan in 1864, appointed to the Mudirieh in 1877, removed by Gordon in February 1884, and immediately reinstated by the Egyptian Government. He was, politically, a doubtful character and, personally, seemed disposed to swing from side to side; but the situation of his province required him to be carefully considered.

or omitted. He seems to have thought that the Mudir's virtues were his own, his offences those of the Turks and Bashi-Bazouks who formed his environment. " The Mudir ", he wrote, " is an absolute sovereign, and although feared, is respected for his victories and revered for his religious fervour. He is a man I cannot help admiring, notwithstanding his *mesquine* appearance and his want of physique. His force of character impresses me, and his earnest faith in the religion he professes. This faith gives him the highest and truest courage. They say that in action he is always in front and takes up handfuls of sand and throws it towards the enemy, which demoralises them."[1] For the moment he even accepted the Mudir's suggestion that the Mahdi might be successfully persuaded to make peace and give up his European and Egyptian prisoners, if recognised as Sultan of Kordofan ;[2] he wrote home that he thought the Mahdi, as a mahdi, was played out.

The stories of a dejected Mahdi, Herbert Stewart's splendid progress with the training of the Camel Corps which he commanded, the north wind which was impelling the river craft forward, combined to raise the Commander-in-Chief's spirits, although the delays in forwarding men and material from Assouan caused him to make a dash down to Halfa to confer with Buller. The desert ride was not without risk ; Wolseley was only accompanied by two A.D.C.'s and an Arab guide, and although he had confided his intention to no one but Buller and Wood, who did not inform any even of their staff, the rumour that

---

[1] " If you can imagine Lord Carnarvon turned fakir, and dressed in a long black reach-me-down paletot, with a native shirt and no shirt-collar, a fez on head, black shiny alpacka-like (*sic*) trousers, and a pair of thin patent-leather, but curiously designed, French boots with elastic sides on—such is my Mudir of Dongola."—W. to Lady Wolseley.

[2] This suggestion had been previously made by Gordon.

the great General was on the desert track was on every native's lips.

Just as he was starting from Dongola, Reuter's news announced that the Franchise Bill had passed the third reading without a division. "Now comes the crisis", Wolseley wrote. "Will the Lords be firm? Shall I find upon my return home that I have no longer a voice in the Legislature?" It is characteristic of an agile mind that the first question he asked when he arrived, travel-stained and dropping with fatigue, at Halfa, was, "What has happened in the Lords?"

The delay on the river was largely due to the lack of coal for the steamers, a matter which Buller unfortunately assumed had been attended to before his arrival. "I blame myself too," Wolseley wrote to Lady Wolseley; "for although I trust Buller fully, I should not have relied upon my trust in him on such a vital question, and ought personally to have gone into it. In dealing with a Chief of the Staff in whom one has every confidence I feel too much inclined, I know, to give him a free hand. I know, from my own personal experience when I was a Staff Officer, how inconvenient and difficult it was to serve a General who wished to command and to be his own Staff Officer at the same time. At the beginning I told Buller I looked to him for all details, which I left unreservedly in his hands, and that I had no intention of keeping a dog and barking myself. The result has been, in this one respect, unfortunate. However, the difficulty is now over; but instead of having the army concentrated at Ambukol about the middle of December it cannot possibly be so until the 7th or 10th January."

Wolseley spent but one day at Halfa, and travelled by day and night—notwithstanding a heavy fall from a camel, a beast he heartily detested—back to Dongola, to find that the Mudir had spoken impertinently to Wilson and written impudently to Kitchener. The offence was dealt with leniently, for Wolseley, true to his promise to the Government, was at this moment so imbued with the idea of saving Gordon by negotiation rather than by force, that he actually sounded the Mudir as to the possibility and feasibility of his succeeding Gordon as an hereditary and independent Sultan.

The difficulty of communicating with Khartoum was increased ten-fold because the cyphers had been lost with Stewart, and Wolseley was at his wits' end as to how to keep Gordon correctly informed. His last letter was, of course, unintelligible, and he could only now write to him in clear. He sent him a cypher page from the *Soldiers' Pocket Book*, the keys being the Christian name of his mother's father, and the number of cash in a stated number of " taels ", with the day of the month in which Gordon was born added. He also ingeniously gave him the date of the proposed concentration at Ambukol by telling him it will be so many days from this year's anniversary of his being made a Major-General.

Lord Wolseley now issued two orders : one, an appeal to the soldiers to strain every nerve to rescue Gordon, for the literary style of which he consulted Brackenbury on the wire. "It is a difficult thing", he told Lady Wolseley, " for an Englishman to compose an order of this sort. For a Frenchman, and perhaps all other foreigners, the task is easy ; he can afford to be heroic and pompous in his expressions without being thought ridiculous. With us it is very different, and I have no doubt the *Pall Mall Gazette* and *St. James's Gazette*, who are nothing if not cynical, will find fault with my grammar and hold up my appeal to all that is good in the British soldier—and there is certainly plenty of good in him—to the ridicule of their readers. However, that will concern me very

SILVER MODEL OF A NILE WHALER.

The Wolseley Prize, 1885, won by 1st Battalion Royal Irish Regiment (now in R.U.S.I. Museum).

To face page 193.

little if I can but get to the heart of those under my command. This labour on the river in this climate is very great, and if I cannot infuse some heroic zeal into my men, this army will be little better than a poor emaciated body without any spirit or soul in it."

The second order announced a prize of £100 to the battalion which made the best time on the river between Serah and Ambukol, with a further promise that the successful battalion should have a front place for the march on Khartoum.[1] "When I was a young man, if any General had addressed an order like mine of to-day to any army I was serving with, it would have made every nerve in my body tingle, and have sent the blood pounding through my veins, until I should have longed to have gone forth and fought the Mahdi by myself. But, there, I was always very impressionable, which I owe to my Irish education and early Irish surroundings."[2]

By December 10th the whole fighting force had passed Halfa except the Cameron Highlanders, who remained at Korosko to present a pistol at Abu-Hamed. The opportunist Mudir confided to Wolseley that he had just had two dreams to the effect that the Nile was filled with salt water, which, being interpreted, meant the surface of the river was covered by the boats of the English, who had come across the ocean, and that the British General was resting on the banks of the Nile after a great victory. The visions, whether or not they were pure inventions, were taken in good part by Wolseley, who replied that his own vision was that he would be in Khartoum before the end of January.

On December 13th Lord Wolseley left Dongola for what he had determined should be his advanced

---

[1] The prize was won by the 1st Bn. 18th Royal Irish Regiment, who decided to have a silver model of a "whaler" made as a memorial of their achievement.

[2] Private Letter.

base at Korti, whither the Mudir wanted to accompany him. Dongola he had come to detest, and the Mudir he had begun to distrust. "If I want him I can always send for him," Wolseley bluntly remarked, "and in dealing with Easterns of his nature one must pay no regard to their feelings on such points, but learn to throw them over when you don't want their services any longer, just as they do one to the other."

Korti was reached on the 16th, and Wolseley, anxious to avail himself of a full moon, planned to send Herbert Stewart on the 28th with the Camel Corps, half the 19th Hussars, a battery of field artillery, and 400 men of the Sussex Regiment, across the desert to Gakdul, half-way between Korti and Matammeh, where there was water in plenty. By then a river force under Major-General Earle would be in process of concentrating at Handab for an advance into the Monasir country and upon Abu-Hamed. But it was not until the 30th that Stewart could leave for the half-way house, whence he was instructed to return with unloaded camels to fetch supplies.

Wolseley's intention was, as soon as a depot of supplies had been formed at Gakdul, to seize Matammeh on the Nile, and then, with any steamers or boats which might be found there and manned by Beresford and his sailors, to make a dash for Khartoum. He proposed to accompany Stewart's column himself, and orders were issued to that effect, but in deference to a strongly worded telegram from Lord Hartington he reluctantly gave up his desire to be present personally at what he hoped would be the relief of Gordon. His reasons for dividing his force he gave in a letter of December 29th to Hartington : "By next week's post I shall send you an official letter explaining in general terms my plans for movements in advance of this place and giving my reasons for embarking in this desert expedition. I shall not state one of my principal reasons, as I don't think the Government would like it made known, viz., that this Nile expedition, which was proposed in April, was only seriously considered in July. Such valuable time was lost that, if I were to adhere to the Nile route for all the force, I should risk Gordon having to surrender from want of food and ammunition, and I should most certainly have to extend our operations so far into the heart of the summer, that the loss of life in the little army would be very great. The Nile route would be the surest, safest, and least expensive; but I find myself in such a position now, with such a short period of fine weather, that I am forced into a land operation on camels for a small part of the troops."

This little letter was brought to Lord Wolseley at Korti by an Arab rolled up in the hem of his clothing

Kartum all right 14.12.84 CGG

It was one of the very last messages General Gordon sent from Khartoum.

New Year's Eve brought serious news. There arrived from Meroe in the evening a picket-boat with a messenger who had left Khartoum on December 14th, bringing a scrap of paper, the size of a postage stamp, with Gordon's Arabic seal on one side, and " Kartum all right " on the other. This was not so bad, but the verbal message was a long, rambling, urgent demand that the British troops must come quickly and in real strength as the enemy was very numerous; it contained a warning that Berber should be taken before an advance was made to Khartoum. The day had passed for a mere demonstration of British strength at the gates of the beleaguered city to overawe the Mahdi; the Mahdi had evidently made himself ready for battle, and genuine force was needed to crush him.

Wolseley rose before dawn the next morning,

roused up Buller, with instructions to halt the half of the 19th Hussars under orders to march to Meroe, and returned to his tent to reconsider the position. "All along", he wrote, " I have been counting on an expression which occurs more than once in Gordon's letters, that the whole attack upon Khartoum would collapse if he had a few hundred determined soldiers upon whom he could depend. I have been basing my calculations on this *aperçu* of the position, and had therefore determined upon forcing my way into Khartoum with about 1500 of the finest men in our Army or any other army. Now this messenger tells me from him not to advance unless I am strong." [1]

The messenger brought some personal news of Gordon ; it was his habit apparently to spend much of the day on the top of one of the two palaces, whence he viewed, with a telescope, the enemy's position. He took a certain amount of sleep in the afternoon, but was up all night going round the works and keeping every one up to the mark. Besides his 18,000 soldiers, he had to look after a civil population of 27,000 souls ; food was more than scanty, but Gordon was still able to indulge his one appetite for smoking, and had even been able to offer the messenger a cigarette. Wolseley had not forgotten his friend's taste, and in his own baggage was a consignment of cigarettes which, with a solitary bottle of champagne, he looked forward to offering him at their first meeting.

A further study of the situation, with all its complexities of distances and dates, decided Wolseley to adhere to the main lines of his plan of relief. With a garrison at Matammeh it should be possible to communicate direct by steamer with Gordon and concert for the final advance on Khartoum. Earle could hurry to Abu-Hamed, where he would leave

[1] W. to Lady W.

half a battalion, and then press on to attack Berber, in which operation Gordon's steamers, manned by the Naval Brigade, might lend a helping hand. Berber taken, Earle would join Wolseley at Matammeh, and the united force move on Khartoum.

The Government, now really anxious, invited his opinion as to the value of an expedition from Suakin, and received the obvious reply, that such an operation could not assist directly the relief of Khartoum, but would tend to the final settlement of the country ; the extermination of Osman Digna being a *sine qua non* for the tranquillity of the Eastern Soudan. There was a further invitation to reaffirm his confidence of success, and in doing so Wolseley made the proviso that Gordon could hold on until the river force should reach Matammeh. In parrying an indirect query as to the effect of a military reverse, he assumed that the capture of Gordon and the fall of Khartoum would be so terrible a disaster as to throw into shadow the risk attendant on the mounted force in its rush across the desert to relieve him. A rider was added that on the question of risk the Government itself ought to express an opinion. " Of course, they won't," Wolseley noted in his diary ; "but, at any rate, I have asked for it, and my request is on record. I shall doubtless receive some enigmatical phrase concocted by Mr. Gladstone, and worded so as to save himself, but carefully avoiding the question I have put."

On January 3rd Earle left for Handab, and five days later Herbert Stewart—who had brought in his convoy of unloaded camels on January 2nd— returned to Gakdul, taking with him a proportion of the Naval Brigade, who had cheerfully hoisted themselves on to camels, and were led by Lord Charles Beresford, mounted on a small white donkey, which he destined to draw his Gardner gun. Colonel Sir Charles Wilson was sent with the column to help

Stewart in his dealings with the tribesmen and to go on with Beresford in the steamers to Khartoum.

Days of acute anxiety were now in store for Wolseley. He had committed his two forces and sacrificed what he chiefly prized, the direct control of them. Later he was heard to say that, looking back, he felt the greatest strain he had ever had on his nervous system was the interval of seven days between the date of receiving the news of Abu-Klea and that of the fight on the river on January 19th. He had led three storming-parties and had had many a bad quarter of an hour of intense suspense since he had been a General, but all that was nothing when compared to these seven days of almost intolerable strain. Anxiety for the safety of his troops included a personal anxiety for the safety of Gordon and of Stewart, his two dearest friends, the latter being perhaps the only man in whom he reposed unlimited confidence. He was beset, too, by troubles which he would have brushed aside had he himself been in contact with the enemy. Buller, just at the moment, was a source of irritation as well as a tower of strength. He would " build up " imaginary difficulties, he was unnecessarily contradictory, he laid claim to something like infallibility. The newspaper correspondents and the chaplains were alike on his nerves. There was to hand an autograph letter from the Queen, the tone and text of which had wounded the recipient to the quick.[1] He was even threatened with a visit—officially winked at —from Arabi's champion, Mr. Wilfrid Blunt, and he was incessantly worried by useless questions from home as to whether the Suakin-Berber route

[1] Her Majesty objected to Wolseley's offer of a money reward, and hinted plainly that British soldiers did not require bribing to do their duty. Nothing was in fact further from Wolseley's thought. £100 would not go far amongst a battalion of infantry. He wished to give the troops the stimulus of competing for a prize, and intended the money to be put just to the use made of it by the Royal Irish.

would not have been more advantageously followed.
" Napoleon ", he curtly wrote, " said the strongest
frontier a country could have is a desert.   Now for all
practical purposes the 250 miles between Suakin and
Berber is nothing but a howling desert.   To have
placed a fighting force of 5000 men at the latter
place, and to have fed it there, would have required
50,000 camels.   So that, if the question is gone into
minutely by one accustomed to arrange for the march
of even small armies through hostile countries, the
operation would be put down as almost impossible ;
for where are 50,000 camels to be found ? "

On January 17th, thinking that Herbert Stewart
would be hammer-and-tongs with the dervishes, the
distracted Commander-in-Chief spent the day at
Twelve Mile Hill (in the desert south of Korti) with
a strange satisfaction that he was that distance
nearer the point of interest than he would be in his
tent.   He had to contend with an almost irresistible
longing to take one A.D.C. and traverse the desert
to see how things were going, but remembered, among
other objections, that the Headquarters Staff would
say they had been left in the lurch while he careered
about in front for his own amusement.

Four days later a courier, who had negotiated
150 miles in three days, arrived with Stewart's
report of the battle of Abu-Klea.   There had been
a fierce fight on January 17th—the fight which induced von Moltke to speak of the desert column as
" a band, not of soldiers, but of heroes ;" Wolseley's
blood must have tingled in his veins as he read the
story.   The enemy had attacked with fanatical fury,
and at more than one point, and at one moment, had
penetrated through gaps into the British square.[1]
Before they were flung out and finally flung back,

---

[1] The Arab theory was that the square had been deliberately
opened to let the Dervishes in, and then closed to kill every one.
The latter part was anyhow correct, as no Dervish emerged from
the square.

their weapons had done some deadly work, especially among the heavy cavalry. The redoubtable
Burnaby, whose personality and procedure had
rendered him unpopular at Court but a favourite in
camp, had been killed. Stewart's horse had been
shot under him, but, *laus Deo*, Stewart was safe, and
he would move on Matammeh at once, and hoped to
occupy it with little resistance ; if the enemy should
fight, he would cut in either above or below it, water
his camels, form a post for his baggage, and attack
the mud forts on the 19th. So far all was well,
and for the next three days Wolseley could feed on
hopes of confirmed success and early contact with
Gordon.

Then the " No news ", which he tried to believe
must be " Good news ", gnawed, as he said, at his
heart-strings. He reminded himself that Stewart
had no more Bashi-Bazouks with him, and that an
English messenger was likely to be less expeditious
than a native. He rode or sent an A.D.C. far into
the desert each day, to strain his eyes for a camelman.

A satisfactory report from Earle, who was making
excellent progress up the river, was no set-off to the
suspense about Stewart. " It drives the blood from
my heart. God have mercy on me." So runs an
entry in Wolseley's diary. On January 28th, waking
long before dawn, he lit his candle to read the day's
Psalms, and heard the grunting of a camel outside
his tent. At last the messenger had come, in the
person of Colonel Piggott, " A fine, gallant fellow,
who had lost his way in the desert, but had made up
for it by sprinting over 140 miles in twenty-nine
hours ". His report spoke of no reverse, but
Stewart had been wounded in a fight near the river
on the 19th, and Wolseley instinctively knew that
he had been mortally stricken. Although Matammeh
had not been taken, the desert column was established
on the Nile at Gubat. Brisk fighting had occurred,

though the enemy had shrunk from close quarters, and had relied on their rifles.

Wolseley determined he must take Matammeh, though the price would be much higher than if it had fallen to Wilson, who had succeeded Stewart in command.[1]   Buller was detailed to proceed at once to the scene of action and assume command, with Kitchener as his intelligence officer, and he was to take the Royal Irish and Royal West Kent Regiments, who cheerfully agreed to foot it across the desert ; Evelyn Wood was to take over his duties as Chief of the Staff, delegating the lines of communication to Grenfell.   Wolseley also issued a bogus letter, written in French, to the renegade Olivier Pain, who was in the Mahdi's camp.   The letter referred to previous correspondence, and a moneyed agreement as to handing over the Mahdi to the British as a prisoner. It referred to sheikhs whose names the Frenchman was understood to have sent him, and it enclosed a proclamation in Arabic reminding them of British good faith in keeping bargains.   Stress was laid on the heaps of dead Dervishes left on the two battle-fields, and care was taken that the missive should fall into the Mahdi's hands, thus causing him to suspect not only the villainous Gaul, but also his own entourage.

So far, even if Stewart were lost, Gordon was safe, but to the end of his days Wolseley always looked back on the 4th February as the saddest of them. " I was certainly knocked out of time ", he wrote

---

[1] Wilson, as it seemed to Wolseley, had made a foolish attack on Matammeh, moving his men about in square and then falling back, a line of conduct likely to encourage the enemy.   During this operation four steamers had arrived from up river and landed men and guns to co-operate in the attack on the village.   On the 22nd Shendy had been reconnoitred by steamers, but nothing of any importance took place.   The enemy had one gun there and two or three in Matammeh, but little ammunition, and but few of their shells had burst.

that evening, " by the dreadful intelligence that Khartoum was taken by the Mahdi's troops on January 26th, and that Gordon's fate was uncertain, but he was said to have been killed." Prayer with Wolseley was a constant habit, and his first prayer was that his friend might have been swiftly killed. To Gordon " death was always looked forward to as the beginning of a new life, whereas if he be alive he may be kept for years in durance by this cruel monster Mohammed Ahmed ".

The news of the fall of Khartoum reached London, but the secret of it was kept four days at Korti. Wolseley never explained the reason for this reticence,[1] but he may have entertained some lingering doubt as to the consummation of the tragedy, or he may have wished to have some indication as to the temper of the Government with regard to future operations before telling his army that they were " too late ". The same evening, however, messengers were sent to halt Earle and to tell Buller to hold his hand as regards assaulting Matammeh, which he had announced his intention of taking at all costs. Buller was informed that everything now depended on the attitude of the Government. There was no longer any " mission " to accomplish ; the British Government might have little stomach for the conquest of the Soudan ; the season was too late for any hazardous undertaking ; a British force could scarcely maintain itself at Matammeh unless supported by the local tribes, who might swerve somewhat from their allegiance and follow the example of Sheikh Saleh, who had already withdrawn his promised supply of camels.

The mind of the Government was made up with unusual rapidity and unexpected bent. " Of all the surprises I have had," Wolseley wrote to

[1] For some time afterwards the Mudir and a great many sheikhs expressed their disbelief in the Mahdi's triumph.

his wife, " this has been the greatest. They have actually plucked up enough courage to tell me to protect from the Mahdi the districts now undisturbed. They don't wish any retrograde movement, and are prepared to support me in every possible way."

The General asked for a more explicit declaration of policy. Was the Mahdi's power to be destroyed ? If not, any advance from Berber would be a political rather than a sound military movement. His military sense may have exulted in the prospect of an autumn campaign with the motive of avenging the men who could no longer be saved ; his common sense apprehended immediately that such a campaign might well be fraught with much more grief than glory.[1] So long as Khartoum stood, Wolseley might have attacked and beaten his enemy in detail ; now he would have to meet an army in bulk six times as large as his own, and with seven times as many guns. The strength and prestige of the Mahdi had been largely enhanced by his capture of Khartoum, and, before even crossing swords with him, the mortality among British troops undergoing tropical heat in adverse circumstances would run high. Nor could he forget that the sentiments of men after six months of enforced inaction and with no heroic Gordon to succour and save might well differ from the military spirit, burning to accomplish a glorious mission. A minor anxiety was relieved by the arrival in camp on February 9th of Sir Charles Wilson, who brought with him the last part of Gordon's

[1] " I am looking forward with intense interest to the campaign before us in the autumn. This Soudan war will be the most serious since Waterloo. As the General destined to command, I am naturally delighted. As an Englishman I most deeply deplore this necessity. I don't like to see Great Britain embarking on an enterprise of which I cannot foresee the end. I would prefer spending our money in strengthening our coaling stations and in aims towards the consolidation of our Empire. This Soudan can never pay its expenses if ruled according to English notions, and the Radical party will insist on representative government. . . ."
[W. to Lady Wolseley.]

journal and several letters from Gordon to Wolseley; but this intelligence destroyed the last flicker of hope as to the safety of his friend, or of any of his devoted followers. Wilson had left Gubat on January 24th, in a steamer which had been repaired by Lord Charles Beresford and his sailors, and after an adventurous journey had got sufficiently close to Khartoum to be certain that it was in the enemy's hands, and to gain reliable intelligence that it had fallen two days before.

Berber was now the immediate objective; it might be taken, so it seemed, by a converging attack of Earle from the north and Buller from the south. But on February 10th Brackenbury, himself in command of the river column, announced that in a successful fight at Kirbekan the gallant Earle, who had unduly exposed himself, had been killed. The British losses had been trifling and the success conspicuous, and Brackenbury was ordered to push on towards Berber.

Gordon's journal, which had to be digested before being sent home, was melancholy reading,[1] and the

[1] " This affair seems to me like a nightmare. At one time I could almost feel Charlie Gordon's hand in mine; his relief seemed, humanly speaking, a certainty, and his relief meant the destruction of the Mahdi's power. Now all is changed, and England has decided on embarking on a war here the end of which it is not easy to foresee. What an irony of fate that Mr. Gladstone should end his public life as a man of war, fighting all round because he had not the statesman's grasp of public affairs to tell him that a policy of cant and cowardice must sooner or later plunge the nation that resorts to it into a slough of war and trouble! "—W. to Lady W.
To Gordon's brother Wolseley wrote later: " I have postponed writing to you from week to week, hoping I might have, if not good news, at least some definite information to give you about your heroic brother. By and by we shall be able to ascertain more particulars about his death, for dead there can be little doubt he is. Had Mohammed Ahmed caught him alive he would, I think, have kept him a prisoner for his own political purposes, but he was killed before that fellow could catch him. Besides, I don't think he would ever have allowed himself to be taken alive. In his journal he discusses the propriety of blowing himself up. I have read through the six volumes of his journal which came into my hands, and it was indeed sad reading for me to think that, if Mr. Gladstone

Government selected this moment to send him a secret telegram asking who should receive a dormant commission in the event of himself becoming a casualty. The reply was prompt. "Buller, certainly; next Greaves, next Wood. Graham is a good fighting man, but not enough brains to command in chief."[1]

Wood was now sent to Gubat to conduct the

had sent us out a month, aye, a week earlier, your brother would now in all probability be alive and well. Believe me, my dear Gordon, we all have done everything we could to save him. When poor General Stewart was wounded some valuable time was lost, for the steamer ought to have started at daybreak on 22nd, and not to have waited till 7 A.M. on the 24th. This might have made all the difference. I always thought that the appearance of one or two steamers, with British soldiers on board, at Khartoum would at any time have saved the place. My plans were based on this conviction. I sent a camel-load of red clothing across the desert in order to dress up the detachment of the Sussex Regt. that I had ordered Wilson to take with him to Khartum, as soon as he could after reaching the Nile near Shandy. I find from your brother's diary that he thought the arrival of such a steamer would also have saved him. Just think how nearly all these plans succeeded, and then picture to yourself our horror when Wilson returned with the news that Khartoum had been taken and your brother killed. Sorrow and rage was in every man's heart; sorrow for the gallant soul who had striven with might and main to save the place, and rage at the Minister whose folly had prevented the effort to reach Khartoum from being undertaken earlier. Well, he is gone from amongst us, and I shall never know his like again; and, indeed, many generations may come and go without producing a Charlie Gordon. His example will be one that every father will hold up to their sons in England, and as long as any faith in God remains to us as a nation, and that we continue to be manly enough to revere the highest form of courage and devotion to duty, so long will your brother be quoted and referred to as the luminous embodiment of all manly and Christian virtue. I hope his journal will be published *in extenso*."

[1] The reversion to command was a matter which Wolseley always carefully considered, and in Ashanti, being mistrustful of the physical powers of his next senior, he had privately arranged with the principal medical officer that this officer, in the event of himself being shot, should be placed compulsorily on the sick list, so that the command should vest in the individual whom he believed most eligible for the post. He had intended Burnaby to succeed Stewart with the desert column, and had provided Brackenbury for the river force, if, as actually happened, Earle became a casualty. To the end of his life he blamed himself for not having provided a third successor to Herbert Stewart and Burnaby, and refused to countenance the attempt to make a scapegoat of Sir Charles Wilson, whose duties were intended to be political rather than military.

withdrawal of the garrisons from the desert to Korti, in case Buller—who had evidently found Matammeh a much harder nut to crack than he had anticipated—could march on Berber. Wood had hardly started when a letter arrived from Buller with a sorry description of his position. The steamers were worn out, the camels so weak as to be nearly useless, whilst if he dismounted his camelry so as to use the weary beasts to carry provisions, the men's boots were too worn to last more than a few days' march.

Buller was still disposed to be confident as to taking Berber, but Wolseley telegraphed home that he was more than doubtful as to this being feasible; moreover, to capture it before the hot weather would still leave an almost insuperable difficulty as to supplies for its garrison. So the forward movement was postponed. On the 13th February Buller sent back a convoy of sick and wounded, among whom was Herbert Stewart;[1] at dawn the next day, having burnt all the stores which could not be carried away and thrown his equipment into the river, he marched out of Gubat, and reached Abu-Klea with little interference. He had intended to make a general halt there to clear the posts, but the water supply proved to be quite insufficient for a large force. He therefore sent on to Jakdul the Heavy and Guards Camel Corps and 19th Hussars,

[1] Sir Herbert Stewart died on February 16th, and was buried in a ravine at Yakdul the next morning. " After dinner a letter reached me from Reggy Talbot announcing the death of poor Stewart. I feel as if I have lost my right arm in this business, and I cannot hope to see his like again. He was out and out the best man I had about me, and to all his military acquirements and qualities he added the rare advantage of being a universal favourite and of being the very pleasantest official to do business with. It is at moments like this that a loathing comes over me for war, that science and art in the study and practice of which I have spent my whole life, and to which I have devoted all my energy and whatever brain power God had gifted me with. This valuable life is an addition to the holocaust offered on the altar of Mr. Gladstone's self-opinionated ignorance."—W. to Lady W.

and stood fast with the remainder of his force—although daily harassed by the enemy—until the 23rd, when he received positive orders to return to Korti, whither the river column was also summoned. His quiet evacuation of his camps, under the pressing attention of the enemy, and his retreat across the desert, were highly commended by Wolseley.[1]

Wolseley now suggested to Baring that it would be politic to make him Governor-General of the Soudan, as his acts and proclamations would have greater weight than if emanating from only a General in Command. He pressed this proposal repeatedly, and finally in a telegram of the 11th March : " Please tell Lord Granville I cannot wait any longer. I must issue proclamations, and will do so on my own responsibility if I do not receive answer to this by 14th instant." Within forty-eight hours there came a " most confidential " telegram from Lord Hartington explaining that the position with Russia and Afghanistan was so critical that it was not expedient for the moment to make any proclamation in the Soudan, or appoint a Governor-General. Wolseley was further sounded as to whether his present safety and prospective advance would be gravely affected if Graham's force were sent on to India before or after the defeat of Osman Digna. He replied, in what he alluded to as a very expensive telegram, protesting against such a course, and painting the absurdity of contemplating a war with Russia when the question of removing or retaining 5000 soldiers at Suakin was a matter of grave moment. If war with Russia were a necessity, Wolseley could only propose the twin measures of calling out the Reserves in England and going, cash in hand, to the Sultan to ask him to tackle the Mahdi with an army of 30,000 men.

---

[1] Buller's move was facilitated by an impromptu reconnaissance of Major Wardrop, whose tiny handful of men judiciously disposed was taken by the Dervishes for the advanced guard of a force.

By the middle of March Brackenbury had drifted downstream to Korti, the footsore and fine-drawn desert column had been shepherded by Sir Evelyn Wood back into that camp, and Wolseley, bending his mind to the autumn campaign, had made personal inspections of possible sites for summer camps.

On March 24th Wolseley embarked in one of his whalers for his proposed summer quarters at Dongola, where he found letters from Ministers saying that the Nile campaign was viewed askance at home, and that only Mr. Gladstone's personal influence could secure the consent of the political party in power to carry it on. Wolseley recognised, and indeed shared, the apprehension of the Government as to the early capture and permanent tenure of Khartoum. He surmised that the Tories would ally themselves with the Radicals in opposition to the war; but he reminded them that we were in Egypt and we could not get out of it, and that our presence imposed on us the necessity of defending it and maintaining order, both of which were impossibilities until Mohammed Ahmed was disposed of. Wolseley's argument was sound, but thirteen years were to elapse before Khartoum was taken, the Mahdi smashed, Gordon avenged, and the stain of " too late " wiped out by the grim perseverance of Kitchener and the crowning mercy of Omdurman.

The Commander-in-Chief was hardly settled at Dongola when the War Secretary wired that it would be more convenient for him to be in Cairo, especially as he might have to take a view of things at Suakin. Wolseley replied that he was prepared to start for Suakin at an hour's notice, but that he disliked the idea of lodging in a Cairene palace while his men frizzled on the sand. Hartington, however, had no scruples on this score, and ordered the reluctant Commander to proceed to the capital at once, Reuter's telegrams at the same time alluding to great naval preparations in England, and hinting that a fleet was to be immediately equipped for the Baltic.[1]

Wolseley reached Cairo on April 11th, his journey downstream not having been sweetened by digesting the military criticisms and comments in the newspapers, which hitherto he had only had time to skim. Nor could he refrain from gloomy reflections as to the narrow margin which stood between the rescue and the fate of Gordon, for he never accepted the theory of the Mahdi's power to work his malignant will at an earlier date.

At Bulak station he was met by Lady Wolseley and his daughter, who had arrived for a short stay in Egypt two days earlier, and took up his lodgings in the Kasr-el-Noussa Palace, which the Khedive again offered him. Three days later came a secret message from the War Office. Imperial interests might necessitate an immediate withdrawal from the Soudan ; secret preparations were to be made at once for the concentration in Egypt of all troops now up the Nile. Wolseley could only protest, although he knew his protest would be brushed aside.[2] He

---

[1] What was known as the " Penjdeh incident " aroused an alarm of war with Russia, which was undoubtedly used by the Government to enable them to get out of the Soudan.

[2] Wolseley's first impulse was to draft a telegram to Hartington : " Yours of to-day. Relying on your declared intention of breaking up the Mahdi's power at Khartoum, I announced to the pashas, Government officers, and people in the Soudan your determination. You now tell me that in the present condition of public affairs you must abandon this policy, and that I must prepare to evacuate the troops now on the Upper Nile so as to have them available for other service. I cannot bring myself to carry out a policy which I believe in a military sense to be as unwise as it is derogatory to the nation, and which, as far as my knowledge of our national exigencies extends, seems uncalled for. I must, therefore, ask you to lay before the Queen the resignation of my position here, and beg to be relieved of my command at the earliest possible date ". Happily, he consulted Lady Wolseley, who was in Cairo, before sending this telegram. On this occasion, as on many others, although she never interfered in the slightest degree with his official life, she exhibited sound judgement in persuading him not to take the step he proposed.

asked anxiously what frontier was to be kept, and urged, as a minimum, that Korosko and Wady Halfa should be held as outposts, and that the bulk of the force should be lodged at Assouan. He rehearsed, in the strongest possible terms, the military reasons against evacuating the Province of Dongola.

The telegram was followed by a private letter from Hartington to the effect that the Government were determined to get out of the Soudan campaign, and were casting about for some good reason to do so, but nothing could be done until the Queen's approval of their foreign policy had been obtained. The Queen was at Aix-les-Bains : some confusion or delay seems to have occurred in her correspondence, and meanwhile Wolseley, as he grimly remarked, must send up the Nile tons-weight of rails, provisions, and stores for operations in the Soudan which had already been cancelled in Downing Street.

Wolseley himself thought that Russia would not declare war,[1] as she was far from equipped for it, and with Afghanistan friendly to Great Britain and Turkey neutral, she would stand to lose in territory and prestige. The policy he outlined was to keep the Russian question open for another year, meanwhile pushing the railway forward to Kandahar, or even to Farah ; to consolidate our alliance with the Ameer, and equip him to stand to arms with us against Russia. The Sultan should be subsidised with money, nourished with suggestions as to Kars and Batoum, and induced to take over Suakin and the Soudan. He himself, in October, would march on Berber and Khartoum, eradicate the Mahdi, establish the Turk, and bring the British force back to Cairo in the spring of 1886, by which time an army of 20,000 British would be assembled at

---

[1] He also said it would be real treason for the Government to begin a war with a great power like Russia when we had no army to put in the field.

Quetta, when a direct challenge could be offered to Russia.

Early on April 21st, Wolseley heard from Harting-ton that the Government would that day explain in Parliament their so-called Soudan policy. Graham's force was to be withdrawn, leaving sufficient men to protect Suakin ; all action against the Mahdi was to be suspended ; troops were to be withdrawn from the Province of Dongola, and concentrated for national requirements, the southern frontier of Egypt being defended by a brigade at Assouan, with outposts at Korosko and Wady Halfa.[1] The die was cast, although Wolseley once more represented that retreat from Dongola meant not only to hand over that province to the Mahdi, but to lose the loyalty of the frontier tribes, and eventually to incur heavy cost in men and money.[2]

At this time he took advantage of his right as a Commander-in-Chief in the field to correspond direct with the Secretary of State, to bring before Lord Hartington a question to which he had in vain invited the Duke's attention. On April 16th he penned a momentous note from Cairo :

" There are now serving under my command some regimental Lieut.-Colonels who are entirely unfit for their positions—men who, although en-trusted by Regulations with the command of over 800 soldiers of all ranks, could not, with due regard for the lives of those soldiers and the honour and interest of the State, be allowed any independent command before an enemy.

" To the Brigadier or General under whose immediate orders they serve, these officers are a

[1] An attempt was first made, but in vain, to induce the sheikhs to afford protection to the railway line.

[2] He had just received an autograph letter from the Queen which had evidently touched him. " Poor lady, she is wellnigh heartbroken at having her kingdom made ducks and drakes of by Mr. Gladstone and Co."—W. to Lady W.

source of constant anxiety. Owing to their ignorance of the first principles of tactics or of the military art, it is always necessary for him, in order to avoid disaster, to keep them under his own personal observation, or to send some well-trained staff officer to take care of them.

" The army in the Soudan is no exceptional case. It was the same in the army I commanded in Egypt in 1882. It has been the same in every military expedition I have been entrusted with, and it was the same in every army in the field I ever served with as a junior officer. I have often on active service seen splendid battalions kept in the rear, or broken up for work along the line of communication, whilst others of inferior quality were sent to the front, because the General commanding did not dare to employ against the enemy corps whose commanding officers were manifestly incompetent.

" The time has now come, I think, for plain speaking on this most important subject, a subject of real national moment.

" The purchase system gave to officers an undefined and unwritten, but a practically recognised, right to obtain the command of regiments without reference to whether they were or were not fitted for the position. That system was abolished at a cost to the nation of some millions, and in my opinion it is but right that the nation should obtain in return the reform it expected and had a right to expect, namely, that none but competent and properly educated officers should be selected for the position of Lieut.-Colonel. And this is of even more importance for our Army than it is for those of other European Powers. For our Army is chiefly employed on small wars, and consequently in small units. The officer commanding a battalion may at any moment fall into the chief command, and under our present method of promotion there is nothing to prevent the safety and success of the whole expedition depending upon a man of notorious incompetence. I hold that it is criminal to hand over in action the care of the lives of gallant soldiers to men who are deplorably ignorant of the elements of their profession. A system must be entirely and radically wrong under which officers of this stamp can obtain the position of Lieut.-Colonels in H.M.'s Army. If from no other motive but the dictates of humanity it appears the bounden duty of those to whom the interests and welfare of the Army are confided to do all that care and judgement can do to prevent inefficient men from being promoted to important and responsible posts. In a system of promotion by seniority neither care nor judgement need be exercised, and the fitness of an officer for his position is, in the main, left to chance. At present the tactical knowledge and the general military capacity of the senior officers of a regiment are in peace time rarely if ever tested. The Lieut.-Colonel commanding a battalion of infantry or a regiment of cavalry retires, and unless there is something glaringly against the character of the next senior officer, he obtains the vacancy, and the Major becomes a Lieut.-Colonel. An officer thus arrives at the highest position in a regiment, not in consequence of his qualifications, but simply in consequence of his place in the regimental list, frequently in the face of known disqualifications for such a position. This is the rule, and it is very rarely departed from. I would ask your Lordship what would be the condition of any other of the great professions if the higher posts were filled upon similar principles.

"In the Navy—the sister service to the Army—the officers to command ships are selected with the greatest care. What reason can be alleged should not equal care be taken in choosing an officer to command a regiment or battalion. The principle of selection is in no way foreign to our Army—it underlies it from its very foundation. It is well worthy of observation that the same officer who perhaps asks for a rigid adherence to seniority in their own case is the first to disregard it directly they require efficiency from those under them. All the non-commissioned officers of our Army—than whom a more valuable and respectable body of men does not exist—are selected for their positions. Adjutants are selected ; Quartermasters are selected ; every regimental post, which may from time to time be instituted, such as regimental transport officer, or baggage master, is filled by selection—and all these selections are made by the same man who has perhaps maintained that for the position he himself fills, that namely of officer commanding a regiment, seniority should be the sole standard. . . .

" There is no greater difficulty in selecting an officer for regimental Lieut.-Colonel than there is for any post on the staff. The real reason which has prevented selection being carried out in the first instance are, in the fear of the unpopularity of the measure, and in the outcry which would ensue. I will not say that this fear is wholly unfounded, but I can assure your Lordship that the outcry will be far less than is anticipated. A certain amount of grumbling and complaining there will be, but the change will be supported by the young, the able, and the vigorous throughout the services, since it is directly to their advantage. With these on our side, I do not think we need fear the dissent of those officers whose only cause of complaint is that they are not put into positions they are thought to hold, nor allowed when on active service to learn the first rudiments of war at the expense of the lives of the gallant soldiers who have the misfortune to be under their command.

" On behalf of these brave men, as well as in the

interest of the Army and the State, I make this appeal to your Lordship. The subject is too serious to be passed by any longer, and I should not deserve to be regarded as comrade by those with whom I so often serve if I did not press it upon your attention with all the earnestness of which I am capable."

This letter marks the change from preliminary skirmishes to a definite offer of one more battle in the cause of efficiency.

On April 29th, Wolseley, who was suffering from something very like dysentery, having made the evacuation arrangements with Buller over the wire, and bidden good-bye to a very perturbed and depressed Khedive, left Suez for Suakin, which he reached on May 2nd. He professed himself amused, but evidently was at first annoyed by what he described as an attempt of Granville to secure an expert opinion agreeable to that of the Government, in respect to the retreat from Dongola. " I am to obtain ", he wrote privately, " the views of Wilson and Kitchener, one a Colonel, the other a Captain on the Staff of the army I command. This is another effort which is being made to invest Wilson with the duties of a political officer, which I would sooner resign than permit. However, I said I would telegraph to Buller and desire him to obtain the views of those two officers, and to send them forward with his own. Called in to bless, they have cursed the evacuation policy in louder terms than I ever did, and Baring has, in consequence, desired Nubar not to order the evacuation for the present, and the subject will be discussed to-day by the Cabinet. Such a Government to serve ! "

Wolseley remained a fortnight at Suakin, where he could honestly eulogise the military dispositions and the admirable turn-out of all the men, with the exception of one battalion of the Guards, his admittedly just comments on which provoked a splutter of wrath from the Commander-in-Chief at home.[1]

Before leaving he issued in a " special order " his farewell to the soldiers, sailors, and marines of the army in the Soudan, and on his arrival at Cairo very reasonably suggested to the Government that he might as well go home, but was bidden to sit tight for the moment.[2]

The Queen's birthday on May 24th brought a cordial message from the Sovereign. Her Majesty's telegram was followed by a special mark of favour : the ribbon of the Patrick was to be bestowed on Wolseley, who admitted himself to be pleased and " flattered ". " Vanity, vanity ", he wrote to Lady Wolseley in a strain of self-defence ; " most truly all is naught but vanity in this world. Even my hero

[1] Besides inspecting the troops and satisfying himself as to conditions at Suakin, Wolseley was charged with a duty which he strongly resented : " In accordance with your directions ", he wrote to the War Secretary, " I will enquire into the general conduct of the operations on March 22nd, but I strongly deprecate (save in the most extreme cases) enquiring too rigorously into the conduct of commanders after unsatisfactory engagements. It is hopeless to expect to find a General who does not make mistakes. The history of war shows that the greatest generals have done so often. There may be cases in which the mistakes are of such a character as to call for the immediate removal of their author from his command. But, short of this, to examine too minutely into any faulty dispositions that have been made, and to publish to the world a condemnation of them, simply takes away from the general implicated all the confidence of his troops, without, as far as I can see, any corresponding good result whatever."

[2] He also heard indirectly that in the event of war the Government proposed to send him with all the troops that could be collected to Riga to raise the Poles. " If given a sufficient force ", he wrote, " this would be an operation entirely after my own heart, but I fear it would be one entirely beyond the military strength of England, as our nation is now constituted. Such a policy would bring the Germans and Austrians on our backs sooner or later, and without having studied the operation it would seem to be one of great risk lest before we could get at the Poles our army near Riga should be crushed by numbers. To be successful in any such great undertaking a very different form of Government to our present one would be necessary. In democracies like ours, it has always been found necessary to create a Dictator in time of great national danger."

Gordon, whom I served when he lived and whose memory I shall always cherish, even he, great and glorious, had his vanities. I knew him so well that I saw them crop up here and there, although he was unconscious of them. I, who was not worthy of being his servant, may therefore be well excused for my innocent pleasure in having this new distinction conferred upon me."

On June 10th news came that the Government had been defeated on the Budget, and that the Queen, who was at Balmoral, had sent for Lord Salisbury. " I wish that dear, good lady would go south at once ", Wolseley commented. " She is inconsiderate upon these points, having been badly educated upon them by Prince Albert."

The defeat of Mr. Gladstone was balm to Wolseley's wounded spirit, but its immediate consequences were that Hartington could give no instructions for the return either of the Commander-in-Chief, or of the Guards, who had been held up in Cairo. Waterloo Day had an exultant note in Wolseley's diary. " I am glad to find that several of my telegrams and despatches condemning the Government's policy have been published, and have had some effect. They will, at least, show the world that I have had the courage of my opinions." [1]

Wolseley's days at Cairo—the one place in Egypt where he never felt well—were drawing to an end. His long early morning rides were his only pleasure, otherwise his enforced idleness irritated him and caused him to chew the cud of his bitter disappointment ; he had neither the means nor the mind to settle down even to such work as the revision of his *Soldiers' Pocket Book.*

[1] Wolseley certainly had the courage of his opinions in his resolute insistence on the publication of his despatch bearing on " Selection in the Army ", which the Duke of Cambridge considered an attack upon himself, a compromise being effected by the elimination of two or three sentences which did not affect the argument.

One of the last straws of his burden lay in the refusal of the Mahdi to give up his European prisoners, that truculent potentate coolly asserting that his captives were quite happy, having all become Moslems, and that he was perfectly indifferent as to the fate of the members of his own family who were prisoners at Halfa. Wolseley was, however, considerably heartened by a graceful and most complimentary telegram of June 25th from Lord Salisbury, announcing that he had accepted the seals of office. "How different from the Party just retired, from whom I have not had a line of thanks. Of course, Lord Spencer has given me the K.P., and perhaps that was intended to be a recognition from the Government collectively of the exertions I had made to save Khartoum. By this little 'touch' Salisbury has shown that he understands men and human nature, for the promptness and unexpectedness of his telegram has 'fetched' me a good deal, and would do so still more with most other men." [1]

There was to be one last spasm of hope as to a British occupation of Dongola. On June 26th came a telegram from the new War Secretary, Mr. W. H. Smith, asking for a full exposition of his views, both as to the present position and possible policy in Egypt, and inquiring how far north our troops had already retreated. Wolseley's reply was a reaffirmation of what he had over and over again laid down ; his telegram, he was told, would be considered at a Cabinet three days later, and meanwhile, he was to hold on to Dongola and state what troops would be required for that purpose, apart from any question of an advance to Khartoum. The pleasing prospect was soon to be swept away, for on July 2nd came the definite dictum of the

[1] "It is curious how few Prime Ministers have realised what a few timely words of encouragement mean to a harassed Commander-in-Chief in the field."—Postscript, W. to Lady W.

Government that, although they condemned the evacuation of Dongola, it was impossible for the time being, at any rate, to retain the place. They left it to military judgement to decide to what point the railway should be held south of Halfa, and Wolseley, after consultation with Baring, designated Akash, with the strong and prophetic reminder that an extension to Firkit, above the difficult cataracts, would be found of infinite value in the event of future operations.

Wolseley's recommendations as to the railway were his " swan song " in Egypt.

It only remained to receive the report of the evacuation of Dongola on the 5th July, to pay the visits of ceremony to Ministers, to wish the Khedive good-bye at Alexandria and hear his professions of profound " Anglophilism ", and to embark — once more on the *Iris*—for Venice. "So ends my un-successful expedition for the relief of Khartoum ", Wolseley wrote as his train neared London. But there are failures of finer stuff than any success, and the Sovereign and her people were disposed to reward with honour the man who had failed as nobly as, in the same country but in happier circumstances, he had succeeded. The vote of thanks moved by Parliament rang with cordial praise, and the *Gazette* announced that Baron Wolseley of Cairo and Wolseley had been raised to a Viscountcy.

BUTTON, THE 18TH ROYAL IRISH REGIMENT.

CHAPTER IX

THE WAR OFFICE AND PREPARATION FOR WAR, 1885–1890

TIRED and disappointed, Lord Wolseley on his return had little taste for fresh polemics. He was under the natural reaction after prolonged strain ; he was saddened by the memory of the friends who had been sacrificed ; he was depressed by the sense of a personal failure ; and he was smarting under his first experience of a check in the field. But he was to find abundant evidence that those who really knew the facts were agreed he had done all that man could do. Hartington, who knew best of all, wrote heavily but with genuine ring : " As to your recent campaign, you know I think, that although we have just missed success, I had never had the slightest thought of attributing our failure to any fault either of design or execution on your own part or on that of your officers and men. I shall always feel most grateful to you for the advice and assistance you gave me last summer and autumn, and also for the way in which you at once, at my request, undertook the responsibility and labour of the command of so novel and uncertain an enterprise. I believe that since that time everything has been done which could have been done to ensure its success, and it is satisfactory to know that although the actual object was not attained, there was not, as far as I know, a single failure either in the administrative arrangements for the despatch of the expedition, or of the military dispositions in its execution."

Wolseley was braced also by a brief holiday, and by an interesting mission to Germany. At Berlin he was deputed to represent the Queen at the Jubilee of the Emperor William I. The old Kaiser he had met before, but he now came for the first time into touch with Bismarck and von Moltke. "These three men", he wrote, "created the German Empire. That it should have been the work of a trinity and not of one leader, marks it out from other great national creations. When you meet the three men it is easy to see how indispensable each was to the other. The old king the heart; Bismarck the cold, calculating brain; Moltke the maker of the instrument." Bismarck he found very friendly but aged and worn. He was suffering from lumbago, and "his clothes hung about him as if he were a scarecrow". He told Wolseley: "After a man passes seventy, he must receive every extra year's existence as a free gift from God, and be thankful accordingly". He asked many questions about Egypt, but characteristically gave no hint of his own views. With von Moltke Wolseley was charmed. The shrewd old Prussian won his heart with many compliments on Tel-el-Kebir, and warm admiration for the gallantry of Stewart—of whom he seemed to know a good deal—and his men at Abu-Klea. But pleasant speeches did not cloud Wolseley's judgement. "Moltke", he told Maurice, "is a great man, a great patriot, a great thinker, and a good Christian, but he is not the heaven-born, invincible General they think him here, and most of our people think him too. What Moltke has done is to inspire the German army from top to bottom with the conviction that hard work and hard study are just as necessary in the military as in any other profession, and to convince the German people that preparation and organisation take you more than half-way to victory. He and Roon[1] have thought out a system which suits the German character and the German people. That is what we've got to do. We copy slavishly the army which is the fashion of the day. When I entered the Army the French were the great military people, and we wore a cap like the French kepi, and our trousers in wrinkles ; now the Germans are the military gods, and we strap down our overalls and wear a feeble imitation of the German ' pickelhaube '. If our officers would copy the Germans as regards work and leave their clothes and their methods alone,[2] and our politicians would understand that war is a serious business which has to be prepared for, we need never be afraid of the Germans."

Three years later Wolseley toured the battlefields of the Franco-German War. His friend, Mr. Edmund Gosse, drew from him a promise to record his impressions. Wolseley wrote to him on October 4th, 1889 : " I postponed writing to you until my tour round the battlefields should have finished, as I could not tell what to write upon the subject until I had studied the ground. I need scarcely tell you that I knew the chief episodes of each great fight very well before I came abroad. The German account of events is so very full and truthful that no student of war has any excuse for ignorance. With that book, and maps and plans, I have care-

[1] The German War Minister in 1870.
[2] " I am glad to hear that the young Prince has taken to his drill kindly. Has he the same German tutor still ? I can't say that I like the German soldier's dress. Ours is bad enough, but theirs is ridiculous. I think the Russian soldier so much better dressed, for his clothes are loose and he can work in them. How the German officer ever gets in and out of his breeches [the word is drawn, not written], I cannot imagine ; they are so tight that they cling to him as if they are woven on him. I don't think it is boastful to say that our most ordinary line officer could—in sporting parlance —give him many pounds in weight, and beat him easily at every manly exercise, and this on foot or on horseback."—Wolseley to Duchess of Edinburgh.

fully studied every phase of every battlefield from Sedan in the North to Strassburg in the South, and I find I could not write upon the subject without expressions of opinion that would be very unpleasant to many men now alive. The Germans outnumbered the French in nearly all those battles to a large extent, and though the French allowed themselves to be surprised, and their leaders committed every possible mistake, the errors of the Germans were very glaring upon many occasions. Almost all their battles were not only fought in a manner entirely different from what was intended, but, in nearly every case, they were brought on without, and in some occasions contrary to, the positive orders and intentions of the Generals." [1]

Wolseley was writing and speaking years before the publication of the French official history of the war had produced in English military circles a more sober estimate of the triumphs of von Moltke and his army; if he was unwilling at the time to challenge accepted beliefs, his visit to the military demi-gods of Europe decided him to apply the good in German teaching without imitating German methods.

One of his first acts on resuming his chair at the War Office was to contrive an extension and magnification of the Intelligence Department. Hitherto that Department had consisted of a handful of officers working in a small apartment

[1] At home Mr. Gosse found him even more positive in conversation. " He had realised to his great surprise that the Germans, whose luck had been incredible, had more than once or twice been very nearly defeated, and he had been particularly excited by his inspection of the battlefield of Gravelotte. ' If that battle had not been won by what was really a " fluke ", the day would have closed upon the German Army in about the most unfortunate position an army could possibly be placed in.' All this struck me, ignorant of tactics as I am, as so very interesting that I entreated him to change his mind and write a complete record of his observations on the battlefields. But he said the praise of German strategy had reached such a pitch of infatuation in England that he should be ' accused of all sorts of things '."— *Some Aspects and Impressions,* Mr. Edmund Gosse.

in Queen Anne's Gate, and regarded as a harmless but rather useless appendage to the War Office. Wolseley persuaded a willing War Minister [1] to press an unwilling Treasury for the necessary funds. He insisted that the main and vitally important function of the intelligence officers was the study of preparation for war. He gave to the head of the Department the rank of Major-General, with the title first of D.Q.M.G. and then of Director of Military Intelligence, and he nominated as that head Brackenbury, whom he then described as "not one of the cleverest, but *the* cleverest man in the British Army". He instructed Brackenbury to draft a full and precise programme showing the exact number of men, horses, and guns, and the amount of transport and material of all kinds, required to mobilise at home a force of two army corps and a cavalry division, the exact size of the Expeditionary Force of 1914, and, during the next year worked incessantly to make good the large gaps between the paper plan and the actual provision.

He had shocked the Duke and offended regimental officers by his mode of collecting volunteers and picking men for his expeditions, but these had been improvisations from the means available to meet needs as they arose. Nothing was further from his mind than to perpetuate the trials of a British General—trials he had tasted to the full—in command of "an army hastily thrown together, without cohesion between its component parts, and with no organised transport".[2] To complete the component parts of a well-organised expeditionary force, he urged that eleven battalions of infantry should be added to the army by the creation of third and fourth battalions in certain regiments ; that the artillery should be increased by seven batteries ;

[1] Mr. Campbell-Bannerman, War Minister, January to July 1886.
[2] See p. 153, footnote.

THE WAR OFFICE, PALL MALL, 1885.

To face page 224.

and the engineers by six companies. At the same time he asked for regular annual training of the Army Reserve. Many of these increases he did not obtain until the South African War convinced both Ministers and public that the demands, which they were disposed to think had been pressed with undue insistence and advocated in unnecessarily plain language during the thirteen years which preceded President Kruger's invasion of Natal, had been neither excessive nor untimely.

No organisation for war can suffice if only brought into existence with the advent of the war itself. For many years the military organisation in Great Britain and Ireland was in districts, and the number of troops in any district, determined mainly for reasons of administrative convenience, had no connection with any formation which could be used in battle. Thus ninety-nine regimental officers out of a hundred did not look, and had no reason to look, beyond their own cavalry regiment, infantry battalion or artillery battery, and there prevailed the vaguest ideas as to co-operation between the various parts of an army. Wolseley would have the troops trained in brigades and divisions in peace time by the men who would command them in war. On September 20th, 1887, he wrote : "I have just been to an Alma Day parade. It is a fine thing to keep alive the memory of those old battles, if we really remember how and why they were won. They are damnably mischievous if we think because they were won we must always win again. Half the Army is still living, not on the memory of the Crimea, for which God be praised, but of the Peninsula, yet in the regiments which justly swell with pride at the mention of Badajos, Salamanca, and the Pyrenees, it is rare to find a man who knows that it took Wellington, with all the advantage of Moore's work before him, four years to make the army which

drove the French out of Spain from the scraps which
were thrown to him. I suppose if we were mad
enough to embark on a big war, as the politicians
have talked of doing at least three times in the last
eight years, it would take us about two years to
make an army, and that's the amount of progress
we've made since the Peninsular War. We have
now in the Army plenty of men of intelligence
and experience who think, but they are sat on by
bow-and-arrow generals. If we could get the troops
into the formations in which they would have to
fight in war, and there is nothing but crass stupidity
and blind conservatism against it, the regimental
officers would soon see the point, and we should not
weaken the regimental spirit which I'm always supposed to be destroying, but add an army spirit to it." [1]

Commissions were to sit, War Ministers were to
come and go, scheme after scheme was to be
drawn up and torn up, before the mantle of
Cardwell fell upon the broad shoulders of Mr.
Haldane, and the plan here advocated by Wolseley
was fully adopted. But with Wolseley as Adjutant-
General a beginning was made at Aldershot, where
brigades complete with commanders and staffs
were formed, and this after a grandiose scheme,
with which he had nothing to do, for the mobilisation of the regulars, militia, and volunteers in eight
army corps, a scheme which consisted largely of
blanks, had been published in the *Army Lists* of
1881, and laughed out of court.

At the end of 1887 Wolseley's normal term of
office as Adjutant-General was due to expire, and
his future was under discussion. The command at

[1] Letter to Maurice. See also *Soldiers' Pocket Book*, 1886 edition:
" No man who knew soldiers or their peculiar ways of thinking, or
who was acquainted with the many little trifles that go to make up
pride of regiment and that form, as it were, the link between it
and discipline, would deprive a soldier of any peculiarity that he
prided himself on without some overpowering reason for doing so ".

Aldershot would have been tempting. It would be a satisfaction to put into practice much of what he had proposed on paper. Malta was dangled before him, but was not attractive. He wrote in February to the Duchess of Edinburgh : " It is very possible I may have to succeed Simmons next year as Governor of Malta. I don't care about the place, and I know my wife would hate it, but I cannot afford to be idle, and my tenure of office as Adjutant-General expires next year. At present nothing is thought or talked of but the great question of peace or war. . . .

" I am glad to say that, in our small way, we have never in our history been so ready for war as now. I shall leave my post next year with the proud feeling that after over ten years of struggling against every species of opposition, I leave everything ready for the rapid mobilisation of two Army Corps—about 65,000 men, or twice the force we landed in the Crimea in 1854. If we have, by any mischance, to fight this year, we can land this little army in a very perfect condition as soon as ships for their conveyance can be obtained."

But as the year wore on the Government became more and more reluctant to let him leave Pall Mall, and the Duke himself urged that he should remain. An extension of two years was agreed upon. Evelyn Wood, whom Wolseley specified as the best trainer of troops he knew, was sent to the premier military station to initiate that training for war which was only to become general when Boer rifles had roughly emphasised the truth of Wolseley's precepts.

In clearing out the dust-encumbered purlieus of the War Office, the Adjutant-General did not limit the use of his besom to the departments of organisation and training. He thrust it into every corner. He had come back from the Nile burning with indignation because the munitions supplied to his

troops in the Soudan had been bad ; cartridges had
been defective, swords and bayonets had been known
to bend. " I will hang these rogues as high as
Haman," he wrote in fury, " even if I have to appeal
to the last court—public opinion." In 1887, at his
instance, a " Committee on Organisation of Army
Manufacturing Departments " was convened. Its
blunt criticism of the prevailing system shocked the
Secretary of State into immediate compliance with
their recommendations. The design and inspection
of munitions of war was divorced from their manufacture, and the former was healthily placed in the
hands of the Navy and Army.

These activities, superadded to the normal routine
of an important office, might well exhaust the energy
of most men, but Wolseley was a glutton for work.
He rose at six every morning, boiled himself a cup
of cocoa on the spirit stove he took with him on
active service, and, like the Duke of Wellington,
wrote for three hours. Thus he began, in 1886, to
work upon his *Life of Marlborough*—whom he voted
the greatest of English Generals—and in the same
year he completed a further edition of his *Soldiers'
Pocket Book*. This modest volume had become
very popular, because it was so very practical.
It was clear that the writer's head was not in the
clouds ; for the renaissance of the Army the humbler
parts of the military machine had to be carefully
tended. " The Army ", he wrote, " exists far too
much for the officers, and as long as they are satisfied,
Pall Mall is satisfied too." His main purpose was
to bring officers and men closer together, and of the
former there were still a good many of the temper of
the young Guardsman who, on being ordered to an
inconvenient parade, said : " The Army would be a
jolly good place if it consisted only of the Mess and

the band ". " In our intercourse with the rank and file ", said Wolseley in the *Pocket Book*, " we must make them realise that all our interests are identical, causing the last-joined recruit to feel that success is of as much real moment to him as it can be to the General. Upon all occasions appeal to their honour and chivalrous feeling ; show them that you have confidence in them and trust them. Cease to treat them as unreasoning children unable to take care of themselves. You will then create in their breasts feelings of honour even if they had been previously devoid of them."

When, in 1888, he contrived to bring the control of the food supplies of the Army under the Commander-in-Chief,[1] his first care was to improve the messing, and to vest responsibility for the material comfort of the men with the regimental officers. The new War Office whim—as it was termed—caught on, and for a time the proper management of swill tubs and the profit-able disposal of refuse for the messing fund seemed to matter more than hitting the bull's-eye.

Wolseley justly recognised that the regimental officer had much to excuse him for the very moderate interest which he was apt to take in his profession. " The British officer is never, or at least very rarely, a loafer, as he is supposed to be by those who talk easily about the emptiness of life in a garrison at home. He is not lazy, but is far too intelligent to spend his time upon nothing but pipe-clay and hurdy-gurdy parades. Give him a chance of interesting himself in the training and welfare of the men, and he will work as hard as any one. I never knew any body of men work harder than the regimental officers who were with me on the Nile. Why ? Because they had something worth working for."[2]

[1] See p. 171.
[2] Private Letter, Jan. 10th, 1887.

Therefore, he would have training more practical and interesting. In December 1887 the Adjutant-General's somewhat contemptuous reference to barrack-square drill as the end-all and be-all of military training made at a military meeting with reporters present provoked the Duke to stern remonstrance. " It is always with the deepest regret ", ran the reply, " that I find my views on military subjects in any way opposed to those held by Your Royal Highness. In the present instance, however, there is no divergence of opinion upon the point named in Your Royal Highness's note to me, namely, the necessity for and importance of ' drill '. I go even so far as to say that our men, and especially our officers, do not get enough of it. Throughout the length and breadth of our Army there is, however, a very strong feeling as to the *quality*, not the quantity, of our drill. I have been always in touch with the officers who advocate progress and who attach the greatest importance to military *training*, that is, to the highest form of drill. With them I have always surrounded myself when on active service, and I am glad to see them coming to the front on all sides.

" These men think our military training is too much sacrificed to show parade movements, and that the soldier can be better disciplined both in body and mind by being taught the duties and evolutions he *must* practise before an enemy, than by parade movements only possible in peace.

" In these views, which I hear on all sides, I entirely agree."

The Duke replied with dignity and reason, if in rather indifferent prose :

" MY DEAR WOLSELEY—With reference to the letter I have just received from you, and in which you say that you, in the main, agree with me, though you adhere to your views, I really don't think there can be much, if any, difference at all between us, as the more that drill is adapted daily to the details of intended movements, the more I shall be pleased. But that is certainly not my reading of the movements referred to, and which give the public, I feel assured, an entirely different view of your ideas on Military subjects from those entertained by myself and the great bulk of experienced officers. I am at all times most willing to attend to any suggestions or recommendations you think it right to make training or equipment in any way more adapted to modern requirements. What I really do object to is that in public addresses made from time to time, very disparaging expressions occur of our old system as compared with what you would wish to have done, and this I think a great misfortune, producing friction of feeling and thought where I think none ought to exist, at all events not in a manner to become known to the public or to the Army.

" I feel assured that on consideration you will think me right in this aspect, and I should be sorry if my views should produce anything but the most satisfactory results, as preventing friction of all kinds.

" One difficulty our Army has always to contend with compared to all others is that we have not sufficient space near our Barracks or Stations to apply extended drill as we should wish or desire, and this fact cannot be lost sight of.—I remain, yours most sincerely, GEORGE."

Unquestionably Wolseley's Irish temperament and his fretting at opposition to what he knew to be beneficial proposals led him sometimes to say on a platform what was imprudent, if true, while his pen was not always under due control. But the regulations which then governed the speeches and writings of officers on full pay were indefinite, and it was possible to keep within the letter of the law and yet comment publicly upon military affairs. Thus Brackenbury, on becoming Director of the Military Intelligence Department, one of the most confidential of the State offices, found it advisable to obtain a written agreement from every officer that, while employed in the department, he would make no communication to the Press. Wolseley took all advantage of this latitude to broadcast his views when those views were set aside in the War Office, and in a periodical for January 1889 published an exceptionally biting article on the shortcomings of our military administration. Then arose a first-class storm. The Duke seized his pen for a severe reprimand :

" MY DEAR WOLSELEY—I am sure that you will feel with me, that the Adjutant-General of the Army, when writing in public periodicals on Military subjects, carries great weight in his utterances, and that it is not desirable that in that capacity he should express himself on controversial matters, which are sure to elicit comment of various kinds. I have had a conversation with Mr. Stanhope,[1] whose attention I have drawn to this point, and he fully concurs with me that it is undesirable for officers of the Army on full pay expressing their opinions in any other way than by the legitimate channels of communication to the Commander-in-Chief. I hope you will therefore agree with me in thinking that it would be well for the Adjutant-General of the Army to set a good example in this respect by forgoing in future all such writings, by which you would greatly oblige.— Yours most sincerely,   GEORGE."

Wolseley could do no less than offer his resignation :

" As Adjutant-General, I feel I have the duty laid upon me of doing my best according to my views

[1] Then Secretary of State for War.

for Her Majesty's Army. I should fail in my duty if I did not advocate the style of training which appears to me to be *necessary*, after a lengthened experience in war, to enable the Army to cope with other forces it may have to meet. I should also fail in loyalty and sincerity to the Queen and to Your Royal Highness if I did not point out in what respect our present system of training is unsuited to secure that object.

"I always put these views before Your Royal Highness with outspoken candour, although the consciousness that they do not coincide with the views you hold makes me regret to have to do so. Were I to hold other language in public, or to be entirely silent, on what my experience tells me are points of vital importance to the State, I should not feel that I was acting honestly by the Army or by my country which pays me.

"It is to me a matter of deepest regret that such divergence of opinion should exist between an officer in my position and the Commander-in-Chief, and it must rest with Your Royal Highness and the S. of S. to decide whether the divergence demands that I should cease to occupy the post of Adjutant-General.

"To write this letter is very painful to me, but the terms in which Your Royal Highness's letter is couched have compelled me to write it."

Wolseley spoke and wrote with a single eye to the public interest, and there can be traced to him no word of personal complaint or recrimination; but to hold up for exhibition the divergences between the highest military authorities sometimes did more harm than good to the cause he had at heart, and he made enemies where a more tactful presentation of his case might have won supporters.

The storm blew over, but the storm clouds drifted about. Wolseley, with the country's danger in his eye, could brook no delay ; the Duke would stand fast till change was forced upon him. At one of his last functions as Commander-in-Chief the Duke said : "Gentlemen, there have been great changes in my time—great changes. But I can say this. Every change has been made at the right time, and the right time is when you cannot help it." Wolseley was continually engaged in convincing the Duke that the time had come when he could not help it. The Duke was every bit as sincere as Wolseley. Soon after he left the War Office for good he wrote to his successor urging him to be cautious in making changes : "My anxiety is, believe me, because I LOVE the Army, and not with a view to making, on the contrary to AVOID, troubles, as I have had the experience of thirty-nine years to guide my thoughts on these large subjects. It is easy enough to upset matters, but not easy to make afresh what is supposed to be better to take the place of the past."

No one doubted the Duke's love for the Army, least of all Wolseley, who wrote of him after he too had left the War Office :

"Educated to believe in the Army as he found it, because it had been made by the great Duke of Wellington, he honestly and firmly believed that what had been created by such a master of war must be the best for all time. He had not apparently taken in fully the great changes which the system of universal military service had produced in European armies. He refused to believe in an Army Reserve, and honestly looked upon our endeavours to create one here as not only a mad folly but as a crime against the State. No more loyal and devoted Englishman ever wore a red coat, but nothing would or could convince him that an Army Reserve in this country would be forthcoming when wanted. Recent experience has proved how absolutely wrong the old school of officers were on this point, and no man more than His Royal Highness has ever been more thoroughly converted to modern views on this point.

" I have mentioned this about a Royal Personage under whom I was long privileged to work, because I liked him more and more the better I knew him. Indeed no one who served so many years on his staff could fail to love his amiable qualities, or to admire his manliness of feeling. His honesty of purpose, loyalty to the Army, devotion to duty, sincere patriotism, and deep and real attachment to his Queen and country pervaded all he did." [1]

To represent the Duke and Wolseley as animated by constant personal hostility would be quite untrue, but upon many subjects it was impossible to bring their minds into agreement. For instance, as to the value of military education Wolseley's ideas were sharply defined : " I have no more desire than the Duke has for what he calls ' military bookworms '. Any boy who has mastered the first book of Euclid can learn and understand the theories of Jomini and Clausewitz and be a perfectly useless soldier afterwards unless by hard thought he learns how to apply their theories to the ever-changing conditions of war ; and how are you going to train a man to think unless you encourage him to read ? The idle and the ignorant say that an ounce of experience is worth a pound of military history. Well, I say that the story of every great commander of whom I know gives the lie to that. It is often said that a man who writes well cannot be a good soldier ; most of the great commanders, from King David, Xenophon, and Caesar to Wellington, not only wrote well, but extremely well."

To make the officer a student of his profession was Wolseley's dream, and he did his best to make

---

[1] *Story of a Soldier's Life*, Wolseley, vol. ii. p. 234.

the Staff College a live centre of military study. He sent Maurice there to teach military history, and later chose as his successor Colonel Henderson, the brilliant author of *Stonewall Jackson*. Henderson was a captain in the York and Lancaster Regiment when Wolseley's attention was drawn to his book on the *Campaign of Fredericksburg*, and he named him in 1889 to be an instructor at Sandhurst. Both men did much to free the Staff College from its somewhat pedantic atmosphere; they sought to make it attractive as well as instructive, and under their tuition came most of the commanders in the Great War. The Duke had no faith in the Staff College; his distrust of the place was increased when at his inspections he found some of the officers turned out less smartly than he liked. Wolseley once put up to him a memorandum asking that a vacant appointment should be given to a Staff College officer. " Staff College officer," grunted the Duke, " what does he want a Staff College officer for ? I know those Staff College officers. They are very ugly officers and very dirty officers."

Another point of perennial difference was the system of promotion. Wolseley urged in season and out of season that merit should have precedence over seniority. He begged the Duke when there was a question of promoting an officer of doubtful value in the field : " Give him orders and ribbons, but don't give him men's lives to lose ". Capacity to command troops in war, he protested, should be the one test of fitness for promotion in an army. This seems *prima facie* indisputable, but the problem was far from being as simple as it appeared. The counter - argument ran that peace training often provided a very inadequate proof of capacity to lead in the field, and that a process of selection might open the door to favouritism and jobbery. By sheer pertinacity Wolseley induced a tentative system of selection for the promotion of generals, a system subsequently made permanent.

On one subject of first-class importance—the care of sick and wounded in war—the Duke and Wolseley saw eye to eye. In the Soudan the British Red Cross Society, then clumsily termed " The British National Aid Society to the Sick and Wounded in War ", had for the first time ministered largely to British troops in the field. The services of the Red Cross were under the direction of Sir Robert Loyd-Lindsay,[1] a V.C. of the Crimea, who with his wife's powerful help was instrumental in supplying a number of nurses for the hospitals on the Nile. On his return home Wolseley had written to his friend : " I shall not attempt to enter upon any detail of the numerous benefits conferred, or the good effected by the Society, but I must not pass over in silence the fact that it is to those who have directed its affairs that the Army is mainly indebted for the hospital nurses who are now, I am glad to say, a recognised part of our military hospital establishment both at home and abroad. It would be impossible to overestimate the boon these nurses have been to every force in the field with which they have been associated, they have earned for themselves the respect and heartfelt gratitude of all ranks. Before dismissing this subject may I venture to add that my experience leads me to believe that the higher the social position of the nurses the greater their usefulness ? " The order of voluntary nurses, thus founded and fostered, was to grow in merit and importance until it issued in the Voluntary Aid Detachments of the Great War.

Such were perhaps the outstanding military problems which exercised Wolseley's mind during years pregnant with good for the future of the Army ; but there arose questions of wider scope and higher

[1] Created Lord Wantage.

237

importance to the solution of which he brought important contributions. In January 1888 the country was startled by Lord Charles Beresford's resignation from the Board of Admiralty. Lord Charles promptly presented himself as a candidate for Parliament, and told the electors that he had resigned simply because he had found in the Admiralty a lack of system and of preparation for war which he could do nothing to remedy. Wolseley was quick to support his friend. " I have been working most of my life ", he told him, " to try and make the Army efficient, something which will give the taxpayer value for his money. But if we had an efficient Army without an efficient Navy we should be like a man with only a left arm. Because I want the left arm strong I don't want the right arm weak. If we are to be in the beggarly position of having only one arm, I'd rather have a right arm than a left, but we can never either win a war or defend ourselves without both. There is, however, something more important than having two lusty arms, that is that they should work together. In every campaign in which I have fought, except the Mutiny, and the Red River, the Navy and the Army have had to work together, or at least they ought to have worked together, but generally have worked separately. The sailors have been given jobs to do of which they knew nothing, and of which they naturally made a mess. The soldiers don't understand the language the sailors talk, and there has been confusion and muddling where there ought to have been co-operation. The root of the trouble is that neither the War Office nor the Admiralty know what the other is doing or thinking, and there is no one to bring them together." But at the moment, the first necessity being to make " the right arm strong ", Wolseley did all he could do to help Beresford in his campaign. At a private dinner he spoke very emphatically on the weakness of Navy and Army to a body of men eager as he was to repair our defensive armour : " The answer to the question why the Navy and the Army are not so strong as they ought to be is to be found in the system of our government by party—that curse of modern England—which is sapping and undermining the foundations of our country—which is depriving our statesmen of the manly honesty which was once their characteristic. What do we see when any new Administration comes into office ? What directly takes place ? It is the same in all parties. The first thing is an endeavour made by the Minister in office to obtain some claptrap reputation by cutting down the expenses of the Army and Navy Estimates, and if he is able to produce an Army and Navy Estimate which represents in some degree a smaller sum than that of his predecessor, he plumes himself upon the victory he has gained . . . and as he chuckles over his success he says : ' See what a good boy am I '."

The prime purpose of this diatribe was to remove national defence from the sphere of party influences. A report of the speech leaked out and caused an angry stir. Lord Salisbury, then Prime Minister, read it as an attack upon the Government, and on the floor of the House declaimed bitterly against a practice adopted " by some who ought to be distinguished authorities on military affairs ". " I allude ", the Prime Minister said, " to the practice of making statements against the Government under whom they serve, and making them in places where they cannot be answered." This gave Wolseley an opportunity. The Duke of Cambridge used occasionally to address the House from the cross-benches on military matters, and Wolseley had consequently been careful to refrain from taking any part in debate. But he was certainly entitled to reply to an attack, and he determined to use the opening thus afforded him to make known his views on an occasion which would give them the widest publicity. He went, therefore, with some trepidation, to Westminster to make his first important speech from his place as a Peer.

The interest which a personal statement always arouses in Parliament had filled the benches, and the Commons crowded to the Bar. Wolseley, after declaring that his remarks at the private dinner were levelled against a system and not against the existing, or any other, Government, and apologising for them in so far as they might be capable of that interpretation, went on : " The noble Marquess has forced from me what I may call an exposition of faith. I give it freely for what it is worth. I give it in plain and unmistakable terms, without entering into any of those particulars which the noble Marquess so pointedly objected to last Friday. When I make this statement I am fully aware of the responsibility I incur. My statement is as follows : That as long as the Navy is as weak as it is at this moment, Her Majesty's Army cannot hold its own over the world, dispersed as it is ; that our defences at home and abroad are at this moment in an unsatisfactory condition, and that our military forces are not organised or equipped as they should be to guarantee even the safety of the Capital in which we are at the present moment." [1]

Such a pronouncement, before such an audience, coupled with Beresford's campaign, was decisive. In 1888 the Imperial Defence Act, providing for the defence of our harbours and coasting stations at home and abroad, was passed, and in the following spring the Naval Defence Act, 1889, became law, and a systematic increase of the Navy followed. These were the public measures taken to allay the grave anxiety which had been aroused. A less ostentatious

[1] Hansard, House of Lords, May 14th, 1888.

but hardly less important step was the appointment of a Commission, with the Marquess of Hartington as chairman, to enquire into our organisation for national defence. The report of that Commission was published in March 1890,[1] but the evidence was suppressed, probably because the differences of opinion in high places were so acute as to render publication indiscreet.[2] Many of the recommendations of what is popularly known as the Hartington Commission proved to be impracticable, but it was the first serious attempt to co-ordinate national defence ; it stands a text-book for the serious student, and to it may be traced, among other creations, the Committee of Imperial Defence and the General Staff for the Army. Wolseley took great pains with the preparation of the evidence he was to give before so important a body ;[3] the opinions he expressed not only reflect the man's mind at the time but have lost little of their interest to-day, as they concern questions which are still the subject of debate.

" The first essential for success ", he said, " in either offensive or defensive war is that all its operations, whether by land or sea, should be directed by one man. . . . Except on matters concerning the movement of troops by sea from station to station, there is no direct official communication between our Army Headquarters Staff and the Naval authorities at the Admiralty. All other correspondence is of a formal character, through the medium

[1] Report of the Royal Commissioners appointed to enquire into the Civil and Professional Administration of the Naval and Military Departments and the relation of these Departments to each other and to the Treasury. C.-5979. 1890.

[2] The departments of the Admiralty, War Office, and Home Office have allowed the authors access to Lord Wolseley's evidence, and have permitted its publication.

[3] The Commissioners were the Marquess of Hartington, chairman, Lord Randolph Churchill, Lord Revelstoke, Mr. W. H. Smith, Mr. Campbell-Bannerman, Sir Richard Temple, Sir F. Richards, General Brackenbury, and Mr. Ismay.

R

of the Permanent Under-Secretary of State for War and the Secretary to the Admiralty. For example, the bombardment of Alexandria would probably never have taken place had there been a Minister of Defence with the Army and Navy directly under him. I have been over and over again in consultation where the two departments were concerned, and there never seemed to be any possibility of coming to anything like a decision on either side. We held one view and the Admiralty another, and the Admiralty never gave way an inch from anything like the old ideas they had. Any change has always been by concession of the War Office. The Admiralty has never, to my recollection, conceded anything, no matter how small, to us. I would strongly advocate the creation of a Minister of National Defence, who should be the connecting link between the War Office and the Admiralty. He should be—if not the Prime Minister—one of the strongest and most influential men in the Cabinet ; I would abolish the posts of the Secretary of State for War and the First Lord, and place the Army and War Office under a commanding chief assisted by an Army Council, and the Navy and Admiralty under a Lord High Admiral assisted by a Naval Council. To assist the Minister of National Defence in Parliament there should be an Under-Secretary of State to represent each of the two services. To assist that Minister professionally there should be a Council of National Defence Department consisting of :

Minister
- Army
  - Commander-in-Chief.
  - Chief of Staff.
  - Accountant-General.
- Navy
  - Lord High Admiral.
  - An Admiral as Chief of the Staff.
  - Accountant-General.
  - Director of Ordnance Factories."

One of the first functions of the Council of Defence, Wolseley said, should be " to define the objects for which our Army exists, and the general military requirements of the Empire ". This done, it would be easy to calculate what should be the normal strength of the Army to secure the fulfilment of these requirements. That most important point, the normal strength, should be fixed without delay ; it should be subject to revision every five or six years, and special consideration should be given in such event as the acquisition of new territory, or the conclusion of a political agreement which might release garrisons or entail fresh obligations. Thus there would be removed from the arena of party politics the most important point which has now to be decided by the Secretary of State, a point on which year by year the Commander-in-Chief had reason to complain. Thus, also, there would be reduced to a minimum the causes of disagreement between the Secretary of State and the Commander-in-Chief. The amount of arms, ammunition, military stores, etc., to be always ready for issue must also be determined. " It is some-times urged ", he said, " that it would be impossible to satisfy the craving of a Commander-in-Chief for more men. My experience of the War Office is entirely at variance with this theory. All we ask is that the military requirements of the Empire may be carefully examined by some Commission outside the Army and the influence of party politics ; this Commission, having laid down what those require-ments are, should determine the number of officers and men required to fulfil them. This would prevent the scandal of a Commander-in-Chief and his military advisers asserting that the Army is not strong enough, and the Government of the day refusing to raise the additional numbers of men said to be necessary."

Lord Wolseley was not less emphatic upon the need for a General Staff. Hartington asked him :

" Do you know of any reason in the constitution of our military organisation why the Secretary of State, who is always a civilian, requires the Chief of Staff Department less than any other European nation ? " The answer ran : " I think we require it more than any nation abroad, owing to the peculiar constitution of our Army, and to its being scattered all over the world, owing to the numerous responsibilities which devolve upon it, and to the numerous phases of war for which it must be prepared. Other nations, when once they have laid down their schemes for offence and defence, have only to keep them going. We have all sorts of curious combinations that may befall us, and which may require special schemes to be made on the spur of the moment. These schemes should be made by some one occupying the same position as the Chief of Staff of foreign armies, who has always at his fingers' ends the consideration of these big subjects. . . ." There is, Wolseley went on, " a scheme for the defence of the country which, if worked out, would absolutely put us in a position such that no foreign country would ever dare to attack us, and that at no great cost ; but there is no authority in existence capable of completing such a scheme or of giving it effect ".

The need for a General Staff was warmly pressed by Sir Charles Dilke and Mr. Spenser Wilkinson in a series of articles and publications,[1] and a public opinion in its favour was gradually created both within and without the Army ; but here again the experiences of the South African War were needed to bring about a change which was not wrought till Wolseley's days of office were over.

Wolseley declared that the more financial control and responsibility were given to military officers, the

[1] Cf. *The Brain of an Army*, by Spenser Wilkinson, an account of the German General Staff system of which Wolseley strongly approved.

better it would be for the State. " It was ", he said,
" perhaps as difficult as it was necessary to prevent
financial control becoming an executive and directing
power in purely military matters, even of a technical
character." He recalled how the Parliamentary
Secretary to the Treasury, before the Select Committee on Army Estimates, when asked about his
responsibility for a grant of money made for a
" position finder " of a peculiar design, the value of
which could only be gauged by highly scientific
officers, said that he thought it necessary to see it
for himself, and to the best of his judgement form
an opinion as to the merits of the invention. This
functionary added, with some pride : " I have done
my best to form a judgement of my own as to
whether it ought to be agreed to ". Thus a civilian,
who had never studied any of the military arts or
sciences, assumed responsibility for advising the
Government whether or no an instrument of a very
complex and scientific character should be acquired.

The Duke and Wolseley were agreed in advocating
a Minister and a Council of National Defence, and
in demanding that military patronage should apper-
tain to the head of the Army and the Crown. " I
am telling the Commission ", Wolseley wrote, " that
neither the political head of the Admiralty nor of
the War Office should have anything to do with
the selection of officers for promotion or employment.
I can see that Ministers are anxious to get as much
patronage into their hands as possible, with the idea
that it will give them greater control over the forces.
But if we have soldiers and sailors looking to political
chiefs for advancement, we shall sooner or later get
into the state in which the French army is, and have
political services rewarded by military command." [1]

In the autumn of 1890 these strenuous years
in the War Office came to an end. During them

[1] Private Letter, January 1889.

nearly every modern development which has tended to the efficiency of the Army had its origin. A real system of mobilisation was prepared, though it was many years before the means were obtained to make the system effective; the machinery for supplying the Army with food and munitions was overhauled and remodelled; training began to take a practical form; the comfort and welfare of the private soldier were considered as never before; a fresh impulse was given to military education; and, most important of all, the minds of statesmen, soldiers, and sailors were, at last, seriously directed to the major problems of national defence. No one man could have effected all this unaided; but many of Wolseley's select band had won for themselves positions of authority and influence. Within the War Office Buller, first as Deputy Adjutant-General, then as Quartermaster-General; Brackenbury in the enlarged Intelligence Department; Biddulph as Director of Military Education; and Coleridge Grove and Hildyard [1] in the Adjutant-General's own office, had forwarded his work as whole-heartedly in peace as many of them had done in war, whilst outside, Wood, Grenfell, Greaves, Butler, and Baker Russell were spreading the gospel of progress and efficiency. In these years the reformers fought and won their decisive battles; the fruits of victory were not quickly garnered, but they were in the main secured in time for the great test to which the nation was to be put.

Work was so absorbing that recreation—apart from a short daily ride—was fitful, and was chiefly found in books and—curiously enough—in converse with bookish people. With Andrew Lang, Henry James, and Edmund Gosse, Lord Wolseley had formed

[1] Afterwards General Sir Henry Hildyard.

a real friendship, and this perhaps gave him access to literary circles to which otherwise he might not have had entry. He loved to talk to men of letters, though he would modestly disclaim any other than specialised knowledge, and never talked of books which he had not read ; and the men of letters never talked down to him, never let him feel himself as a stranger among them, and certainly never alluded to the slips in spelling and lack of " style " which sometimes marked his own written and spoken words. The Poet Laureate, Alfred Austin, was another intimate, though Wolseley cared little for his, or any other poetry. For the theatre he had no affection ; there are notes in his diary that *Faust* distressed him, and the *Dame aux Camélias* went near to disgusting him : he sat uneasily through a tragedy, but rather enjoyed a screaming farce. He read little fiction, but maintained a constant correspondence with his friend Miss Rhoda Broughton, pathetically entreating her to make patriotism the note of some of her novels, and taking pains to be on familiar terms with her characters. What was denied to him, and what he seems to have panted for, was a fair share of country air and country pursuits, apart from the stereotyped country-house life, which he detested.[1] A house in Hill Street was for some years his home. It lacked the desired space and quiet, and was, moreover,

---

1 " *6th August* 1888.
From WADDESDON.

" We have had that disgusting Dilke trial ; quite apart from the horrors that surrounded those principally concerned in its nauseous details, it was sad to see an Englishman forswear himself as he did. . . .

" All the countryside is to assemble to-morrow to see the Prince, and have tea in a tent, and dance on a canvas sheet laid down on a lawn. The parsons and their wives from far and near will arrive in one-horse shays, the wives in cotton gloves, the children in short frocks and red legs. To-morrow the whole party will go to church, some in carriages, the men walking in tall hats, their trousers turned up, and with an air of morality and martyrdom over their black coats and ruddy faces."—Wolseley to the Duchess of Edinburgh.

expensive to keep going. Expense was, at this time, a serious consideration, for the grant of £30,000 for Tel-el-Kebir had vanished in an unfortunate invest- ment. The Queen, knowing all the circumstances, and now most graciously disposed, made a timely offer of the Ranger's House at Greenwich ;[1] here, in pleasant surroundings, Lord and Lady Wolseley delighted to gather their friends and acquaintances, and more especially those who were steeped in literature and art.

[1] 22nd August 1888. " It was very very good of the Queen giving this place to me, and I feel extremely grateful to her. I never saw her looking better than when I was at Osborne last week." —Wolseley to the Duchess of Edinburgh.

OLIVER CROMWELL'S WATCH.
From the Wolseley Collection, R.U.S.I.

THE RANGER'S HOUSE, GREENWICH PARK, 1888.

To face page 248.

CHAPTER X

IN COMMAND IN IRELAND

IN April 1890, proposals were afoot that Wolseley should take over in the autumn from Sir Frederick Roberts the Indian command. Ten years before, when he scented trouble across the North-West Frontier, he had coveted and laid some claim to the post. But the hour had passed, and with it the allurement of high command in the East; India now attracted him scarcely more than the Governorship of Victoria, which he had unhesitatingly declined two years earlier. He felt it was too late in life for him to be responsible for a large and complex machine with which he had little acquaintance; he knew that any suggestions he might make for its improvement would be heavily frowned on. He could gain nothing by the novel experience, and stood to lose what might be his if he remained with the Army he knew by heart. Domestic circumstances reinforced this view, and he submitted a measured refusal with the reservation, " Were any national interests involved, I should have no hesitation in accepting ". The War Minister fastened on the phrase, and, invoking a soldier's sense of duty, tried to wring from Wolseley a consent to follow the wishes of the Cabinet. But the soldier was not to be so easily snared :

" Before replying to your note of the 3rd instant ", he wrote to Mr. Stanhope, " I thought it essential to ask the advice of some friends. This, and a more than usually sharp attack of Indian fever, has hindered my answering you sooner. Your letter puts the question of the Indian command in an entirely new light. I am now asked to accept it on national grounds, and to meet an emergent state of affairs in the East. May I venture to remind you that, when you first spoke to me on this subject some months ago, you urged no national grounds as a reason why I should accept the Indian, in preference to any other command. Again, in acknowledging my letter of the 29th ulto., in which I declined the offer of India and gave my reasons at length, you accepted those reasons as natural on my part, and urged no question of national emergency as a reason why I should alter my determination. I know of nothing that has taken place in India since then to make the position critical either in Afghanistan or in Persia. As far as I know, everything in Central Asia remains now as it was then. I cannot realise that it is because a strong man is wanted that I am asked to go there, when it is intended to bring home Sir F. Roberts, who has passed his whole life in the study of Indian military problems. If danger threatens in India, surely Sir F. R., who is now on the spot, thoroughly understands how to meet it. If he were not in India and fit and willing to remain there to meet the emergency, the case might be different : but when apparently—as far as the public and I know—profound peace reigns in India, to go there would be to me professional suicide. As already explained in my previous letter, there are, in my opinion, apart from all family considerations, the very strongest public and professional reasons why I should not go there. My whole career tells you that, were it a question of active service, or were war imminent, I should long to share in it. If there were paramount national reasons why I should now go to India, my past life puts it beyond question that I would go at once, and with the utmost pleasure, and at any personal sacrifice. But as I cannot realise that any national considerations are really involved in my decision, I feel the strongest reluctance to undertake this command which you have so kindly offered to me.

" I will only add this : in the event of my not going to India, I presume it will be offered to Sir E. Wood ; Aldershot, as well as Ireland, would thus become vacant for H.R.H. the Duke of Connaught to take either of these two commands, as might be arranged between the Cabinet and himself. I should be perfectly content to serve in whichever command the Duke of Connaught might leave open."

The letter proved conclusive, and the War Secretary addressed himself to the easier task of inducing Roberts to remain for a further period in India, and to relinquish his candidature for the Adjutant-Generalship, a candidature for some reason opposed by the Commander-in-Chief. Three years later Wolseley was to press the Duke of Connaught's qualifications for the command at Aldershot ; meanwhile that Prince expressed a praiseworthy wish to remain where he was, and on the 12th July Wolseley was writing to Miss Rhoda Broughton : " Just a line, to my dear friend, to say that it is settled I am to go to Ireland. Much as I dislike the idea, I should dislike still more being left unemployed."

Wolseley found the Sovereign in cheerful acquiescence with him. " The Queen thanks you for allowing her to read your letter ", Sir Henry Ponsonby wrote on the 5th May. " She cannot say she thinks you are wrong in declining the offer, and she is at a loss to understand why Sir F. Roberts should not be continued in India. She is grateful to you for the kind way in which you have treated the Duke of Connaught."

The succession to Prince Edward of Saxe-Weimar may not have been very alluring to an energetic soldier, but it would mean at least emancipation from servitude at the War Office, where the wear and tear of office work had left their mark on him. For ten long years Wolseley had striven day in and day out to rouse the Army to the magnitude of a task which in time—as he foresaw—surely awaited it. "The world must have a great upheaval before long," he had written two years earlier to a friend, " and assuming this to be inevitable, I wish it would take place before I become too old to act a part in that great drama." Perhaps he scarcely realised how weighty had been the part he had already played ; perhaps he scarcely perceived that the Army was really awakening from its long slumber, and was putting on—or at any rate trying on—its new vesture of efficiency and professional zeal ; and all the while, as it seemed to him, opposition had been his daily fare, and of resentment and reproach he had tasted frequently. No wonder that fatigue had begun to find some lodgement in his body, just as an unjustifiable sense of failure had crept into his mind. "Do you ever feel tired ? " he wrote to Miss Broughton. "I often think I can understand the wearied sensation of the horse who has been hunting for two days consecutively. Steady occupation never tires any one, but it is when a dozen or twenty people come at you open-mouthed in want of various things, and you have to carry your mind from one man's business to that of the others in quick succession, that the spirit flags and the brain becomes fatigued. I am tired and sick of my present position. I thought I would have done more in it, but the resistance of an irremovable Royal Commander-in-Chief has beaten me. Very often I have been getting on well and the prospects for the Army have for a time looked bright, when, Presto ! some party

252

change has removed the War Secretary, and I have
had to begin with another who neither knew Joseph
nor understood his schemes, nor had the least notion
about military affairs." And to the sense of weariness
there was added some feeling of loneliness. He was
never inaccessible, but he had been perhaps a little
remote. " I have just lost the only real man friend I
have ever had. He was a parson and a friend of my
early youth," is an entry in his diary at this time.

Colley and Herbert Stewart, the two soldiers
nearest to his own heart, were sleeping the soldier's
sleep in opposite corners of Africa. Evelyn Wood, for
whose military genius he had profound admiration,
had been a little irritating in his methods and
manners; Butler was too impetuous; Buller was a
little cold; Brackenbury had been personally somewhat unsympathetic; Coleridge Grove was only
beginning to come into his counsels; Maurice was
constant, but not always available. The Duke of
Cambridge had been greatly touched by his subordinate's quick sympathy with him in the illness
and death of his well-loved wife,[1] but between the
Commander-in-Chief and the Adjutant-General gaps
—if not gulfs—occurred too frequently to render
intercourse altogether easy.

He did not feel any man's hand in his own, and
he had a lurking fear that those who had not gathered
with him would be apt to scatter when he had gone.
And if the recommendations of the Hartington
Commission [2] were to be carried out, he would never
hold supreme office wherein to polish the weapon of
war which he had striven to forge. He would never,

[1] " You have taken so kindly an interest in my beloved one's
illness that I must tell you myself that dearest Mrs. FitzGeorge
passed away very peacefully this morning in my presence, and
surrounded by her children. I know I shall have your sympathy
in this to me most severe affliction."—The Duke to W.

[2] The Commission had recommended the abolition of the office
of Commander-in-Chief and the creation of a Chief of the Staff.

he reflected ruefully, be more than *primus inter pares* ; his authority would be always open to question, and his recommendations to refusal. Clouds of doubt and difficulty seemed to hang about him, and change of scene and work would be helpful, even if not needful, to renew his youth and health.

The summer and early autumn were largely spent, apart from the routine of "winding up", in final attendances on the Duke at the formal inspections which Wolseley detested,[1] at manœuvres, which he thoroughly enjoyed, as the guest of Lord and Lady Wantage, and at Osborne, where he was summoned to meet the German Emperor. The Duke had be-taken himself to German baths before Wolseley gave over his portfolio to Buller, but he wrote pleasantly, if a little inconsistently, at Michaelmas :

"As to-morrow is your last day of office at Headquarters, I must tell you how much I have at all times appreciated the assistance I have derived from you as Adjutant-General of the Army. The changes that have so constantly taken place—and alas, we live in an age of perpetual change—have rendered the duties of your office especially arduous, and I have always admired the characteristic vigour and energy you have thrown into them. Though we have at times differed in our military methods and conclusions, we have still been thoroughly convinced, at the same time, of the sincerity of our respective wishes for the interests of Government and Services, and we have been able to keep pace with the times, though perhaps as far as I am con-cerned we have gone rather faster than I have thought judicious.

[1] "I have just returned from one of those most tiresome field days in which the Duke of Cambridge delights, but which to me are hateful in the extreme. I am not good as a dissembler, and I keep my temper with difficulty when I see and hear so much that tends to rub up the wrong way every military instinct I possess."—Wolseley to the Duchess of Edinburgh.

" In taking up new and important duties, let me assure you that you will find me at all times ready to support you in a not altogether easy position.

" You leave the Adjutant-General's office in good hands with Sir R. Buller, and I doubt not that in the future, as in the past, our intercourse will continue on the same agreeable footing as hitherto. Wishing you and Lady Wolseley every happiness, and with sincere good wishes for yourself, I remain, my dear Wolseley—Yours very sincerely,

" GEORGE."

The glowing terms of the penultimate paragraph were perhaps scarcely borne out by history, and the picture of the Duke as a progressive may have provoked a smile ; but the letter marked the under-current of friendly feeling which really ran strong, and their later correspondence, maintained till the Duke's death, showed increasing cordiality, the nearly illegible writing of the elder man being always a fair set-off to the faulty spelling of the younger.

Wolseley's name and fame had preceded him to Ireland, and the crowd at the Dublin railway station on the 2nd October was very large and very vocal, while a pile of messages of welcome and invitations awaited him at the hotel where he proposed to stay. The Royal Hospital was undergoing much-needed repairs, and Lady Wolseley chose to remain at the Ranger's House until they were completed, her husband consulting her on every detail of the new arrangements of the house, and drafting for her con-sideration a precise table of what their prospective expenses would be.

For the next three months Lord Wolseley depended largely on the companionship of his aide-de-camp, Lord Edward Cecil, the selection of

255

whom showed that the breeze with Lord Salisbury had completely blown over. A plethora of social engagements was repugnant to the man to whom home life was specially dear,[1] and he restricted himself at first to the acceptance of purely official invitations, though later he did not fail to appreciate at its true value the genuine Irish hospitality offered to him wherever he went. Some of his earlier experiences were apparently not quite happy. "At an awful dinner-party", he tells Lady Wolseley, "I took in an official lady, and felt as if I had given my arm to one of the iron rails extracted from the rails before the house, and that its nakedness had been barely hidden up by a Toby ruff at the top and some black muslin rags below." On a more agreeable occasion, however, he writes to Miss Broughton: "I sat at dinner next to the Provost of Trinity College, one of the most agreeable men, as well as one of the most eminent mathematicians. He devours novels, and is said to be the best judge of a novel in the country; he says *Alas!* is quite the best novel you have written."

The autumn was not to pass without a further tussle with the Duke, who angrily resented Wolseley's recommendation that economy, without prejudice to efficiency, could be effected by a reduction of the staff in Ireland. A redundant staff, especially where staff duties overlapped, was always a *bête noire* to him. He had gained some of his earlier unpopularity by sending home unnecessary Staff Officers from South Africa, and, on assuming the post of Adjutant-General, he had said that if the intentions of Mr. Cardwell were carried out, a very considerable

---

[1] "I think with you", he had written to Lady Wolseley in Germany, "that in Ireland we shall be very happy. I shall see so much more of you than I can ever do in London, and that alone is sure to make me happy. I am arranging to make a long tour round all the military stations during October, so shall kill one month of the four in which I am to be roofless."

saving of expense in the matter of the staff of the War Office might be achieved.

A little later he wrote : " I have written so often and so often spoken to H.R.H. on this subject, that I have long given up all hope of expecting any reform".

The reply to Wolseley's pruning proposals from Dublin was warmly worded. There was trotted out the usual protest that the Army had undergone so many changes lately that further dislocations were of themselves undesirable. The Duke was prepared to make certain concessions, " the changes to be effectual as opportunities offer for carrying them out ", but rejected the programme submitted. He professed himself as anxious as Wolseley to be economical, but could not agree with him that it was wasteful in time of peace to maintain more staff officers than were actually required. " The Duke ", Wolseley wrote rather sadly to his wife, " asked me to take back my letter and modify my views to suit his. He who knows nothing of war, asks me to think only as he is pleased to think. It was necessary for me at the outset to put down my foot and show my individuality. He has ruined the Army as far as he has been able to do so by keeping it back and retaining its theatrical aspect, with detriment to true military training."

Christmas that year found the Royal Hospital semi-roofless and wholly comfortless, and Wolseley, braving a murmured remonstrance from the War Office, repaired for a short while to Ranger's House, having asked that Döllinger's *Essays, With Essex in Ireland*, and *Warren Hastings* should be laid in for his holiday reading.

A more agreeable matter had now to be discussed, and one on which the Duke and Lord Wolseley for once entirely agreed. The Duke of Clarence, the eldest son of the Prince of Wales, was an officer in the 10th Hussars, then under orders for the Curragh, and every effort was to be made to give the young Prince a thorough military training, so that his promotion, if accelerated, might be justified by a full measure of proficiency. But before this could take place, there was announced to the general satisfaction the engagement of the Duke of Clarence to the Princess of Teck—the future Queen Consort. Wolseley rose to the occasion, and in his letter of congratulation hinted that a visit to Ireland in the course of the wedding tour would be intensely popular, and further made bold to urge that nothing could be more beneficial to Ireland than that the future Heir to the Throne should be the next Viceroy. The proposal was not lightly dismissed, and the Prince himself in his reply said : " All that you say about my taking the post of Lord-Lieutenant would no doubt be a popular move in many quarters, although I know it would be a very difficult position for me to fill adequately ". Two months later, with swift and sudden stroke, death had laid low a most amiable and attractive Prince, who was said to be guiltless of an unkind word and incapable of an ungenerous action.

The Commander-in-Chief's first tour of inspection was the preliminary to a thorough overhauling of the military régime of Ireland. He made himself acquainted with the inner history of every unit which came under his command, and he specially enjoyed facilities for educating personally many of the younger officers with whom he brought himself into touch by a system of constant hospitality which took something like the form of open house. He was an excellent host, and thoroughly enjoyed the opportunity of showing himself as such. Economical by habit, he would spare no expense or trouble in the entertainment of his friends, just as he had always been generous to a fault at his Headquarters Mess on campaigns.

He had no personal desire for luxury, and preferred for himself the simplest habits of life and daily fare. But he understood the points of a menu, and would criticise a cuisine which was ambitious and failed to be good. " The food poisonous ", he writes to Lady Wolseley from a country house. " I think the coachman does the cooking, and the kitchenmaid, dressed in livery, does the waiting." And if he enjoyed dispensing hospitality, he also enjoyed—even if he did not admit it—the popularity which in Ireland he quickly earned. He liked to think he was liked for himself as well as esteemed for his reputation ; and indeed, underlying a thin crust of reserve, there lay always the warm, impulsive nature which craved, though it would not ask, for affection in return. In all this there was also a distinct military aim.

"No one loved Wellington ", he once wrote, " except some women. His soldiers certainly never did, although they had undoubted confidence in him ; whereas all Caesar's soldiers worshipped him. Whatever may be the reason for it, it is nevertheless a fact that up to the present we have never had an English commander who succeeded in calling forth any great enthusiasm for himself or the cause in hand. It is not true that Englishmen are not capable of such high sentiments, but it is only special nourishment and treatment that will develop feelings so long ignored. Let any general arise who knows how to do so, a new era will be arrived at in British history."

In the Irish Command he instituted annual manœuvres as the culmination of a progressive system of training, and he was in constant correspondence with Wood at Aldershot, to whom he wrote in October 1891 : " No man has in my time effected more useful military work than you, and the Army is beginning to realise that as fully as I do ". Wood sent him all the latest " tips ", and these he applied with the zest of a keen mind putting into practice ideas long entertained. The subalterns were delighted to find that they received, instead of the hectoring lectures and explosive abuse too often associated with generals and "brass hats", sympathetic encouragement when they had done well, and sensible explanation of how and why they had erred when they had gone wrong. "A leader", he said, "must lead, not drive." It was noticed that on field days the Commander-in-Chief would walk his horse up behind some subaltern whose men were not carrying out some part of the manœuvres to his liking, would call him aside and tell him quietly how this or that should be done or left undone, showing him especially where danger would be incurred to the lives of his men in real warfare by neglect of some appropriate precaution. The purpose in all this was to convince young soldiers that their profession was fully as interesting and absorbing as any other, and that manœuvres were something more than an irksome duty. He was ceaseless in his efforts to reduce the number of guards and unnecessary duties in order that the number of men available for training should be increased ; he created a real flutter by proposing to abolish his own guard at the Royal Hospital. Lord Wolseley would only give way on this point when it was represented to him that, in the disturbed state of Ireland, it was very necessary to maintain the dignity of the position of the Commander-in-Chief. He entirely relished blending social with military life, and as the political conditions served to discount socially the Lord-Lieutenant, the entertainments at the Royal Hospital had special vogue if not pride of place. He constantly invited his soldier friends to stay with him, and sought to stimulate keenness among the officers for whom he was responsible by making them rub shoulders with men who had seen sharp fighting or who had been through the Staff College. From most of his military visitors he exacted contributions in return for his hospitality. He revived the Military Society of Ireland and induced the best men to lecture at its meetings, the discussions at which he almost invariably led. A garbled report of a lecture on barracks annoyed Mr. Stanhope, and in reply to an inquiry from Buller, Wolseley remarked: "In the first place, I wish to warn you against any newspaper reports of our Military Society's proceedings until these reports have been corrected. Any one who has ever spoken at any of our meetings will tell you how ridiculous the newspaper reports of our proceedings are. Maurice will tell you what a mess they made over his lectures, and as for my remarks, I can seldom recognise my own words. During the discussion much had been said as to the propriety of having our men housed, on the score of discipline, a point which I thoroughly endorsed, adding, there were many barracks which were a disgrace to our nation, that had been reported upon for years, but that nothing had been done to provide others, until the present Government had taken the matter up, and that much still remained to be done. You say, 'Cui bono?' The truth is always good on such points, for it keeps them before our eyes."

These comparatively quiet years in Ireland were occasionally disturbed by the aftermath of his old struggles in Pall Mall, and in 1891 he was called across the Channel once more to do battle for short service. Yet another Commission on the Army was in session, this time under the chairmanship of Lord Wantage, and charged with an inquiry into the terms of service in the Army. There were many who asserted that Cardwell's creation had broken down, that the drafts sent to India were unsatisfactory, and that the battalions of boys at home were too weak to be of any value. With the latter opinion Wolseley was in entire agreement, and before the Commission he stated that, after sending drafts abroad, our regiments at home were " like a lemon when all the juice is squeezed out of it ". But he would not allow cold water to be thrown on Cardwell's work. "It cannot be repeated too often or be too strenuously drummed into the heads of outsiders ", he wrote to Sir Arthur Haliburton,[1] " that it is not Mr. Cardwell's system that has broken down, but that all our present difficulties and misfortunes have arisen and are at present directly attributable to the fact that his system has been glaringly and most injudiciously departed from. His system was based upon a balance between the number of units kept at home and those kept abroad. In his time it was 71 battalions of infantry at home and 70 abroad : now we have 65 at home and 76 abroad. He intended we should have 833 rank and file at home for every 1000 we maintained abroad—now we have only 731 at home for the 1000 abroad." He went on to apply his old remedy of increasing the number of troops at home, so as to provide for a systematic mobilisation of two army corps and balance the increased garrisons abroad. He continued : "We want our Army for war. For the duties it has to perform during peace, it is, as at present constituted, fully capable. I grant you it does not gladden the heart of the old-fashioned inspecting Generals who want a theatrical or circus display. It is composed of growing lads who, when twenty-two, will be superior, man for man, to the soldiers of any army. The stuff and the untruths that are brought forward by those who don't like the work our present system entails is simply sickening to men who know the truth ; who know

---

[1] Afterwards Lord Haliburton, Permanent Under-Secretary of State at the War Office.

that a great deal of it is said to please and curry favour with H.R.H., but especially because they had little to do in the old chaos Army and have a considerable amount to do in our short service system.

"I joined at Chatham in 1852. It was full of recruits, all waiting for conveyance to India. As regards age, they were all boys, and not nearly such nice-looking or such good boys as we now get. I was nearly nineteen myself, and thought myself a man, but I remember that I regarded the recruits around me as boys, that is, as much younger than I was. We never did enlist *men* in this century. We used to enlist men long ago. Cromwell's army was composed entirely of men, and even in Charles II.'s reign we had men as soldiers. But then we competed for men with men's wages in a very restricted labour market. If we don't take recruits at their present age, we shall not get the numbers we require, even if we give the extra sixpence which I would like to see given."

Short service and promotion continued to be the battle-grounds on which the young school was wont to meet and challenge the old school. Promotion other than by seniority—or occasional special favour—was still to the Duke of Cambridge sheer and damnable heresy, and on the Promotion Board he would pour his vials of scorn and wrath. Wolseley, from across the Irish Channel, sustained his chant that merit, and merit only, should be the passport for preferment; the work, he urged, must be entrusted to the best workmen available; the quality—not the length—of his service must be the test of an officer, and this above all when there was any question of command in the field. He knew to his satisfaction that Buller had been found no pliant instrument in the matter, and on more than one occasion had withstood the Commander-in-Chief to the face. "I cannot recognise", Wolseley wrote to him in 1893, "any officer's right to be ever made a Colonel, still less a General. I think it is positively wicked to give a man command of a regiment unless you have every reason to believe he is likely to make a good C.O. But when we approach the general officers, we add grotesqueness to our wickedness if we make a Major-General of a Colonel whom no one would entrust with any command in the field. If you will tell those who now encumber the Major-Generals' list that you never mean to employ them, they will take their retiring pension and make vacancies for a sufficient number of selected Colonels to fill. Why on earth make such a man as . . ., for example, a Major-General, when you know it would be a crime to employ him in the field, and a joke to give him a Command-in-Chief ? '' And in tone of entreaty he writes to the War Minister : '' Will you lift us out of the slough of Seniority Promotion ? You can easily do so, and the Army—all that is best in it— will bless you. The British Army wants a spurt of reform ; there is growing up a feeling of hopeless- ness ; that good, hard work and ability are kept in the background, and that the idle and stupid—of whom it is thought they have friends in high quarters —enjoy as good, if not a better, chance of preferment. The young school want to make the Army a real profession, in which the best men, made by their own exertions, rise to the top, as do lawyers, doctors, civil engineers, etc.'' To Wolseley, Campbell-Banner- man [1] always lent a willing ear. For the soldier who took his profession seriously, he had the greatest respect, and in the special War Office reform, over which he was just now busy, he leaned largely on the best military advice he could secure.

What went to spoil in some degree Wolseley's

[1] Mr. Campbell-Bannerman became Secretary of State for War, a second time, in Mr. Gladstone's last Administration after the General Election of 1892.

enjoyment of his service in Ireland, and caused him finally to say that he left the country without regret, was that the climate did not suit him [1] and was wholly uncongenial to Lady Wolseley, who suffered there —and there only—from incorrigible insomnia. She found it impossible to reside for any length of time at the Royal Hospital, and could scarcely take her full part in the activities which went to make up the routine. Her chief pleasure, with which she soon infected her husband, was in the pursuit of old furniture and works of art. Here she seemed both indefatigable and something like infallible. She could measure herself with the most astute dealer —though it was not dealers to whom she often addressed herself—and gain his admiration for her *flair* and her bland refusal to be gulled. She added to knowledge—itself the result of considerable study —something like intuition as to what was genuine and what was faked. She was willing to pay a fair price for the former, and scorned to be even attracted by the latter; no small proportion of the fine objects which later found their home in Hampton Court Palace were drawn from Ireland.

It had been thought by his friends that, after his feverishly busy days at the War Office, Wolseley would find time hang heavy on his hands in Ireland; his energies would not have sufficient outlet, his hunger for hard work could scarcely be appeased. His letters, however—and he was a voluminous letter-writer,—go to show that his spare hours were happily occupied in books, for which at long last he found the coveted leisure, and in preparing his *Life of Marlborough*. For this, no pains were too great; he read eagerly every work which dealt with the

---

[1] " I am horribly seedy from indigestion ; I suffer the pains of hell and these ignorant doctors cannot cure me. However, I shall be fifty-nine years old on June 4th, and have had the best of health all my life, so I cannot complain, even if I never get rid of this inconvenience."—Private Letter.

great soldier who was the subject of his ardent but critical admiration. He wrote and rewrote his own pages, referring them sometimes to Miss Broughton and other writers, so as to secure ease and style ; he repaired to Blenheim, where, under rather difficult conditions, he pored over every available paper, and he finally produced a standard work, polished and complete to a point, which unfortunately subsequent ill-health prevented him from finishing. A smaller book published at the time was the *Decline and Fall of Napoleon,* and he contributed to the *United Service Magazine* articles on von Moltke and Sherman. He urged and helped his officers to read well and wisely ; he started in Dublin a lending library of sound literary works in connection with his Military Society ; he took every opportunity to provide the private with recreation of mind and body, and tried to improve reading-rooms within and without barracks. Here a little trouble arose. The Soldiers' Homes in Ireland were managed by Protestants, who were accused by the Irish priests of proselytising. Wolseley wrote to the Duke : " Some of the men whose names appear on the Committees are very objectionable to the priests, because, I am told, these gentlemen are very outspoken in their loyalty, and belong to that violent class of Protestant who denounces Roman Catholicism as idolatry. I wish I could get rid of them, and will try to do so. Of course it will be impossible to please the Irish priests unless they are allowed to manage all institutions in Ireland, but the only really sound line of conduct they can take up is to start Soldiers' Homes themselves, and manage after their own fashion. I shall be only too pleased to support the movement and to subscribe towards the annual cost of their maintenance. I know that these Homes, when worked by ladies, do so much good in keeping men from drink and in civilising them, that

I would gladly support a Mohammedan or a Buddhist home for soldiers. We fight the public-house by means of these Homes, and the public-house in Ireland is ten times worse than it is in England, for it is not only an emporium of drink, but it is a hotbed of disloyalty and sedition." Nor was he attacked by the priests only, for in 1894 the Protestant Alliance roundly upbraided him for permitting soldiers in uniform to attend a Roman Catholic ceremony and to salute at the elevation of the Host. Wolseley promptly wrote to the priest concerned :

"I am much obliged for your note about the services in your church which some, not very wise, people have thought fit to complain about. The matter was referred to me by the War Office and explained, I believe, to the satisfaction of the Secretary of State for War. I told him in my letter that I made it a rule to encourage all soldiers to frequent their places of worship, and that the more they did so, the better soldiers they generally were. As far as I am personally concerned, I hope that next year the same annual festival in your church at Rathmines may be even still more loyally attended by men in Her Majesty's uniform.

"From a military point of view the only mistake made was in the few Catholics of the Royal Dragoons drawing their swords when at a voluntary service, but that will not occur again to give cavillers occasion to complain.

"I feel that all who wish well to our Army owe you so much for the good you do amongst the Queen's Catholic soldiers, that it will always be a pleasure to help your good work to the best of our ability."

A staunch Protestant and an Irishman closely interested in Ulster, Wolseley was no bigot in religion, but did not extend toleration to politics, and the political situation in Ireland, after the fall of the Tory Government in 1892, sorely oppressed him.

Home Rule was to him a hateful schism, and he feared then the contingency which ten years later was to occur. " I have given Ponsonby my views," he wrote to Lady Wolseley, " and intimated that I could not stop here if civil war took place. I fear the worry of the Home Rule Bill will kill the Queen. If so, Mr. Gladstone will have another, and a very great sin to answer for." He took counsel as to whether he might speak, or even vote on the Bill in the House of Lords, and refrained from doing either on being reminded that Lord Hardinge, in the Upper Chamber, never took part in anything like political debate, except on the occasion of the repeal of the Navigation Laws.

It was just now that two opportunities occurred to pay just honour to a distinguished soldier, both of which were held up for some time. Early in 1893 Sir Patrick Grant tendered his resignation of the Colonelcy of the Royal Horse Guards. No one could be more eligible for the succession than Wolseley, but the Duke of Cambridge was so opposed to the idea that Sir Patrick was urged—or rather ordered—to retain his post, and it was not until after his death two years later that the " Blues " were offered to Wolseley, the regiment to his great pleasure being then under command of Colonel Brocklehurst, the intimate friend of Charles Gordon.

Then the question of pay had been the peg on which to hang a delay in conferring a Field-Marshal's baton, but on the 22nd May 1894, the War Secretary wrote pleasantly : " Few events could give me greater pleasure than that you should reach the highest rank in the Army while I am S. of S.,— and this, I hope, will happen on Saturday next. But there is a difficulty. I wanted you to have a paid Field-Marshalship, but it turns out that there is not one vacant. So that what must be done is to make it without pay at present, which of course makes no difference to you while you are employed, with the promise that you succeed to the first vacancy."

In the late summer of 1894 there was an agreeable interlude. An old friend, Sir John Pender, invited him for a cruise on his yacht as far as Constantinople. Wolseley, who had just then been ordered rest and change of scene, availed himself quickly of the suggestion. Constantinople itself did not much appeal to him, and he wrote disdainfully of the Sultan as a " little, cowardly black man ", nor could he understand his host's scarcely veiled eagerness to be invited to the Palace. But he had long wanted to revisit the Crimea. Alma, Inkerman, Balaclava, the Monastery of St. George, all teemed with interest for him, and he had Evelyn Wood as a wholly sympathetic companion in going over the ground which recalled memories of just half a century ago. Nor was his interest altogether confined to the past. There is an entry in his diary : " Wood and I start off early this morning for a bay on the Black Sea an hour and a half's ride from Therapia, where the Russians will land when they try to take Constantinople ".[1] On his return he delighted the Duke of Cambridge with comments specially prepared for him on the campaign in which both had served :

" This month it is exactly forty years since I embarked here in Dublin with my battalion for the Crimea : what changes are to be seen everywhere except in that place itself ! Your Royal Highness asks me several questions which it would take a small volume to answer fully. Had we marched directly upon the Star Fort and the works north of

[1] In 1915 a Russian force was waiting near Odessa to land at this bay during our attacks upon the Dardanelles.

269

Sebastopol Harbour, we might, I think, have taken them by a *coup de main*. But as there was no harbour near them from which we could draw supplies of food and ammunition, the operation would have been, with our small Allied army, too risky. What I have always thought we should have done was to have taken the works, then just begun, on the south side at the Malakoff, Bastion du Mât, etc.; this would have given cover to our men for the winter, and we could have drawn our supplies from Kamish and Kazatch Bays.

"We unfortunately halted to wait for our siege guns to be landed, to *knock down works* that did not exist upon our first arrival, and which were actually built during the time that we squandered in landing guns, etc., and in bringing them to the front for our *October* bombardment. I don't know if I am right, but I have always in my own mind blamed Sir John Burgoyne for this delay, and for not having gone in and taken Sebastopol on the south of the Harbour the morning after we had crossed the Tchernaya River.

"Of course, in my opinion, *the* great fault of the campaign was having failed to pursue *at once* when we took the heights over the Alma. Had we driven the Russians before us all that evening of the 20th September, we should have taken a great deal of the Russian guns, etc., and have so thoroughly de-moralised their army that the assault of the Malakoff, Redan, etc., would have been comparatively easy. Once in our hands, we could have very easily destroyed the Russian Black Sea Fleet, and the docks, etc., on which it depended. That is, we could, and I think ought to have done all this before the first week in October. We could then either have re-embarked for Turkey, or have housed ourselves for the winter in Sebastopol city and its suburbs.

"At the Alma it would seem, from the absence

270

of any pursuit, in fact of any previous plan of operations in the event of victory, that we squandered the most valuable hours, perplexed as to how we should dispose of our wounded. Did we expect to fight a battle and have no wounded ? There was no forethought displayed from first to last in all this war, and our poor Army was ordered about by a number of politicians, so called a Cabinet, who were about the most incompetent set of fellows who ever ruled over any country in difficult times."

Before the end of 1894 the War Secretary was addressing himself to the reorganisation of the War Office ; he had taken down the report of the Hartington Commission from its shelf, dusted its pages, and decided to put some of its provisions into immediate effect. The creation of a Naval and Military Council had already been ruled out ; the appointment of a Chief of the Staff he did not favour.

His own plan, which, roughly speaking, found acceptance with his colleagues in the Cabinet and the subordinates whom he consulted at the War Office, laid down that the Commander-in-Chief should be Chairman of an Army Board on which would sit the heads of the principal military Departments. The Board would select officers alike for promotion and for staff appointments, would make proposals for estimates, and deal with all questions referred to it by the Secretary of State ; it would also form part of a War Office consultative Council in conjunction with the Under-Secretary of State, the Financial Secretary, and other specially nominated officers, this Council to be itself under the direct control of the Secretary of State. The part of the scheme immediately open to criticism was to be found in the divided responsibility inherent in it.

The Commander-in-Chief would issue orders to the Army and be responsible for all military decisions arrived at, as well as for the preparation and observance of military plans, but the high military officials would have direct access to the War Minister, and " would thus constitute a deliberative Council, so that the Secretary of State, when he gave his decisions, would be guided and supported by the expressed opinions of all the experienced officers by whom he was surrounded ".[1] Thus the man who was charged with something like full responsibility would not be vested with anything like full authority. Wolseley himself was moved to remark, when he was Commander-in-Chief, that the Adjutant-General and the Quartermaster-General were no longer his staff officers, but those of a civilian Secretary of State.

By May 1895 the War Minister's scheme had taken definite shape, and it was realised that underlying it was the necessity of inviting, or otherwise inducing, the resignation of the Duke of Cambridge. Campbell-Bannerman was the last to belittle the services of a Prince whose sincerity of purpose had been of a piece with his unreserved devotion to the Crown and country ; but although limitations were to be put to the new Supreme Command, it was evident that the command had already outgrown the present commander, and if the Army were to be fitted for the work which awaited it, old things must be made new, and a vigorous hand would be required to brush away some still adhesive cobwebs. The Commander-in-Chief was, unfortunately, reluctant to bow to the decree, delicately as it was conveyed to him. He protested, and honestly believed, that he was still quite equal to the performance of his duties. " I never anticipated ", he wrote, " such a decision being come to without my willing consent. I must

[1] Mr. Campbell-Bannerman, House of Commons, June 21st, 1895.—Hansard.

submit as best I can to the inevitable, but I own that I am disgusted with this, to my mind, most unjustifiable proceeding, though Mr. Campbell-Bannerman was most amiable in all he said."

The Duke at once took the correct constitutional step by placing himself unreservedly in the hands of the Sovereign. The Queen, who but a few months earlier had believed that the Hartington Commission was dead instead of only sleeping, could scarcely view with favour the decision of the Cabinet to limit to five years the tenure of the Commander-in-Chief's post; the pleasing illusion could no longer exist that this high military functionary was the deputy of the monarch. No personal consideration was, however, allowed to weigh, and the Queen quickly wrote to the Duke : " Considerable changes in the distribution of duties among the Headquarters of my Army are desirable. These cannot be effected without reconstituting the particular duties assigned to the Commander-in-Chief, and so, though with much pain, I have arrived at the decision that for your own sake, as well as in the public interest, it is inexpedient that you should much longer retain that position, from which I think you might be relieved at the end of your autumn duties."

Although the retirement of the Duke of Cambridge was not to take place for some months, the question of his successor admitted of no delay, and neither the public nor the Army had much doubt as to who would be the Government's nominee. Wolseley himself, who was in London at the end of April, wrote to his wife : " The Duke of Cambridge, who was extremely civil, said to me the papers were filled with stories of the Commander-in-Chief. I turned the conversation, and said I had not remarked it, but had read a great attack upon Army administration in the *Times*. We then discussed that subject. I have not had any talk with Buller or Gipps about the

Duke, but I think the feeling is that his reign is nearly over, and I think it is generally agreed that I shall soon be in the War Office once again." But for some reason never wholly explained, Campbell-Bannerman decided to appoint not the leader but the follower, not the teacher but the pupil ; in other words, not Wolseley but Buller. The prospective appointment was formally approved by the Sovereign —though it was wholly without her personal influence —and it would have been announced before the rising of Parliament had not Campbell-Bannerman suddenly succumbed to a blow dealt to him by his own eventual successor in office.[1] The uncertainties of public life were curiously exemplified on June 21st, 1895. The War Minister had scarcely resumed his seat after delivering his farewell eulogy of the outgoing Commander-in-Chief, and explaining the functions of his successor, when the Member for the Guildford division of Surrey rose to his feet, and in a few rapid sentences convicted him of a shortage of the prescribed munitions of war, and by a majority of seven secured the formal reduction of his salary.

The Prime Minister, Lord Rosebery, accepted the incident as the defeat of his Government, and with cheerful alacrity resigned the cares of office, which were daily becoming more complicated, and retired into dignified leisure and literature. For the third time, Lord Salisbury was called upon to form a Ministry, and his first step was to secure the seals from the outgoing War Minister, and thus arrest the patent presumably in preparation for Buller.[2]

No other choice for the Commander-in-Chiefship than Wolseley probably occurred to him, but before committing himself the Premier wished to discuss

---

[1] The Hon. St. John Brodrick.

[2] This was the cause of some acrimony. Lord Kimberley accused Lord Salisbury of " sending his private secretary very much as he might have sent his footman to ask for Mr. Campbell-Bannerman's seal ".—Hansard, House of Lords, June 27th, 1895.

its new status with Lord Lansdowne, to whom he handed the portfolio for War. Wolseley had cause to think that the late Government had set him aside ; he had some reason to complain of Buller's lack of frankness in not disclosing to the man who had done so much for him the overtures that had been made ; he had no knowledge of Lord Lansdowne's reversal of his predecessor's appointment, and late in July he was writing to Colonel Childers : " There is an intrigue on foot to make Sir Redvers Buller Commander-in-Chief when the Duke of Cambridge retires. That means military extinction for me. The 1st October will be the end of a career devoted to the reform of the Army, which finally I am not deemed worthy to command. . . . It is a horrible finish to my career, to be superseded by one of my own lieutenants, whom I may say I created a General officer."

A few days later the rumour was afloat that the advice of the Duke of Wellington as to the desirability of a Prince of the Blood being appointed to a high command was to be followed, and that the Duke of Connaught was to sit in the seat of his royal relative. The report reached Wolseley's ears, and he at once let it be known that if the Queen wished her son to be Commander-in-Chief, his own candidature for the post should be promptly cancelled. Nothing, he said, would be more repugnant to him than to block the way for the Sovereign's son, whose military merits, moreover, and sturdy common sense he very highly appraised. In such case, however, he thought that the Viceroyalty of India or the Embassy at Berlin might be open to him. In India he believed that as a soldier he might be able effectually to check the growing military expenditure, which would be a difficult matter for a civilian Viceroy, who might be unable to withstand a Commander - in - Chief heavily backed by military opinion. In Germany, on the other hand, he might keep vigilant watch over the military preparations, which even then went far to suggest that a great trial of strength was in contemplation.

As a matter of fact, the name of the Duke of Connaught had not been officially considered. Early in August Lord Lansdowne wrote to Lord Salisbury: "It has never occurred to me to propose the Duke of Connaught for C.-in-C., and I have never mentioned his name to any one in connection with the appointment. I should say he had much better make up his mind to wait. But within the last days it has been evident to me that his candidature is being vigorously promoted. I hope that you will join with me in concluding from all this that the sooner the new C.-in-C. is selected the better. Could you see me before you go to Osborne? It might be profitable for you to get the Queen's consent: (1) to the new scheme of War Office organisation; (2) to the selection of Wolseley for C.-in-C. I don't know if you would care to send him to Berlin, and I can express no opinion as to his fitness. I am circulating to the Cabinet a memo. on the new W.O. arrangements. If it is agreed to in principle, I should like to select a new C.-in-C. at once, and consult him as to the precise manner in which the different changes should be carried out. There are innumerable pitfalls, and we must try to follow, or seem to follow, the main recommendations of the Hartington Commission. A possible solution of the personal question might be to make Wolseley C.-in-C., to send Buller to Aldershot, and to bring the Duke of Connaught in as A.-G. vice Buller. This might reassure the Queen, who positively fears that the appointment of Wolseley means side-tracking the Duke of Connaught." A few days later the appointment, with its new limitations, was definitely offered to Wolseley. Meanwhile, the notion of giving him charge of the Embassy at Berlin had found favour alike with the Queen and the German Emperor, and Lord Salisbury was asked to induce him to exchange a military for a diplomatic appointment. But, the Duke of Connaught's candidature for the supreme command cancelled, Berlin had disappeared from Wolseley's purview. " Before I received your extremely kind and considerate letter ", he wrote to Lord Salisbury, " I had a cipher message from Lord Lansdowne, conveying to me a message from the Queen about Berlin. My only object in proposing Berlin was to make it easier for you to pass me over had you intended to make H.R.H. the Duke of Connaught Commander-in-Chief, having learnt on what seemed good authority that I was the main difficulty in the way of that arrangement. To occupy that position has been my ambition, and I was vain enough to think I might do some good in it. I hope, therefore, that I do not entail any fresh trouble on you or Lord Lansdowne by adhering, if you will allow me, to the decision I communicated to Lord Lansdowne by letter on the 8th. The gracious terms in which you offer me Berlin are deeply appreciated by me. I have never had a greater compliment paid me." The Sovereign made no sort of demur, and it only remained for Lord Lansdowne to telegraph to Wolseley : " You must clearly understand that the changes in the position of the Commander-in-Chief are inevitable. Their precise extent is not yet decided, but I think they will be on the lines indicated by the late S. of S. in his House of Commons statement. I shall, of course, give you full opportunity of discussing these with me, but it is necessary for me to have a free hand, and I could not agree to any conditions which might afterwards embarrass the Government in carrying out the desired reform."

CHAPTER XI

COMMANDER-IN-CHIEF, 1895–1900

"THANK God for all his mercies", is an entry in Wolseley's diary for August 8th, 1895. "He has been good and gracious to me, and I hope to show my gratitude by walking more firmly along the road He has marked out for those who wish to serve Him faithfully." The Duke, it seemed to him, had stood, stolid and four-square, the obstacle to progress in the Army, or at any rate to progress at Wolseley's pace. With the Duke as a benevolent onlooker, his successor's hand would be free to finish the work to which he had given himself. His great opportunity had come at long last. True, he must act within restrictions—unless or until those restrictions could be relaxed—which might limit his power for good, but he was determined that a fair trial should be given to the new order, and he set himself loyally to his duties as defined. Lord Lansdowne had sent to him, in Ireland, the proposed distribution of functions amongst the military chiefs in the War Office, and he replied in August:

"I have thought over the paper you showed me yesterday, containing the new proposals for the distribution of duties in the War Office, and would strongly recommend a few emendations. They are as follows: First, the duties and responsibilities of the C.-in-C. According to my notion of an army, whether in the field or on a peace establishment,

CHANGING GUARD AT THE HORSE GUARDS.

From Cartoon by Mr. Linley Sambourne.　By permission of the Proprietors of *Punch*.

To face page 278.

his first duty to the Queen and country is, that the army under his command should always be a thoroughly efficient fighting machine. This is a responsibility he cannot divide or share with an Adjutant-General or any one else. It is a function inherent in the position of a General in command of an army during peace or war; indeed, it is *the* most important of his functions, according to a soldier's notions. According to my recollection of your proposed draft, it would leave the Army in doubt as to whom it should regard as primarily responsible to the Secretary of State for its fighting efficiency. This would be unfortunate, according to my knowledge of our Army. After the opening expression—I quote from memory—that 'the C.-in-C. shall exercise chief command over H.M.'s military forces at home and abroad', I think it very desirable to insert some words to this effect : ' and shall be responsible for their fighting efficiency '.

"The second proposal I have to make is that, in enumerating the duties of the Adjutant-General, I would adhere to the old and understood expression, that he 'is *charged with* the discipline', etc. etc. It is a vague term, and therefore has value in my eyes in this matter.

"My third proposal refers to the duties of the Military Secretary. I forget the exact words of your draft, but I think it referred to the Military Secretary as 'reporting to the Commander-in-Chief,' and that to him was left the responsibility of selecting officers for promotion and for nomination to all staff appointments. I do not think this is an arrangement which is calculated to work smoothly, for it makes the Military Secretary too independent of his master, the C.-in-C., by giving him by regulations an initiative that with many men would certainly lead to friction.

"I am sure you will forgive these expressions of

opinion on my part. I state them for what they are worth, but with the assurance that I shall use my best endeavours to carry out efficiently and smoothly whatever system of administration you determine upon. The views I have enunciated here would, I feel confident, recommend themselves to 9 out of every 10 experienced officers in our Army.

" It will be difficult to retrace hereafter any false step now made in defining the duties of the officers in the War Office. Remember there was only *one* soldier a member of the Hartington Commission, and, clever and able as General Brackenbury is, he has had absolutely no experience in the administration of the superior offices at the War Office.

" I think it is desirable that the Accountant-General should always be present on the ' Army Board ', for I know from past experience how valuable his views and opinions always were, and how helpful they were to us soldiers when in Council."

The new C.-in-C. had scarcely taken his seat when a disquieting rumour reached him. A proposal had been made to recognise the Duke of Cambridge's long service by conferring on him some such substantial title as Honorary Inspector-General of the Forces. Wolseley at once protested to Lord Lansdowne : " With reference to our conversation of yesterday, the more I think of the proposal to confer any unusual military title or position upon H.R.H. the Duke of Cambridge, the more dangerous it appears to me. I do not enter into any argument as to what may be H.R.H.'s claims, on the score of military services, to some new and hitherto unknown position in the Army; I confine my remarks to the effect it would inevitably have upon all ranks, and to the increased difficulties it would certainly entail upon his successor.

" Before entering on these, however, I may as well

point out that the instance of the Archduke Albrecht, which has been quoted, does not apply in this case, for he never was the Commander-in-Chief of the Austrian army, a position then and still held by the Emperor. There is therefore no real analogy between the position he held and that which I understand the Duke of Cambridge wishes to obtain. Coming now to the effect of the proposed appointment, I would observe that for years past the Army, to its great detriment, has been divided into two schools: the old-fashioned school, strongly opposed to any change, and honestly believing that old ways and methods should be upheld in every possible manner ; and the modern school, which, realising what rapidly moving sciences war and military administration are, is anxious to advance at least as fast as the armies of other countries, which some day or other we may have to meet. The Duke of Cambridge has been for years past the head of the old school, and to give him the position suggested would keep it alive and active for years to come. If let alone, it will soon die out, for all the energy and ability of our Army are on the other side. But with H.R.H. remaining as the titular head, with the power to speak as, to a great extent, the official leader of military thought, all that is most reactionary and most opposed to improvement would be revivified and would get a new lease of life. The effect on the Army would, I am certain, be highly injurious. It would lead to the belief that the present changes were not intended to have any real effect, and that the whole thing was more or less of a make-believe. The more active and hardworking of our officers would lose heart, and the lazier and more careless feel that they had won the day.

" I must now add my own personal objections, for I feel very strongly on the point. If I am to do good in the Army, and to develop it in the way in which I believe it is now ready and anxious to be developed and brought up-to-date, I cannot have my hands strengthened too much. I have not the great power and weight which accompanies the position of a Royal Prince, and the effect of which it is not easy to overestimate. This adds to the difficulties I shall have to encounter, but if over and above them I am, in the eyes of the Army, to be placed under the retiring C.-in-C., either on paper or on parade, my power and my influence will be very seriously lessened. Soldiers are, from their training, specially observant of even the smallest matters connected with rank, precedence, and command, and they would never believe, if the Duke of Cambridge were retained as Honorary Inspector-General of the Army or any other analogous title, that he would not also, in many important ways, be its real head. I need hardly point out how difficult such an impression might make my position.

" Lastly, I come to a point which I approach with great delicacy, but which is so important that I feel bound to draw your attention to it. Knowing as well as I do the personal character of H.R.H., I am certain that, were he given the position under consideration, it would not remain in his hands a purely honorary position. He would inevitably use it as a lever for intervention in matters of all kinds, and especially in that of patronage. I trust that you will understand that I say this in no carping spirit, but solely because I deem it to be a fact, and a serious one which has to be considered. The Duke has been too long the absolute military head of our Army for it to be possible for him to look on and let others now manage it, if he be given the smallest pretext for, or power of, intervention, however nominal. The disposition which could do this is not his. I trust that in all that I say it will be understood that I have no wish to oppose the bestowal upon H.R.H. of some special recognition of his long and important command. But if so, do not let the recognition take the form of making him Honorary Inspector-General of the Forces or anything of that nature. Might I humbly suggest that it should take the form, either of a special pension or of an A.D.C. for life. This would be, I should think, quite as effective and a far more advisable manner of recognising his long and faithful service."

Certainly there was full justification for the claim that the "Modern School" had come by its own, and Wolseley may well have chuckled to find little or no opposition among soldiers to his plans for increasing the efficiency of the service, of which he was in name the head. In 1896 the acquisition of a great part of Salisbury Plain added very materially to the facilities for practical training, and army manœuvres on a large scale became a regular part of the annual military programme; even the drill books grew less formal and pedantic. Wood, as Quartermaster-General, had the old troopships which Wolseley so painfully remembered sent to the scrap-heap; and the up-to-date liners, hired when required, reduced both the discomforts of the Red Sea for the troops and a good deal of the cost for the tax-payer. Military education strode forward, and Wolseley was at special pains to stimulate the Staff College. Henderson wrote delightedly after his first inspection of that institution : " Lord Wolseley took the Staff College by storm. Not even I anticipated that he would fetch the officers as he did. They are quite enthusiastic; the few words he said to them individually settled them. The worst of it is that they have already begun to give themselves airs on the strength of their interview, but that is perhaps no fault. They have been comparing this inspection with the last, when the old hero of many banquets grunted ferociously at the pile of schemes, maps, etc., and then darted off to revel in pork chops and other delicacies, giving us to understand that we were very dull dogs."

Even selection for promotion made steady, if slow, progress, and in October 1896 Wolseley was writing to Sir George White, then Commander-in-Chief in India :

" I am doing all I can to improve the race of Generals and also of C.O.'s, and even to select, as far as I can do, those who are to be 2nd in Command of regiments and battalions. With an army like ours that is scattered over the world, that is no easy task. But to help me and those at Headquarters, the first thing is to obtain the fullest and frankest confidential reports upon all officers. When I was A.-G. I had it laid down that all young officers join the Army upon a three years' trial, during which term of probation they were reported on annually by the three senior officers of their corps present with it, and can be sent about their business at any moment. I am now very anxious to improve generally our present system of confidential reports upon all ranks, and want you very kindly to help me. May I begin by saying that the old officers of the Indian army are generally too lenient : all their geese are swans, and from goodness of heart and anxiety to deal leniently with human failings and intellectual shortcomings, they seldom condemn any one.

" This places the C.-in-C. at home at a great disadvantage. . . . If ever you know of a man who is useless, it would be very kind of you to write privately and tell me of him : [1] and I can assure you that on

---

[1] This was of course subject to the regulation that any adverse report must be communicated to the officer concerned. To this Wolseley referred in another part of this letter.

the other hand, the Army Board will be only too glad to push on those whom you will write to me about, also privately, as men whom you feel sure it would pay the State to push on. It was only the other day, I may say, that, under pressure, I allowed a Colonel in the Army who had been employed in command of a Brigade, to retire as a Major-General. Not many months afterwards I found that he had been a notorious drunkard for some time : not a suspicion of this had appeared in any of the reports made upon him by his superiors. This would not have occurred at home, but abroad it is not easy to obtain such information."

So closely adjusted also was the system of mobilisation that, in 1898, Wolseley was able to say, amidst the jeers of the incredulous, soon to be confounded by the *fait accompli*, that the Army could make ready two Army Corps [1] for shipment quicker than the Admiralty could provide ships for their conveyance. For if progress within the Army was now steady without being alarmingly rapid, co-operation between the War Office and the Admiralty was still halting and impeded by formality and procedure. A Committee of Defence had indeed been formed with the Duke of Devonshire as chairman, but its functions were nebulous, its meetings irregular, its minutes non-existent, and its influence upon the major problems of defensive policy nugatory. In March 1897 Wolseley was writing to Maurice : " Mahan's books have done the country, and the Navy for that matter too, a world of good. It is a sad reflection that it has taken a Yankee to wake up this generation of Englishmen to the meaning and importance of sea power. But we have still got to convince the Navy that they can't win a war by themselves, and that we are not trying to nab

[1] At this time preparations were well in hand for the mobilisation of a third Army Corps.

the money they ought to have, but want to make our power, what it must be to be effective, amphibious. If we can get the sailors to come in with us in this we shall have some chance with the politicians. But what is the use of our being able to mobilise in a fortnight, as we shall be able to do, I hope before long, if the Navy are going to take a month to find the ships to send the troops where they should go? and what is the good of having the men ready and the ships alongside the quays, if there is no pre-arranged naval and military plan worked out before the need for it arises? Commissions! I am sick of Commissions. I thought in my foolishness that the Hartington Commission was going, at least, to give us the means of making real plans of campaign with statesmen, soldiers, and sailors all working together, and the only use they have made of it is to clip my wings."

Obstruction within the Army had ceased to be a serious factor, and the reformers found themselves to be pushing doors which, if they still creaked on their hinges, were at least open. Obstruction without the Army now became the goad to Wolseley's fighting spirit, which, truth to tell, needed little goading. With the one object of making the Army ready for war, his mind had been concentrated on the task of defeating the " old School " and the Duke as its leader. First in the stress of combat, and then in his joy at getting rid of the chief opponent of progress, he had not observed that His Royal Highness had had another purpose in view besides the postponement of all change; he now found that others had been anxious to get rid of the Duke for very different reasons.

The story of the office of Commander-in-Chief is to a large extent the story of the struggle between Parliament and Crown for control of the military forces of the State. The first Commander-in-Chief was the Earl of Arundel, appointed by Charles I., but his duties were ill defined. After the Restoration, Monk, Duke of Albemarle, became General in Chief Command and acquired very large powers. He was authorised to raise forces and to issue commissions to all officers. He framed Articles of War, signed warrants for the issue of money and stores, and the Secretary at War was little more than his political private secretary for military business. It was not long before Parliament became frightened at the possession of such authority by a nominee of the Crown ; between 1719 and 1793 there was no Commander-in-Chief, Parliament declaring in 1789 that in time of peace no such functionary was necessary.[1] Some years before this, in 1783, Mr. Burke had carried through an Act which, among other things, established the position of the Secretary at War and made him the Minister responsible to Parliament for the military forces of the State. With the beginning of the long war with France, the need for some central military control of the Army resulted in the duties of Commander-in-Chief being assigned to a General, Lord Amherst. From 1793 the functions of the military head of the Army became gradually more important and more clearly defined, partly because the need for such an official became, in the stress of war, to be more clearly recognised, partly because the wise administration of the Duke of York gave to the office authority and power, and partly because the influence of the Crown was always exerted to increase the prestige of the head of the military forces.

The Prince Regent made more than one attempt to arrogate to himself the powers of Commander-in-Chief, but could find no Government to support

[1] Before that, in 1724, Lord Wharton asserted in the House of Lords that if, during the King's absence in Hanover, the command of the Army should be delegated to one person, the liberty and property of the people would be endangered.

him; as George IV. he repeated the demand in 1827, on the death of the Duke of York,[1] only to be repulsed by Lord Liverpool, who in this matter was backed by the Duke of Wellington. In that year Wellington, after holding the office of Commander-in-Chief for a few months, resigned, and was followed by Lord Hill, who, as a hint to the Crown that its authority over the Army was to be exercised through the responsible Minister, was not given the title of Commander-in-Chief, being nominated a General on the Staff at the Horse Guards. In 1837 a Royal Commission, presided over by Lord Howick,[2] was appointed to investigate the administration of the Army. The Commission, while criticising with justice certain very obvious defects in that administration and proposing some useful remedies, had as its prime object an increase in the power of the War Secretary, who was to be a member of the Cabinet, and generally responsible for the entire administration of the Army. The Duke of Wellington protested vigorously against this measure. He asserted that, while it was right and indeed indispensable that control of military expenditure should rest with Parliament through the Secretary at War, the Sovereign was the head of the Army, and exercised authority through the Commander-in-Chief. He insisted that the patronage and discipline of the Army must rest with the Commander-in-Chief, under the direct pleasure of the Crown, so that they might be kept entirely apart from politics.

Queen Victoria shared Wellington's views, and in a letter to Lord Derby dated September 1st, 1858, said: " As to the whole Army, whether English or Indian, there can only be one head and

[1] For a short period, until the appointment of a successor was made, Palmerston as War Minister claimed and exercised the functions of Commander-in-Chief.
[2] Afterwards Earl Grey.

one general command. . . . The advice of the Commander-in-Chief ought to be heard on all matters affecting the troops, and he ought to be kept officially informed of whatever affects the discipline and general efficiency." [1]   The Duke of Cambridge was equally concerned with the Queen to keep military, as distinct from financial, questions in the hands of the Commander-in-Chief and the Crown, but at the time of his appointment in 1856 the authority of the Crown, acting through Ministers, was expressly conserved in the letter of service appointing him " to serve as a general officer upon the Staff of the Army " and " to obey the orders of Her Majesty, the Commander-in-Chief, or any other Your Royal Highness' superior officer ".   The Duke was thus at first General and afterwards Field-Marshal Commanding-in-Chief. He had no control over the artillery or engineers, movements of troops, fortifications, barracks, supplies, or munitions, nor over the auxiliary forces,[2] and not until the Queen's first Jubilee in 1887 was he made Commander-in-Chief. He, like the Duke of York, owing to his long tenure of office, his position as a Royal Prince, and his absolute discretion in his relations with Ministers and Parliament, succeeded in increasing greatly the power and prestige of his office.   The Adjutant-General and the Quartermaster-General were his Staff officers, and in 1888 Mr. Stanhope brought out an Order in Council making the Commander-in-Chief responsible for everything connected with the efficiency of the soldier, that is to say training, discipline, housing, clothing, movements, food, and armament. Thus from 1888 till 1895 the Duke enjoyed powers greater than those of any Commander-in-Chief since the Duke of Albemarle.   He fought to preserve these

---

[1] Martin, *Life of the Prince Consort*, vol. iv. p. 308.
[2] The control of the Army was then organised as described on
p. 5.

U

powers mainly with the object of keeping out political interference in purely military functions, and above all to prevent military patronage from passing into the hands of a Minister who would change with each successive Government.

The Hartington Commission, like that of Lord Howick sixty years earlier, pleaded the facts that training in the Army was not progressing as it should, and that there was congestion of business in the War Office, to suggest that the Commander-in-Chief was overburdened with work, and that over-centralisation was the prime cause of trouble. This was only partially true. The defect in the War Office machinery was not that the responsibilities of the Commander-in-Chief were too great, but that the War Office had taken upon itself business which should and could have been better left to be dealt with in the commands. But the statesmen of both parties, while rejecting many of the recommendations of the Hartington Commission, fastened upon the particular findings which advised a decrease of the powers of the Commander-in-Chief; these they would employ in order to make the position of the Secretary of State for War impregnable. Mr. Campbell-Bannerman, on the eve of the fall of the Government of which he was a member, had sketched the changes which it was proposed to make in the organisation of the War Office; those changes were adopted with little modification by Lord Salisbury's Government and embodied by Lord Lansdowne, as War Minister, in the Order of Council of 1895 under which Lord Wolseley took office. The Commander-in-Chief was made the principal adviser of the Secretary of State on all military questions, and was charged with a general supervision of the Military Departments of the War Office. He was responsible for plans of operations and the Intelligence Department was placed under his care; he directed the distribution and mobilisation of the Forces; he would superintend the appointments to commissions and the promotions and rewards of officers, and control the educational establishments for officers. The discipline, education, and training of the troops and recruiting were in the charge of the Adjutant-General. The Quartermaster - General moved the troops, looked after their food, forage, and quarters, and controlled the Pay Department. The Inspector - General of Fortifications and the Master-General of Ordnance dealt with their separate functions. Each of these high military officials had direct access to the Secretary of State, who was responsible for co-ordinating their work, and was in the pleasing position of being able to choose between his numerous advisers, to set off skilfully one against the other, and thus ensure that no one obtained a dangerously predominant position.

Wolseley had worked as hard as any one to obtain for the Commander-in-Chief the increased powers with which he had been invested in 1888; indeed, it was largely due to his efforts and exhortations that the control of the armaments and food of the troops had been given to the Duke of Cambridge. He had insisted before the Hartington Commission that an army should be commanded by one man, but he had accepted office on the terms of the new Order in Council partly because he, with his mind fixed entirely upon making the Army efficient, had overlooked the political implications of the Order, partly because he was deceived by its terms, and assumed that he would be in reality the principal adviser of the Secretary of State and have a real power of supervising the Military Departments. His disillusionment was speedy. In December 1896 he wrote to Sir E. Collen, then Military Member of the Council of the Viceroy of India :

"What the civilian does is to create a system that, according to his ignorance of war, is good in his eyes for the ordinary humdrum contingencies of peace, and then picks up some rudimentary notions of war as best he can to see how the supposed wants of war could be best provided for under the conditions and establishments he has created for peace.

"This is the reverse of what should be done. We should organise our War Department with a view to war and for a condition of war, and then, working back from the arrangements created to meet the rude exigencies of war, see how they can most conveniently and economically be worked during peace to meet the shallow everyday wants of an army at peace.

"By a multiplication of civilian clerks any system can be made to work in peace, but the first breath of war, and of the real strains of war, will blow the whole fabric to pieces, and very possibly in doing so will entail national disaster.

"During peace the civilian forgets war, but, in the experienced soldier's mind, war has always the most prominent place, even when it seems the most improbable of events. He wishes to create an establishment for purposes of war.

"The system of the War Office of a nation should be the system on which that nation's army is to be worked in the field, and when this is not the case, when there is to be one system at Army Headquarters at home and one entirely different system at Army Headquarters in the field, it will be very difficult indeed to avoid disaster.[1]

"Under a system of Parliamentary Government like ours, it is no easy matter to devise a system that will at one and the same time maintain the Army

[1] Many of Lord Kitchener's difficulties in 1914 were due to the fact that the War Office was organised for administration in peace. Not until Sir W. Robertson came to Whitehall as Chief of the Imperial General Staff was an organisation suitable for war introduced.

upon purely military lines and under the sole command of soldiers, and will also give to the Secretary of State for War that general control over the
Army, its numbers, and the expenditure of the money
voted for it, which is essentially necessary under our
Constitution."

A month later he entered in his diary : " A distressing day. I am vice-chairman of a debating
society. The Secretary of State is the Commander-
in-Chief as far as we have one." The distressing
days were frequent, and produced increasing friction
within the War Office. Wolseley gradually found a
position of nominal responsibility with limited power
to be impossible ; Lord Roberts made the same discovery within a shorter period. The Queen used
all her influence to support her Commander-in-
Chief. She had on his appointment desired him
to write to her fully and frankly, and the correspondence was regular and often voluminous. Upon
one matter only was there a serious difference of
opinion. In October 1897, when Buller left the War
Office to take up the command at Aldershot, Wolseley
was anxious to have Wood as Adjutant-General.
The Queen objected, though she had a high opinion
of and personal liking for Wood, on the ground that
he was a better commander than administrator in
an office, but she gave way to Wolseley's wish to have
a tried comrade at his right hand. Comradeship
could not, however, overcome the defects of a faulty
system of administration, and the difficulties did not
grow smaller. In March 1899 Sir Arthur Bigge
wrote to Wolseley at the Queen's request :

" I have reported to the Queen what you told me
during our conversation yesterday morning. Her
Majesty does not feel at all inclined to let matters
remain in their present unsatisfactory condition, and
she desires me to say that she would like you to see
Lord Salisbury and explain to him your position as

laid down by the Order in Council of 1895, and prove to him that the Commander-in-Chief has practically no control over the discipline of the Army, and that papers dealing with that subject do *not* come to you unless the A.-G. wishes for your opinion or advice. H.M. wishes you further to point out to the Prime Minister that in India and Ireland the Commander-in-Chief is invested with this responsibility, and how inevitably it would at once again come under the British C.-in-C. directly war was declared. The Queen is going to write to Lord Salisbury and desire him to see you."

To this Wolseley answered :

" Lord Wolseley presents his humble duty to the Queen and has learnt with satisfaction from Sir A. Bigge that Her Majesty wishes that the Commander-in-Chief should have charge and be responsible for the Discipline of the Army. Until the Order in Council of 1895 that responsibility had always been one of the most important functions of the Commander-in-Chief. It is still the function of the Commander-in-Chief of all foreign armies, and is so still that of the General Officer Commanding the Army in India and in all our possessions beyond the sea.

" The words of the Order in Council bearing on this matter are : ' The Commander-in-Chief shall exercise general command over Her Majesty's Military Forces at Home and Abroad, shall issue Army Orders, and hold periodical Inspections of Troops. He shall be the principal adviser of the Secretary of State on all military questions, and shall be charged with the general supervision of the Military Departments of the War Office.'

" On the other hand the Order says : ' The Adjutant-General shall be charged with the discipline, etc. etc., of the officers, N.C. officers, and men of the Regular and Reserve Forces '.

" Thus, while the Commander-in-Chief exercises general control, the Adjutant-General is directly charged with and responsible for Discipline, and only one officer in an army can be held responsible for its discipline. That responsibility cannot be shared by two without danger.

" The system now applied to the Army in Great Britain could not be carried out with an Army in the Field. It is, however, an arrangement that Lord Wolseley accepted upon assuming the office he now holds, and therefore, though contrary to his views of sound military organisation, he can have no good personal reason to complain of it. It is Lord Lansdowne's intention, as he has assured the C.-in-C., that the Adjutant-General should invariably consult the C.-in-C. upon all important questions and matters which bear upon the Discipline of the Army, but he does not wish to alter the wording of the Order in Council upon that subject."

Just before Wolseley left the War Office the Queen requested the Prime Minister to invite him to write a memorandum setting forth his opinion of the defects of the Order in Council of 1895.[1] This memorandum, prepared in November 1900, was presented to Parliament, and in it he repeated, in more formal terms, the note made in his diary in January 1897 : " The Commander-in-Chief has become, to use a common expression, the fifth wheel of the coach. He has neither the supreme control exercised by the Secretary of State nor the administrative functions possessed by those below him ; between the Ministerial head on the one hand and the Departmental

---

[1] Lord Salisbury wrote : " The Queen has charged me to ask you whether you will utilise for her your great experience by writing down any suggestions you have to offer for the improvement of the War Office, and especially that part of it which has been under you ; and of the Army generally : including, of course, any matters appertaining to your own office. If you should kindly do this, will you be good enough to send the memorandum when completed to me for submission to Her Majesty ? "

heads on the other, he has been crushed out, and the Secretary of State has become the actual Commander-in-Chief of the Army. . . . The whole principle of Army administration is that of working up through converging channels which finally meet in one man charged with supreme military command." At the same time he wrote : " There is really no difficulty in separating command in the full military sense of the term from such administration as can and should be separated from command, and be in the hands of a civilian minister. He should have complete control of all finance, of the manufacture of munitions and clothing, and of the provision of supplies in accordance with the specification sent him by the soldiers ; he should, I think, also have control of recruiting, for he has to get the consent of Parliament to the numbers of men to be maintained, and in an emergency the Government must decide how many men the Army may have. But for preparation for war, discipline, promotion, appointments, and rewards, the movements of troops, their feeding, their barracks, and the issue and care of all their requirements, one soldier should be ultimately responsible. This is such obvious common sense that I am certain the real object of ministers is not to have an army which will be efficient in war, but an army which they can control in peace. We soldiers have been to blame because we allowed military business to be too much centralised in the War Office, and that enabled the Hartington Commission to say that the Commander-in-Chief was overburdened. If our military business is properly organised, the Commander-in-Chief will not have more on his hands than the general manager of any industrial concern, but I have never heard of any industrial concern which put its affairs into the hands of six general managers." [1]

[1] Private Letter, November 16th, 1900.

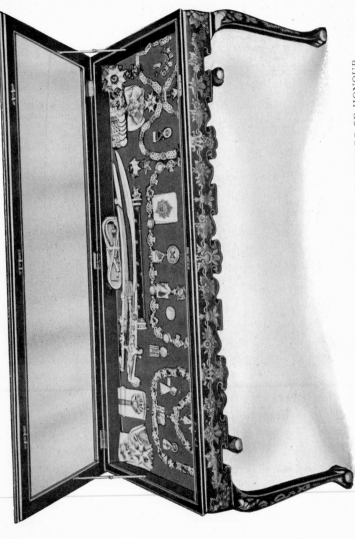

LORD WOLSELEY'S MEDALS, DECORATIONS, AND SWORDS OF HONOUR.

From the Wolseley Collection, R. U. S. I.

To face page 296.

APPENDIX

In March 1901, after he had left office, Wolseley went down to the House of Lords and spoke on the question of War Office administration, which had been raised by the Duke of Bedford. The views he then expressed conveniently summarise those which he formed during the years of his service as Commander-in-Chief : " In 1895 the illustrious Duke, who had been a most popular Commander-in-Chief for nearly forty years, resigned that position, and I was selected to succeed him. The present Secretary of State for Foreign Affairs, in intimating to me that I had been selected to succeed His Royal Highness, informed me that it was intended to introduce regulations which would greatly alter the position of all future Commanders-in-Chief, and it was on that understanding that I accepted the offer. When I subsequently learnt what was the nature of these alterations, I found that they were certainly not to my liking, but I resolved to give them a fair trial. I have done so honestly for the last five years, including a full year of actual war. It is because, after this experience, I believe them to be injurious to the efficiency of the Army and fraught with danger to the highest interests of the Empire, and because I am certain that under their provisions you can never have any effective Army, that I am here to-day in the hope of making my reasons for this opinion evident and clear to your Lordships.

" Allow me now to analyse briefly this experimental Army system of 1895. It follows generally, as I have said already, the plan under which the Navy has long been administered— namely, by a Board. In other words, it divides into what I may call water-tight compartments the responsibility, under the Secretary of State for War, for the fighting efficiency of the Army, a responsibility which in all previous times had been concentrated in the Commander-in-Chief. The heads of these four water-tight compartments have no connection one with the other. They have no military head ; each is singly and individually responsible to the Secretary of State for War for the orders he gives and the work he performs. Each is the adviser of the Secretary of State for War, and in describing their duties and position no reference even is made to the existence of a Commander-in-Chief. Until 1895 the Commander-in-Chief, as I have repeatedly urged, was responsible to the Secretary of State that the Army was thoroughly well trained for war. There is now no one soldier to whom the country can look as directly responsible for the military efficiency of the Army it pays for. It must depend upon the statesman, almost invariably a civilian, whom the Prime Minister may select from among political supporters for the position of Secretary of State for War. I would ask, Is this wise ? Is it business-like ?

" I venture to illustrate this method of Army administration by a homely and familiar analogy. I have lately been engaged in converting an old farmhouse into a little country residence. My first step was to call in an architect, an expert. I left the expert to look after the builder and his men. Under our Constitution the Secretary of State, as the representative of the Cabinet, used to stand to the Commander-in-Chief in much the same position as I did to the architect. The Secretary of State acted as the owner, the Commander-in-Chief as the expert. But mark the difference of procedure : instead of dealing with one expert the Secretary of State asks the opinion of every one of his foremen without the knowledge of the architect, much less consulting him. Had I followed this system, I wonder what sort of a house I should have had—very possibly the stair-case would have been forgotten. One of the foremen—let us say the carpenter foreman—in his anxiety to make perfect his own particular job in which his interest was absorbed, and knowing little or nothing of the general plan of the whole building, might have impressed me with the importance of his own special share in the operation, while the drains might have been overlooked, or some other necessity might have been omitted that would have left the house uninhabitable. Amplifying this, and dealing with it on broader lines, the inconvenience, the mischief, the possible dangers of the present system may be exemplified in another way. Hardly one of the many questions that come up before the Secretary of State for decision is of quite a simple nature. All, as a rule, concern several distinct branches in the War Office. Take for instance the introduction of a new rifle. Here there are intricate technical points affecting all manners of people. The mechanism, range, and precision of fire are within the province of the Director-General of Ordnance ; the weight of the weapon, the carrying power of the soldier, the facility for aiming and firing, involve important questions which concern the Adjutant-General, the Quartermaster-General, and so on. Each of these officers would naturally give the best advice from his own particular branch's point of view, which would often be at variance with the views urged by other departments. How can the political Minister of War, to whom military science is more or less an enigma, usefully hold the balance between such conflicting opinions ? How can he be sure that he is giving due weight to each point, and that he fully realises the force of one and the weakness of the other ? That can only be well done by the trained military expert, the Commander-in-Chief, who knows from experience every technicality, every detail himself. It is the business to which he has been brought up, and he can therefore easily sift out the rubbish and emphasise the good stuff in a way which only an expert can. Then, when he has heard all sides, he will form his opinion, and with the sound judgement of ripe knowledge and wide experience he will lay the case before his official superior, the Minister of War. There can be nothing of this kind under our present military system. The civilian Secretary of State is left in a fog of doubt and indecision, the result of which is the probable shelving of the question, or, still worse, that the wrong course is taken." [1]

[1] Hansard, House of Lords, March 4th, 1901.

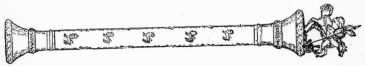

LORD WOLSELEY'S BATON.

CHAPTER XII

FROM Wolseley's first day as Commander-in-Chief to his last, England was engaged in minor campaigns which were to culminate in President Kruger's invasion of Natal. Little wars had marked the Victorian era ; towards its close they seemed to jostle one another to trouble that Sovereign's last years and stain them with her soldiers' blood. The first collision which it fell to Wolseley to direct from the War Office, was in that country which had first brought his name prominently before the public. Prempeh, King of Ashanti, had defied our High Commissioner on the Gold Coast, had refused to pay the balance of the war indemnity which had been exacted from his predecessor, had encouraged the slave trade, and revived the horrible practice of human sacrifice. The Government determined to bring Prempeh to his senses, and Wolseley advised Lansdowne that, as in 1873, the number of British troops should be kept at a minimum, and retained in the fever-stricken country for as short a period as possible ; the bulk of the force should be composed of native troops, guided by a small band of carefully chosen special service officers, and stiffened by a selected body of a few hundred British soldiers. On these lines the expedition was successfully conducted by Sir Francis Scott, but it brought in its train a personal sorrow for the Queen in the death from fever of her son-in-law, Prince Henry of Battenberg, one of the special service officers.

Contemporary trouble occurred on the restless North - West Frontier of India, and the Chitral campaign was followed up by the Tirah expedition which lasted into 1898, and was India's most serious military enterprise since the Mutiny.

Early in 1896 the Government decided on the re-conquest of the Province of Dongola. They had at first wrapped up their decision with the label of Military Demonstration, but the Italian *débâcle* at Adowa nerved them to expose their hand and pronounce for an advance up the valley of the Nile. Wolseley's heart rejoiced ; he knew—even if he were not officially told—that the re-conquest of Dongola was to be the prelude to the redemption of the Soudan. He had himself been unable to save Charles Gordon, but Gordon was to be avenged and the people for and with whom Gordon died were to be released from bondage and misery. No one was more determined than Wolseley that every provision should be made for his former subordinate, Sir Herbert Kitchener, in whom Salisbury and Cromer were alike insistent that command should vest.[1] He had some months before said to Lord Lansdowne, " These sorts of expeditions are half over when all possible eventualities have been discussed, prepared for beforehand, or discounted ", and now he was eager to see that proper provision was made for Kitchener's advance. He wrote to the War Minister (April 2nd, 1896) : " I don't want to force you to go to Dongola or Khartoum, but I want you to have the power to do so should you decide upon it. The provision of steamboats and launches I have recommended you to buy would secure you this power, and I would again urge the subject on your consideration."

[1] General Grenfell, Commander of the British garrison, gracefully agreed.

301

Against his express advice a native brigade was ordered at this moment from India to Suakin to deal with the turbulent Osman Digna, who had taken advantage of the withdrawal of the garrison to renew his impudent raids. The brigade remained at Suakin for several months, to be eaten into by sandflies and scurvy, but without firing a shot; Wolseley took advantage of their dreary mission to expound to the Queen his opinion of the Indian Army, which in some quarters he had been reputed to belittle:[1]

"Ever since the Queen took over the direct government of India, there has been in Lord Wolseley's opinion but one British Army; he draws no, and has never drawn any, distinction between what some people call the Queen's Army and the Indian Army. As regards the officers, the best men in both of those so-called two armies should be brought to the front in all parts of the Queen's dominions. One of the very best officers on the home staff at this moment is General J. Gordon, C.B., of the Indian Army, who is the Assistant Military Secretary here ; an officer who would make a very good Commander-in-Chief in India. As regards the Indian Army generally, Lord Wolseley has written and published more than once his opinions upon it. They were always most highly complimentary, and pointed out that the Indian Cavalry acting with British Cavalry would ride over hordes of Cossacks. Lord Wolseley has in his career fought against the Regular Indian Army when in mutiny, and has fought side by side with them again and again and has charged with Indian Cavalry. He knows and highly appreciates their good and gallant qualities. But when, being examined by a Royal Commission, he was asked if the British Cavalry could not be safely withdrawn or reduced, he felt bound to answer 'No'. This

[1] In consequence of some remarks he made in evidence before a Royal Commission.

answer at once led to the question being put to him by a civilian member of the Commission, 'But are not the Indian Cavalry regiments quite as good as the English regiments?'[1]

"Lord Wolseley is strong on this point, for he believes that the great mutiny of 1857 was to a considerable extent due to the fact that the old East India Company had so pampered its sepoys that they began to believe themselves quite equal to the English soldier. To use an Afghan expression, 'they had got wind in their heads'.

"Lord Wolseley has heard many of the ablest Indian officers now alive deprecate in strong terms the frequent employment of Indian troops out of India, even the bringing home of a few squads of sowars, because they feared it might unduly give them inflated notions of their own importance to the Empire.

"The history of all the great Empires, made up as the Queen's Empire is with auxiliary troops of many races and many creeds, is a warning against allowing the auxiliary to imagine himself his master's equal.

"On the other hand Lord Wolseley is often shocked when he is told of the rudeness and vulgarity of Indian officers and their families to the Princes and gentry of India. It is impossible to do too much to make them feel that we accept them with open arms as our friends and social equals, but he would never flatter the native soldier by allowing him to think himself the equal of the British soldier as a fighting man. Lord Wolseley thinks it would be highly dangerous to the Empire to do so."

[1] In May '97 Wolseley wrote to a correspondent: "I make it a point to answer questions put to me by authority in a straightforward way. I took part in the Crimean War and know that the Russian Army is hard to beat. . . . In the answers I gave before the Indian Commission on army matters I merely stated my opinion, and it is only men who either know little or who wish to attack me who would find anything insulting to our splendid Indian Army in what I said."

For two and a half years Wolseley was to watch with eager approval Kitchener's slow but sure steps on a path parallel to his own fourteen years earlier. Personally he urged in October 1897 that for a very special reason the advance should be expedited :

" I have followed closely all our recent moves in Egypt," he wrote to the War Minister, " and have become much impressed with the conviction that we ought to push on to Khartoum this winter. To do so you would require to move from Berber with a British force of 2 Infantry Brigades, with at least 1 strong regiment of Cavalry, and 2 batteries of Artillery.

" This force, backed up by the Soudanese soldiers of the Egyptian Army, would enable you (1) to destroy the Khalifa's Army to a certainty—if ever there can be certainty in war ; (2) to occupy Khartoum and to occupy the White Nile before the French establish posts there. As far as I can learn, the French are now working hard to forestall us on the Upper Nile, and if they do so we may have to face serious complications with them when we attempt the job in the autumn of 1898.[1]

"We can—badly off as we are for soldiers at present —furnish the 2 Infantry Brigades required, and as to the Cavalry and Artillery required send them out in first-rate order."

The Government, however, was content to wait on Kitchener's deliberate winter progress, and it perhaps took the Good Friday success at the Atbara to convince them that the Khalifa's days were numbered.

"No one", Wolseley said in a letter which followed a prompt telegram of congratulation, " has rejoiced over your victory more than I have done. The whole conception and execution has been with-

---

[1] Kitchener found Marchand at Fashoda in September 1898. He had arrived there on July 10th.

out fault and reflects the greatest credit on all concerned, but beyond all others upon you, the able
Commander in the Field.

" In common I may say with every one here, I have
followed all your moves with intense interest, and
when asked by the Government what answer should
be sent to your telegram ' to fight or not to fight ',[1]
my answer was, ' You have a first-rate man in command, trust him and let him do as he thinks best '.
That was done, and the result was all that the most
critical could desire. Were I in your place, I would
not, however, ask such a question. You must be a far
better judge than Lord Cromer or me or any one else
can be. You have your thumb upon the pulse of
the Army you command, and can best know what
it is capable of. This is my only criticism, and I
give it for what it is worth. Men and governments
at a distance are prone to parries and weak measures
and are never to be trusted, no, not the best of us.
When you advance on Omdurman, if you could feed
an English regiment of cavalry it might be invaluable.
We have also an admirable gun now in the service, I
mean the 5-inch Howitzers, that are worth your
thinking of. We could either send you a Battery of
them complete with mules instead of horses, or make
over to you the guns, waggons, etc., etc., to be
manned by your Egyptian gunners. The shell of
these Howitzers is admirable against Zarebas, Mud
houses, Field Works, and the sort of works you will
have to encounter during your final advance.[2] We
are delighted with the good marching powers of
Gatacre's Brigade. It is a good answer to the silly
stuff propounded by those *intelligent* M.P.'s who style
themselves ' the service members '."

Five months later the news of Omdurman reached

---

[1] Cf. *Life of Lord Kitchener*, vol. i. p. 225.
[2] It was a shell from this howitzer which breached the Mahdi's
tomb.

X

Wolseley when he was on Salisbury Plain superintending Army manœuvres. The entry in his diary runs: " God be praised. We can once more hold up our heads in the Soudan. Cromer can now bring peace and prosperity to that country, if he keeps the Pashas out of it, and that will be Kitchener's best memorial. What a fine fellow he is! I will see that he and the senior officers that he recommends get the promotion they deserve." Here he was as good as his word ; and remembering some of his own difficulties in the past he took into his own hands the matter of arranging for the medals and clasps for the campaign.

The famous rencontre at Fashoda was intense with interest, and Wolseley seized the incident to tighten up the measures for mobilisation, and to call attention, not for the first time, to defects in our coast defences and in the organisation and equipment of the Auxiliary Forces. In November 1897 he had told the War Minister that for the Militia and Volunteers we had only " obsolete guns, mostly old muzzle-loaders, which from want of horses can only be used as guns of position. Their shell fire and range is contemptible, and it would be cruel if not a crime to send these Auxiliary Forces into action with the artillery they possess at this moment." He now added, "We have one hundred and seven Volunteer batteries of position eight of which have no guns at all; the remaining ninety-nine batteries are armed with obsolete guns, some of them being next to useless ". Upon the larger questions of the status of the Auxiliary Forces he minuted the Secretary of State:[1] " Our laws which bear upon the disposal of the Auxiliary Forces of the Crown when war is imminent but not declared are obsolete. They are not suited for these days of steam, and seem based upon an unworthy suspicion of those who had formerly

[1] Dec. 25th, 1898.

306

command of the Army. I have such confidence in the good sense of Parliament that I believe we have only to explain what was our position some two months ago when war seemed near at hand to have this rectified.

" In the Coast Guard the Navy have a splendid Reserve which can at any moment be placed on board ship without any application to Parliament. Any number of ships can similarly be put into commission by orders of the Admiralty. But with regard to those military measures which must be taken for the defence of our home ports and fortified places on the Coast at such a time, the hands of the S. of S. for War are dangerously tied by law.

" In the interests of the country at such moments, it is most desirable, it is essential that the S. of S. for War should be able in a somewhat similar fashion to temporarily dispose of the Auxiliary Forces.

" Under your instructions I had to see all the General Officers in command of our sea-coast defences when war recently threatened, and I can assure you that it was most difficult to arrange for their security under our existing law. The only safe way open to us at such a time of tension is to call Parliament together, an expedient that would be nearly as disastrous as the plague."

But the Fashoda scare as a military warning proved only a flash in the pan, and little or nothing was done to steel the Volunteers until Mr. Haldane gave being and dignity to the Territorial Force.

If the soldier is to give of his best, he must receive of the best—in other words, he must not only be trained to the hour, he must be well fed, suitably dressed, and adequately paid. This was Wolseley's evangel in word, and to the extent of his powers, in deed also. The carefully chosen and generous ration which he had claimed for his troops on the Nile had opened the eyes of the Commissariat, and suggested the future provision which was carried almost to the edge of profusion in the Great War. In 1882 he had encouraged the Duke of Connaught to represent in high quarters how infinitely more appropriate was the khaki of the Indian Contingent than the red and blue in which British troops were then for the last time to take the field; soon after becoming Commander-in-Chief he sought the advocacy of the Heir Apparent [1] — of whose sympathy he was sure — to secure a proper fighting kit for the Army :

" If the Prince would be prepared to take this matter up, it would be a great support to me if he would graciously discuss it with me at some early date to be fixed by himself. As I told you, my dear Ellis,[2] the other day, I am most anxious to work in all Army matters with the Prince and under his orders. Our late C.-in-C. looked at the Army from a parade point of view : I want the Prince to look at the practical and fighting side of this important question."

The Prince of Wales gladly responded to the appeal, and a good many yards of gold lace disappeared from the dress of the officers, but it needed Boer bullets to point and enforce the demand for a wholly serviceable equipment.

Few things ever brought Wolseley's anger to so white a heat as an attempt made at this time to convince the soldier that he was being generously treated by the State when in fact he was being tricked in his accounts. In 1897 there was a pleasant proposal to increase the soldier's pay by giving him threepence a day to cover the amount he had had to pay for groceries ; but it was intended to recoup the State by docking that portion of his earnings kept back and given to

---

[1] June 1896.
[2] General Ellis, the Prince of Wales's equerry.

him on his discharge, known as " deferred pay ". Wolseley bluntly told the War Minister :

" I shall have much to say on the question of ' deferred pay '. The juggle of deducting from it what you mean to give the soldier as a free ration is just the sort of plan that has given the War Office such a bad name in the Army.

" It will be howled at in every mess, and even the small-minded officer who wants to keep the soldier, if he can do so, from leaving the Colours at seven or eight years' service, will scoff at the arrangement.

" The I.G. of recruiting tells me the arrangement will have no appreciable influence upon recruiting. You want to add half an inch to the height of a man's collar and you recoup yourself by cutting the same amount from the tail of his coat. The soldier will see this at once.

" To my mind it is cruel to the soldier to interfere with his deferred pay. You might add to it, but certainly not decrease it. He has earned it, it is his. We preach to him on the subject of thrift and we show how insincere we are by reducing the amount we had laid by for him out of his pay.

" We do this because it is unwisely said that this deferred pay encourages the man to leave the Colours instead of engaging to serve on until he has completed twelve years' service with the Colours. But we at the same time pretend to hold out the bait to him that we are to provide him with employment in the Post Office, etc., when he leaves at seven years' service. Is this logical ?

" There is a strong agitation against the War Office in the air. The whole Army will join in it *con amore*, and most of all the officers who have served here on the Hd. Qr. Staff.

" It has no friends, and as far as I am able to gather of these proposals about deferred pay and the Ration Stoppage, they will intensify this feeling."

In the thick of his work, there came unmistakable
signs that the wounds which scarred his body and
the after effects of cruel climates, superadded to
constant mental strain, had begun to tell on his constitution. He kept this as much as possible to
himself ; he tried without success a short spell of
sea-air ; he struggled through the ceremonies of the
Diamond Jubilee, and then went quietly into a
nursing home for an operation on the glands of his
neck which had become poisoned. He recovered
quickly from the operation, but somehow never
seemed again to reach his former level of health. So
anxious was he to avoid all fussy inquiries that he
confided to no one at the War Office the real reason
for his absence, and the Queen only knew its cause
when a summons to Osborne reached him in hospital.

During these years the clouds in South Africa
were becoming more and more lowering, and Wolseley
was at constant pains to impress upon the authorities
how unready they were for the storm. In 1879, on
leaving South Africa, he had urged that the garrison
in that country should be increased as the surest
means of preventing trouble with the Boers, and
he had repeated that advice as Adjutant-General
in 1888. Almost his first act as Chief Military
adviser to the Government was to ask for the
despatch of reinforcements to the Cape and Natal ;
these " would always be enabled in case of need to
take up a forward position either near Ladysmith or
on Transvaal territory on what is locally known as
the Berg ". In the same month [1] he renewed the
demand which he had made as Adjutant-General that
the infantry should be increased by eleven battalions;
finding that the need for artillery had become

[1] February 1896.

greater, he then asked for an increase of ten batteries, and for complete equipment for twenty batteries. He kept his finger on our weakness in artillery both for the field and for coast defence, and he cried aloud that our infantry were numerically wholly inadequate to meet our increasing obligations. The result of continuous pressure was that in the Army Estimates of 1897 provision was made for adding two battalions to the Guards, one battalion to the Cameron Highlanders, and one battery to the Artillery. Upon this matter of increasing the Guards he had written to the Duke of Connaught in November 1896 :

" I have asked for a very considerable addition to the Army to enable it to fulfil the duties for which it is maintained without reducing the force at home to a hopeless state of inefficiency.

" I hope to get at least a part of what I asked for, but I am begged to put forward a scheme by which the cost and extent of these proposals might be reduced within the narrowest limits. To do this I have revived the old idea of adding two battalions to the Foot Guards. This has long been a hobby of mine, for, from the first I preached to all here that a short service system could never be complete without a strong Guards Division. Besides, in the mobilisation of our three Army Corps for war, it is very desirable that we should have a Guards Division instead of a Brigade of Guards as heretofore.[1]

" Well, I can get those 2 Battalions if the Colonels of the Guards think it desirable, for I think the Queen, who has such a practical mind upon all such matters, will be the first to understand what a benefit this would be to the Brigade : and would therefore not oppose it if the 3 Colonels approved.

" But I can only get this done on terms, and in my humble opinion the terms will afford the Guards

[1] A Guards Division was eventually created by Lord Kitchener in July 1915.

opportunities for taking part in our little wars, which they can never expect to secure in any other way.

"The terms are that three battalions of Guards under a Guards General should form the peace garrison of Gibraltar. If this were approved, I would withdraw the battalion of Guards from Dublin, so that there might continue to be, as at present, six battalions between London and Windsor. . . .

"In the interests of the whole Army, which I know has first weight with you, Sir, this proposal would be a great matter at present. We now have 76 Battalions of the Line abroad, and only 65 at home. If the proposal were carried out, those figures would stand 73 and 68, and if I can get 5 more line battalions they would become 73 abroad and 73 at home. The Army can never be a well working machine until this balance is established during peace. I earnestly hope Your Royal Highness may be able to see your way to supporting this proposal, which would be from a military point of view a great benefit to the Brigade of Guards, and would be of incalculable value to the service generally. The Duke of Cambridge is, I think, practically committed to the scheme, having given in his adherence to the proposal to keep two Battalions of Guards in Egypt."

Even this small increase was slow to materialise, for there was ample opportunity for procrastination after Parliament had voted the necessary supplies. A battalion of Guards went indeed to Gibraltar, but in September 1898, when receiving the freedom of the City of Glasgow, Lord Wolseley found it necessary to prod the Government into action by the statement that only one battalion had been added to the Army since the introduction of the Cardwell system in 1871, and that meanwhile we had been constrained to increase the British garrisons in India, the Mediterranean, and South Africa, and to occupy Egypt. He calculated that the burden placed upon the Army was at least 30 per cent greater than it could bear. The speech had the result that authority was given for the addition of third and fourth battalions to each of three line regiments, but at the time of the outbreak of the South African War only five new battalions had been raised.

While he was slowly and painfully winning his case for an expansion of the Army, Wolseley was simultaneously urging the reinforcement of our garrisons at what he saw to be the points of danger. In April 1896 he wrote to Lord Lansdowne :

"I wish your Cabinet would send a couple of battalions to Cape Town at this moment. If the Boers see we are strong and in earnest we *may* avoid trouble by and by. If they deem us weak and afraid to be great, our hold over the Cape will become very precarious."

In the following July he again wrote to the Secretary of State :

" You put the two following questions to me :

" (1) Am I in favour of immediately strengthening the Natal Garrison ?

" (2) If so, what Force should *now* be sent from England to enable us to hold the position of Lady-smith [1] and even of Laing's Nek ?

" My answer to No. (1) question is ' Yes '.

" My answer to No. (2) is :

> 1 Regiment of Cavalry.
> 1 Battery of R.H.A.
> 2 Battalions of Foot.

[1] Wolseley never, despite allegations later laid, contemplated that Ladysmith should be held defensively. He maintained that if we were forced to fight defensively in Natal, the Biggarsberg position some twenty miles north of that town was that which we should seek to hold, and that, if we were unable to do that, we should fall back behind the Tugela. By "the position of Ladysmith" he meant the Biggarsberg. He knew Natal from end to end, and he considered Ladysmith, lying in a hollow and commanded on all sides by hills, as the last place in which to lock up a garrison.

313

The Regiment of Cavalry could be accounted for as required to take the place of the 7th Hussars sent to Bulawayo : the Battery R.H.A. to replace the two guns of the Mountain Battery sent to the same place. The 2 Battalions of Infantry to eventually find increased garrison for the Mauritius, now being recommended by the Colonial Defence Committee.

" When the 7th Hussars return from Bulawayo we should then have a complete Brigade of Cavalry in Natal, with a Battery of R.H.A. and a Brigade of Foot (3 battalions), with a battery of Mountain guns, all available for the occupation of Biggarsberg position beyond Ladysmith ; whilst we should have 3 companies of Foot for a garrison in Maritzburg."

Wolseley's correspondence and journals are clear evidence that from the early days of 1896 onwards his chief preoccupation was how war with the Boers might be avoided. In April 1896 he wrote to Sir Gordon Sprigg, then Prime Minister at the Cape :

" I confess to feeling uneasy regarding the march of events in South Africa. I have but one great object in the world and that is to maintain the Greatness of our Empire. But apart from my John Bull sentiment upon the point, I firmly believe in doing so I work in the cause of Christianity, of peace, of civilisation, and the happiness of the human race generally. When therefore I hear of the Boers arming and building forts and blustering, and knowing how little it would all be worth if we took the matter up seriously, I feel sorry for England and sorry for a race very kindred with our own and possessing some of our best characteristics. I grieve to think that two peoples that ought to live together in peace and unity are being set against one another, and that the little boy is being taught to talk big to his big brother who could at any moment crush him in the hollow of his hand, if he put forth even a little of his strength.

The big brother is very forbearing and has been seriously angry with the Filibusterers who lately attacked his little brother, and has gone out of his way to let bygones be bygones, for there were serious faults on both sides. I wish the little brother, and he is a very small boy, was as kindly disposed towards his big brother as that brother is towards him. What we want is peace, but peace must be secured on terms that will satisfy the big as well as the little brother."

He was soon convinced that the one way to preserve peace was quietly and unostentatiously to reinforce the garrisons of the Cape and Natal so as to persuade the Boers that it would not be worth their while to put up a fight. His diary in April 1897 has some pathetic entries :

"*April 11th.* Chamberlain wrote to say he would call, so I went and called on him instead. He is most anxious to take strong measures at the Cape, but the Cabinet won't face the cost.

"*April 12th.* Am still pressing the Government to largely augment the force at the Cape. Lansdowne is, and always has been, opposed to it. Chamberlain is for it. Hicks-Beach attended meeting at W.O. Cost of sending 2 batteries R.H.A. and 3 regiments cavalry to the Cape and keeping them there for six months over half a million sterling !

"*April 13th.* Met again at W.O. to discuss South African affairs. New proposal is to occupy and strengthen Laing's Nek, which we could do by sending out two batteries of Field Artillery, and one battalion to Natal. Every one off for the Easter holidays so nothing will be done until the Westminster talking shop meets again. Let us not lead others into temptation should be a daily prayer on the lips of every British Cabinet Minister. It is as wicked to pretend to be weak when we are strong and to leave rich prizes dangling under the noses of ignorant farmers as it is to leave sovereigns about in a room."

A précis of the more important of his subsequent representations is appended, and demonstrates how far performance lagged behind advice.[1] The Commander - in - Chief was fully conscious of the difficulties of a Government, embarrassed by the consequences of the ill-starred Jameson Raid, and anxious to avoid all appearance of desire to precipitate a conflict. Once his policy of silently sending adequate reinforcements to the Cape and to Natal in the years 1896 and 1897 had been rejected, every stage of the crisis was to increase the difficulty and make the Government's task harder, and from 1898 onwards he was at least determined to burn into them that war with the Boers would be a very serious military undertaking.

In April 1898 he again represented to the War Minister that we were not ready for the storm:

" I fully endorse the serious view taken by the Government of the Cape upon our position in South Africa. We may go on for some years as at present, but sooner or later we shall have a violent explosion there. Were we now or at any time in the near future to have any serious trouble with a foreign power that explosion would take place at once. Are we prepared for it ? Any student at the Staff College would say ' No ' to such a question. There is no good reason that I know of why we should not be thoroughly prepared for it."

In a final attempt to awaken the Government to the realities of the situation he wrote, in August 1899, to Lansdowne, who seemed to be nursing some notion of a peaceful issue :

" Your note of 24th is written in so hopeful a spirit of peace in South Africa that I assume the Cabinet has information on the subject not known to

[1] See Appendix to this chapter.

the press. To judge of matters there from the daily papers, it would seem that every preparation is being made by Mr. Kruger for war, and that he is striving to force a war policy upon the O.F. State also. He is a shrewd old fellow who will, I have always thought, make terms at the last moment, and easy terms for us if we have the backbone to exact them, but will prolong the pourparlers and put England to all possible inconvenience and very great expense before he does make terms. It is not for me as a mere military adviser to pronounce when the interruption to business, the unrest caused by the Boers' present policy, and the very great outlay of public money it entails, has become a heavier and a greater and more dangerous burden than would be the actual war for which we are preparing in driblets. The pacific bent of public opinion at home compels us to be careful to avoid measures that might be fairly regarded as ' hurrying the pace ' and forcing on hostilities. The problem before us, according to my light, is by what measures can we most effectually and judiciously make Kruger and Co. fully realise that we mean business unless Sir A. Milner's modest demands are freely conceded ?

" A soldier in power would bring this about by such a display of force as that I have recommended from the first in this matter, and which on a smaller scale I strongly advocated in my note to you of the 17th inst. and in the minute enclosed with it. I write this very early in the morning before I have seen any of the newspapers of the day. But judging the position from all news to hand up to yesterday, I can see no change in Mr. Kruger's attitude towards us. At this moment we are *not* locally prepared for war in South Africa, so that if it comes upon us under present circumstances we shall surrender the initiative to Kruger, and in no recent case that I can think of would, or at least if properly handled could, that loss of initiative be more likely to seriously injure our national prestige or be more hurtful to the party in office, if I may venture upon such a political comment.

" I still believe, perhaps foolishly, that a display of force would be the quickest and the surest way to secure peace."

With a strange disregard of truth the man who day in, day out, was pleading that we should arm ourselves for the fight was accused of having greatly underestimated both the strength of the Boers and the force required to defeat them. As a matter of fact the Intelligence Department, under the able direction of Sir John Ardagh, not only made an accurate estimate of the numbers which the Boers could put in the field, but knew of every gun they possessed, and with that precise information Wolseley supplied the Cabinet. It is true that the force which he recommended, one Army Corps and a Cavalry Division in addition to the troops already in South Africa, proved insufficient, but he had pressed for that force to be mobilised and held ready on Salisbury Plain in June 1899, whereas it was not until October 9th that the actual order for mobilisation was given. The moment that White was known to be in difficulties in Natal, Wolseley pressed for the immediate mobilisation of a second Army Corps, which was not completed until the " Black Week " had alarmed both Cabinet and country. It requires but a modicum of military knowledge to understand that a force recommended as sufficient in June might with the march of circumstances be insufficient in October. Neither to Lord Wolseley at home, nor to Lord Roberts after a year's experience at first hand, was it given to gauge the resistance which the Transvaal and Orange Free State patriots would put up; but to no Government was ever given more timely or more persistent warning of the certain consequences of " putting off " and unpreparedness than Wolseley gave Lord Salisbury and his Cabinet.

The mobilisation tardily ordered was at once a complete success and a triumph for the short service system. The Queen wrote her congratulations, and the Commander-in-Chief proudly answered on October 24th :

" Lord Wolseley presents his humble duty to the Queen and feels very proud indeed that Her Majesty should feel satisfied with the manner in which the Military machinery of the Army has worked during the present mobilisation of one Army Corps and one Division of Cavalry. Lord Wolseley's only regret is that this Mobilisation did not take place two months ago.

" The result up to the present is as follows—on the 7th inst. the Queen's orders for the Mobilisation of the above-mentioned force were issued. The men were given ten days to assemble, the number to whom notices were sent being 14,200. That is the number of reservists belonging to the Regiments of Cavalry and of Infantry, Artillery, etc., to be employed. Of this number 14,108 men rejoined, and of that number 1271 were rejected by the Doctors as unfit for active service. The first detachment embarked on the 20th inst. at Southampton ; five Batns., of whom four constitute the 2nd Brigade of 1st Division and one belongs to the Line of Communications. I never saw five finer Batns., *not one* man under the influence of drink. When the five ships carrying those 5000 men had pushed off from the quays, the men, crowding every possible part of the upper decks, sang ' God save the Queen '. By the evening of yesterday, Monday 23rd inst., some 20,000 men were embarked and had sailed for South Africa.

" This reflects the greatest credit on all the Staff Officers, who had to plan and carry out this operation, by far the largest operation of the sort we have ever attempted before.

" Lord Wolseley regrets very much that they are not in South Africa already, where their services are now sadly needed. The horse ships are very well fitted and I hope the horses may have a comfortable voyage. Everything that could be done to make it so has been carried out and attended to as the Queen desired.

" Lord Wolseley knows the Queen will be glad to hear from him that over two Army Corps could be mobilised *quite easily* in a fortnight, and ready for embarkation if needed. He has urged the Government to call up 36 Batns. of Militia, to raise to war strength at home 7 Regts. of Cavalry, and the 18 Batteries of Artillery we should want for our Second Army Corps. The Cabinet have agreed to this and I think the effect abroad will be good.

" Lord Wolseley is in great hopes that the success of this partial mobilisation may so satisfy all classes of the Queen's subjects that even the old-fashioned Generals, who honestly believed it would not work, may recognise its advantages."

The story of the administrative preparations for the campaign and of the conduct of the war from London has been told in the Official History and in the Report of the Royal Commission on the South African War. Wolseley was not the man to interfere from Pall Mall with a Commander in the Field or to allow others to do so. On hearing that Sir George White in Natal was being pressed to modify his plans to suit local political exigencies, he had telegraphed to him in October 1899 :

" Please understand that we expect you to act strictly in accordance with military requirements of the situation. Governor is in his right in directing your attention to political consequences of your arrangements but responsibility rests entirely with you. You may find steps necessary which run counter to public opinion here and in the Colony, but we shall unhesitatingly support you in adhering to arrangements which seem to you militarily sound."

No clearer indication could have been given that neither Ladysmith nor any other place was to be occupied for political motives; and if there remained any doubts as to Wolseley's views of the functions of the arm-chair strategist, he settled them in a letter to the Queen's private secretary in March 1900 :

" I am sure there is no desire here to interfere in any way with the direction of the War in South Africa. If there was, *I* would not stand it. But I know that the confidence felt in Lord Roberts is so complete that every wish and desire of his is unhesitatingly acceded to. No General in the Field has ever been less questioned by his Govt. at home. Judging according to the imperfect information at my disposal of the present position in Natal and the Orange Free State and the Transvaal, my own private opinion is that Buller and Roberts were in the first instance right, when it was settled to remove Warren's Division from the Tugela to Bloemfontein for an advance across the Vaal. The information upon which Buller subsequently acted was to my mind absurd, namely that Joubert, etc. etc., still meant to drive Buller and the English Army from Natal into the sea. However, no matter what might have been my own views on such a point, I would never set them up against the views of the General on the spot. He *must* be supported and his plans *must* be carried out. I know that Lansdowne had no intention to interfere and no wish to do so. He is far too cautious a man to try to influence a General in the Field, to change his plans about operations regarding which his education has not fitted him to judge. It may be that Roberts and Buller hope to join hands through the Drackensberg passes and cross the Vaal River together. Looking at the position as I do, with the information at my disposal, it would seem to me unwise to leave between thirty and thirty-five thousand troops near Ladysmith doing nothing whilst Roberts fights what may be a final battle on the Vaal River. But I would not upon any account force my opinion upon a General Commanding in the Field.

" I hope Mafeking may be saved, for the place has made a gallant defence and Baden-Powell has proved himself to be an able leader."

From the beginning of the war he, who had been always the first to insist that military training must have as its object preparation for war, was naturally careful to apply at home the lessons learned on the battle-fields of South Africa. In August 1900 he was a spectator at an Aldershot field day which he brought to an abrupt conclusion, and in an address to the officers he alluded sharply to the lack of system and to the make-believe which marked their training. The incident stirred up a good deal of dust, and its sequel was a drastic change in the Aldershot régime. The *Times* was moved to remark, " False standards he felled, the true standard suited to the needs of the occasion he imparted to our home Army ", and Mr. Linley Sambourne was quick to draw a cartoon depicting him as bowling out the stiff and the antiquated.

If the Commander-in-Chief had to keep a steady watch that the needs of the Army in South Africa were promptly met, the soldier responsible for the safety of the country was not blind or deaf to the anti-British propaganda on the Continent which grew in volume and venom as and when our weakness in Oversea war was exposed. Day by day his repre-

FROM CARTOON BY MR. LINLEY SAMBOURNE.

By permission of the Proprietors of *Punch*.

To face page 322.

sentations to the Government as to the paramount importance of raising fresh troops became more urgent in text and tone, and in despair of otherwise being listened to, he wrote to Lord Lansdowne : [1]

" You told me yesterday afternoon that the Cabinet had just decided not to adopt the emergent measures I had proposed to the Defence Committee on December 29th last for the protection of England during the absence of our Standing Army.

" The Regular troops I then asked Ministers to raise from the very many thousands of trained soldiers now in civil life, and the other measures I recommended would, I said, provide us with the minimum Regular Force, which, added to the Militia and Volunteers remaining at home, would enable us to meet an Invading Army with every prospect of success.

" Pressed as to how I proposed to raise these Veteran Regts., I supplied the information required.

" As the Cabinet refuses to adopt the measures by which alone, I believe, you could raise the troops I conceive to be essential for national safety, I feel compelled to resign my position as C.-in-C. I am anxious to communicate to the Queen as soon as possible my reasons for taking this step, and would therefore esteem it a favour if you would kindly let me know at your earliest convenience when I may do so."

For two days the resignation remained in the balance ; Wolseley only withdrew it upon an assurance that proper provision would be made for home defence. This was his last serious collision with the Government. As Great Britain became more and more denuded of troops his anxiety for the safety of the motherland did not diminish, and he did not cease to make that anxiety known to the Cabinet; but during the short period of duty which remained to him his prescriptions received greater attention.

[1] January 1900.

323

On September 30th he learned from Lord Lansdowne that Lord Roberts had been invited to come home to be his successor, and in November, on completion of his five years' tenure of the office of Commander-in-Chief, he left the War Office for ever.   Wolseley's farewell to the Queen ran :

" I cease to be Your Majesty's Commander-in-Chief this evening, and as it would seem that my chance of re-employment in any other public capacity is, I suppose I may say small, I am unwillingly compelled to regard my retirement from office now as final.

" I therefore presume to humbly and respectfully express my heartfelt gratitude for the support and consideration as well as the many acts of gracious kindness and the many rewards I have received from Your Majesty during the nearly forty-nine years I have had the privilege of serving the Crown.

" The pride in being a British soldier is enhanced a hundredfold by the inward satisfaction experienced by all ranks in serving Your Majesty.   This has been felt by no one more keenly than by Your Majesty's most humble and faithful servant."

Two days earlier he had written to Mr. Brodrick, who had succeeded Lord Lansdowne as Secretary of State for War :

" I shall be very glad to dine with you on January 3rd to meet Lord Roberts.   I cease to have any military position the day after to-morrow, so it will not do for me to make the arrangements for keeping the streets, etc. etc., the day Lord Roberts arrives. I shall be at home in the country when Lord Roberts arrives, but will come to town for your dinner, to which you have so kindly invited me.   I shall mention these dates to Sir Coleridge Grove, but to no one else outside my own front door.

" *P.S.*—I open this, for I have just had a letter the writer of which informs me ' upon the very best authority' that I am expected in Government quarters to make an attack on the Government on Army matters, as soon as Parliament meets. I wish to tell you and any one who takes an interest in such a humble individual, that I never had, nor have I now, any such intention.

"I assume that when Parliament meets in February next there will be an 'Army' night, during the session in the House of Lords; if so I shall certainly speak and point out what I know from experience to be the serious effects of the present system of Army administration, but I shall neither attack the Government nor any individual.

"Lord Lansdowne as well as Lord Salisbury are in possession of the points which makes our system differ from that of all other European Powers, for I furnished both with the headings of my argument."

The "Army night" came on March 4th, 1901, when Wolseley exposed the system under which the Army had been administered. His speech,[1] made from the cross-benches, was entirely impersonal; his sole purpose was to remedy defects, not to attack individuals. Lord Lansdowne, now the Foreign Minister, rose to reply. After a cursory defence of an organisation which within a few years was buried unmourned, he went on to make, without notice given, a bitter personal attack upon the ex-Commander-in-Chief. He said that if Lord Wolseley had paid more attention to the duties assigned to him he might have enabled the War Office to turn to better account the large number of auxiliary forces which we had in the country, and which had been not a little neglected during the past five years; he protested that Lord Wolseley might have told the Government before war broke out in South Africa that Ladysmith was

[1] See Appendix, Chapter XI.

not a favourable station for the British forces to occupy, and might have warned them that it would take more than one army corps to subjugate the two South African Republics. The onslaught, wholly unsupported by any evidence, was a deliberate appeal to a public, sadly disillusioned by the setbacks of the war, to condemn the man who had pressed in season and out of season that preparation should be made for the conflict which he had foreseen. The speech was so lacking in the good taste characteristic of the Minister that it might be ascribed to momentary irritation if any apology had followed. In the debate both the Duke of Devonshire and Lord Salisbury sought to remove the unfortunate impression which their colleague had created by denying that Lord Lansdowne had made a personal attack upon Lord Wolseley, but it was obvious that the Foreign Secretary's words had no other meaning, and were intended to have no other meaning, than that Wolseley had failed to perform his duty as Commander-in-Chief.

On March 15th Wolseley moved in the House of Lords for all papers bearing upon the allegations made against him by Lord Lansdowne, and supported his motion in a speech admirable in temper and dignified in tone. The Government made the question a party matter and refused the production of papers on the usual ground that it would involve the publication of War Office minutes of the most secret character. A majority thus obtained was reinforced by the timely circulation in the lobbies of a report, for which there was no foundation, that the publication of the papers would involve Great Britain with foreign powers.

His speech in the House ended, Wolseley never again made public reference to what he privately described as the most unpleasant incident in his life. Confident that the facts would one day be known, he was content to await the judgement of his countrymen upon the evidence which now lies before them.[1]

[1] In August 1903 a monumental Blue Book, the report of the Royal Commission on the War in South Africa, made its appearance. The evidence offered was often very striking, and sometimes bordered on the sensational. Such of it as bore on preparation for war and the state of the Army underlined all that Wolseley had said during his long struggle for efficiency and reform. No testimony proved more interesting in general considerations or in technical detail than his ; he was examined at great length, his replies met with great public favour, and in summing up his remarks he disclosed the prime cause of our military weakness. " I pointed out ", he said, " what was, I thought, a very curious fact regarding a nation like ours which is so often at war in different parts of the world. It was that we have never formulated to ourselves, as a Power, as a People, or as a Government—we had never put on paper to be translated from one Government to another—what were the objects for which our Army was created and maintained."

The one comment of the Commissioners, which could be construed as a criticism of the man who held the office of Commander-in-Chief on the eve of the war, was that the War Office had no plan ready ; a remark which shows that the Commissioners' knowledge of the conduct of war was limited. It is no part of the business of the War Office to prepare plans of operation, in the sense indicated in the report. That is the function of the man appointed to command in the field. The duty of the War Office is to supply him with all needful data and the *pros* and *cons* of various courses. In this case a definite plan of campaign could not be completed until it was known whether or no the Orange Free State would join the Transvaal.

APPENDIX

SOUTH AFRICA, 1899–1900

Précis of Letters and Minutes from
Commander-in-Chief to Secretary of State

June 8, '99.—The C.-in-C. wrote a long letter to S. of S. reviewing affairs in S.A., urging him to prepare for war, to mobilise an Army Corps on Salisbury Plain, and to collect large quantities of food and stores at Cape Town and Maritzburg. *Mobilisation began Oct. 9, four months after this minute. Order for food and stores given Sept. 23.*

July 4, '99.—S. of S. to C.-in-C. proposed that we should be ready to send 10,000 men, an installment of the larger force proposed by him, and asked him to consult with Army Board. *Instead of 10,000 from England, 5700 were sent ten weeks later from India.*

as to its composition, etc., and to get an estimate of the cost. This was done at once. But on receiving the information S. of S. wrote on *July* 12, '99, that the proposal need not be further pursued.

Meantime, on *July* 7, '99, C.-in-C. had written to S. of S. again pressing for the immediate mobilisation of 1 Army Corps and 1 Cavalry Division, 35,000 men at Salisbury or Aldershot, and begging that 10,000 men should be sent to S.A., and that supplies of all sorts for 1 Army Corps and 1 Cavalry Division should be provided, on the intended line of advance. Also that 1300 ponies be purchased in S.A. and that mules (11,000), wagons, carts, etc., be mobilised at home.

S. of S. approved services for supplies for Army Corps, Sept. 22.

First large purchase mules made, Sept. 23.

July 8, '99.—C.-in-C. supplied details of Army Corps he recommended should be mobilised, and urged the sending of officers to mule-raising districts to be ready to buy mules.

Sanction to send officers refused till July 27.

July 10, '99.—C.-in-C. sent to S. of S. details of the proposed mobilisation, and stated the sequence in which the necessary measures should be taken.

On *Aug.* 2, '99, S. of S., ignoring the preceding mins., informed the C.-in-C. that H.M. Government's view was that Natal should be strengthened by a force of 2000 men, 1 Batt. of this force being taken from Cape Colony. *Aug.* 2.—C.-in-C. replied he was glad it was proposed to strengthen Natal. S. of S. on this paper wrote a min. proposing as a " Demonstration " to send ½ Batt. Yorks L.I. from the Cape and a Batt. and Brig. Div. R.A. from England, to which C.-in-C. replied, *Aug.* 3, that as a " Demonstration " this would take in nobody, and advised sending 1 whole Batt. from the Cape and 1 on its way home from India, and the Brig. Div. R.A. from England *with* its horses.

Without horses.

This Brig. Div. had been under orders since early in July, and embarked Sept. 28.

Aug. 18.—C.-in-C. in printed min. for Cabinet reviewed the military situation, strongly

urged Govt. to send to Natal with least possible
delay 1 Inf. Div., 1 Regt. Cav., 2 Brig. Divs.
R.A., and some R.E.—about 10,000 men
altogether—and added that if given a free hand
he could PLACE THIS FORCE IN LADYSMITH in *That is by Oct. 20,*
nine weeks from date of order. He pointed *the date of the battle*
out that Mr. Kruger was making every pre- *of Talana, the first*
paration for war, and that it would be unsafe *action of the war.*
and unwise to delay further action in regard
to the measures he had suggested.

Aug. 24.—S. of S. wrote a very hopeful
min. to which C.-in-C. replied the same day
again pointing out how great were the preparations Mr. Kruger was making, and that
we were not locally prepared for war in South
Africa.

Sept. 1.—C.-in-C. pressed the necessity of
purchasing stores for mobilisation, but *Sept.* 31
S. of S. refused to sanction the purchase.

Sept. 3.—C.-in-C. referred to decision to
bring troops from India, and recommended
provision of khaki serge for troops. Advised
sending ½ Batt. redcoats to Kimberley.

Sept. 5.—On this date C.-in-C. received the
first intimation that negotiations with Transvaal had reached an acute stage. In min. to
S. of S. he urged Govt., as it had lost time in
Mil. preparations, to stave off, by diplomacy,
hostilities for five or six weeks. He added that
he had all along urged the increase of our
Military forces in S.A., and now asked for the
immediate despatch of a Brig. of Foot Guards
to Natal.

Sept. 16.—In reply to a minute of S. of S., *The first troops of*
C.-in-C. wrote urging the *immediate* mobilisa- *the Army Corps em-*
tion and despatch of the Army Corps, Cav. *barked six weeks*
Brig. and Lines of Communication Troops, *later, Oct. 20.*
which was the force he had asked for, in order
to cross the Orange River for an advance on
Pretoria. The force then in S.A. was: Cav.
1172, Infantry 8379, Art. 1066, Departmental
Corps 1169—total, 11,786.

Sept. 28.—C.-in-C. advised S. of S. to postpone for a month any act of hostility ; to obtain authority to spend £939,000 ; to fix date for calling out Reserves ; ascertain attitude of O.F.S.

(a) Date of R. Proclamation ; date Special A.O. 3.11.00, Oct. 26 ; first Mil. Batt. embodied Dec. 12, 1900.

(b) Decided on Oct. 18.

(c) Orders given Dec. 12.

Sept. 30. — C.-in-C. pointed out how denuded England would be of troops when those under orders had embarked, and advised (*a*) calling out 37 Mil. Batts. ; (*b*) raising 7 Regts. Cav. to higher establishment ; (*c*) Do. 19 Batteries H. and F.A.

Nov. 1.—C.-in-C. recommended a further mobilisation, at once, of

Mob. began Dec. 26. at Aldershot . . .

$\left\{\begin{array}{l}\text{1 complete Brig. Cav.}\\ \text{2 Batteries H.A.}\\ \text{1 Brig. Div. F.A.}\\ \text{1 Div. Inf. (5th Div.),}\end{array}\right.$

Mob. began Nov. 13. at the Curragh . . 1 Brig. of Inf.,

and to call out 12 more Batts. of Militia.

Nov. 3.—Having heard by telgm. from Sir Redvers Buller on 2nd that as soon as Gatacre's Div. reaches Cape Town he will send it to Natal, C.-in-C. proposed, if Buller wished to have Gatacre's Div. replaced, to mobilise the 2nd Army Corps and a Cav. Brig. (4th Brig.), this to take the place of his proposals in min. of 3rd inst.

Nov. 4.—C.-in-C. advised S. of S. to prepare for all probable eventualities, and to consider the mobilisation of the 3rd Army Corps, the composition of which he discussed.

These 3 Brig. Divs. were not raised then, but were merged in scheme of 29.12.

He also advised the raising of 3 Brig. Divs. F.A. at once for this Army Corps.

Nov. 12.—C.-in-C. strongly urged mobilisation of 1 Div. for S.A. (5th Div.) to replace troops sent to Natal ;

1 Div. (6th) in Reserve at home ;

1 Brig. for Ireland ;

1 Brig. to replace troops from India if required.

In other words, the 2nd Army Corps.

To this min. he added a *P.S.* on 13th to the effect that Sir R. Buller had asked for another Inf. Div.

Nov. 15.—C.-in-C. supported a proposal by $\frac{079}{9981}$
D.G.O. to send 2 Brig. Divs. F.A. instead of 1 *The 2 Brig. Divs.*
with 5th Div. *were eventually sent.*

Nov. 16.—S. of S. disagreed.

Nov. 28.— In a printed minute for the
Cabinet C.-in-C. once more urged the mobilisation of 6th Div. so that, when 5th Div.
sailed, we might have at least 1 complete Div.
in Great Britain ready for the Field. On the
following day he asked D.G.O. to what extent
he could clothe and equip the 6th, and his reply
was so extremely unsatisfactory that on *Dec.* 1
C.-in-C. addressed a min. to P.U.S. pointing
out our unpreparedness for war, and urging
on the S. of S. the necessity of at once giving
orders for the immediate provision of the
necessary clothing and equipment for the
6th Div. To this the S. of S. replied, *Dec.* 2,
that C.-in-C.'s min. must have been written
under a misapprehension, as the preparation of
the 6th Div. had been approved by the Defence
Committee the previous day.

Dec. 4.—A.A.G.(D.) addressed a min. to $\frac{079}{187}$
C.-in-C. asking whether in event of 6th Div.
going out (1) 7th Div. will be mobilised ; (2)
the Corps Bn. to complete Inf. of 2nd Army
Corps ; (3) a Cav. Brig. and the Corps Regt.
of 2nd Army Corps ; (4) if answer to (1), (2),
(3) is in the affirmative, how many Batteries of
F.A. will be mobilised.

Dec. 5.—C.-in-C. forwarded the above to
P.U.S., and expressed a strong opinion that the
same force of Art. should be sent with 6th as
with 5th Div., viz. 1 Brig. Div. F.A. and 1 Brig.
Div. H.A., and again urged mob. of 4th Cav.
Brig. at Aldershot.

Dec. 7.—S. of S. replied that Sir R. Buller
had not yet accepted offer of 6th Div., but that
as soon as it went it would be desirable to warn
the remainder of Reservists of Classes A, B, and
C ; that he proposed to ascertain Sir R.
Buller's views as to the 2 Brig. Divs. Art.;
that he approved of the Cav. Brig. being

331

mobilised. But on C-in-C. asking him whether the latter, viz. mob. of Cav. Brig., might be carried out at once, *Dec.* 6, he replied that he only contemplated calling out the Reservists of the 3 Regts. C.-in-C. forwarded a minute on subject from A.G. ; asked for approval to purchase or provide (1) the horses ; (2) the equipment ; (3) the clothing ; and (4) $\frac{1}{2}$ Batt. M.I. The Defence Committee, however, decided only to call up the Reservists, and give them their complement of horses.

Dec. 12.—C.-in-C. recommended that Militia, Yeomanry, and Volunteers be employed in S.A.

On this day was fought the battle of Colenso, the culminating event of the " Black Week ".

Dec. 15.—C.-in-C. in a paper to S. of S. repeated the recommendations which he had made verbally, the previous day, at a meeting in Lord Salisbury's room at the F.O. They were as follows :

(*a*) Despatch of Art. and M.I. of 6th Div. with least possible delay.

(*b*) That shipping be taken up for 7th Div. and that it begin to embark Jan. 2.

(*c*) Arrangements to be at once made for mob. of 8th Div.

(*d*) That the additional contingents offered by the Colonies be accepted.

(*e*) That Militia be accepted for service in S.A. up to 10,000 men.

(*f*) That the services of Yeomanry up to 1000 be accepted.

(*g*) That the services of 6000 Volunteers be accepted.

29.11.00.

LORD AND LADY WOLSELEY AT HAMPTON COURT PALACE, 1904.

To face page 333.

AFTERWORD

THE work was over, and the workman could rest if only his mind were easy. But if he could review his own past without any spasm of self-reproach, the future of his country filled him with anxiety—and for the future he must be content to sit in shadow and watch. The Boer campaign dragged on, and Wolseley now gave more credence to Kitchener's broad hint as to its duration than to Roberts's breezy optimism as to the struggle being practically over. Reinforcements might be required again and again, and from what reservoir would they be drawn? And when the resistance of the South African patriots should be overcome, would it be possible to make a peace free from the taint of Majuba, yet such as would win to our side a South Africa *amica* no less than a South Africa *pacificata*? And with peace would the lessons of the war be taken to heart or tossed aside as having no further concern for us? Would Lord Roberts, fortified by his successes in the field, now pronounce from his official chair the imperative necessity for some form of general service? Would he insist on our armoury being so furnished that we could not again be caught at sudden disadvantage,—or would the country lurch back into its easy-going unreadiness, and would a great war find us without an army worth the name, and without the machinery to equip one? Would the British Empire thus and then lie open to the spoiler?

These were some of the thoughts which seemed to have chased one another across the stage of Wolseley's mind, and to have prevented for a while the repose to which the farmhouse Glynde—the place he loved better than any other—invited him. He had lived in many houses, but Glynde alone seems to have been the home where he was on easy terms with life, and where no unwelcome visitor intruded. The house lay in the folds of the Sussex Downs, and Wolseley loved to climb to their heights with some friend—or more happily still with his daughter—for a companion. The keen air acted as wine to his veins, and his friends would say that so exhilarating was his talk he would infect them, however ignorant they might be of military circumstances, with his own enthusiasm. So graphic were his descriptions of strategic movements, so easy did they seem of execution, as he explained and dilated on them with word and gesture, so wholeheartedly did he appear to lift his hearers up to his own level, and to withhold from them no professional secret, that they felt themselves no less ardent soldiers, and scarcely less capable of military exploits, than the old Field-Marshal himself.

And on the other hand, with the laying by of his sword, came the larger indulgence in books and in the taste—keen if uncultivated—for literature. He read more eagerly—though he began to retain less easily—than ever before. Andrew Lang, Edmund Gosse, and Henry James were devoted in companionship and delightful in conversation ; and had they not admitted him to the fellowship of the very elect ? For, to his intense satisfaction, and by virtue of his *Marlborough*, Lord Wolseley had been numbered among the thirty authors who, at the instance of Thomas Hardy, signed a letter of congratulation to George Meredith on his seventieth birthday. It is possible to think that of the honours which in half a century rained thickly upon the soldier, none was more closely cherished than this.

From Glynde he would go with something like reluctance to the stately apartment in Hampton Court Palace, the gift of Queen Victoria not long before her death. Later, when the *meubles* and works of art had been set out there by Lady Wolseley's skilful hands, when each room had become a little treasure-house charged with many memories of the old fighting days, he learnt to appreciate the beauty of the place and to be intensely happy in it. But at first he would speak of it as " my wife's palace "; he would remind her ruefully he was the only male resident in it, and that with the lady tenants of the smaller apartments he had little in common ; the voices of the tourists distracted him, the influx of Sunday visitors distressed him. Eventually what really reconciled him to Hampton Court was Lady Wolseley's delight in it ; on no point could he be out of sympathy with her, for in his last decade her constant companionship was not only his solace and joy, but an indispensable condition of life.

With the new Sovereign came Lord Wolseley's last appointments. He was to be one of the original members of the Order of Merit : he was to carry the Third Sword at the Coronation, and he was to announce the accession of King Edward VII. to the Courts of Austria, Roumania, Servia, and Greece, as well as to the potentate from whom he would willingly have averted his eyes, the Sultan of Turkey.

Wolseley at first hesitated a little as to the acceptance of the mission. He pleaded the Royal Commission, before which he would have to give evidence ; that his day was over, and a younger man would better adorn the duty ; that he was prone to fatigue. But the King gracefully insisted ; [1]

[1] " My reception at Marlboro' House was most cordial. I made my reverence and kissed the kingly hand in due form. I sat with

the date could be made to suit his convenience; so distinguished a soldier could not be excused from so important an errand; every arrangement would be made to facilitate his journey; and from the Sovereigns he was to visit he would receive an honourable welcome. The result proved King Edward to be right. Wolseley thoroughly enjoyed his tour; the warmest greetings awaited him from the Monarchs, and the richest jewels—for his family as well as for himself—from the Sultan; he wrote his most animated and descriptive letters to his wife, and apparently his only disappointment was to miss at Bucharest the Crown Princess of Roumania, of whom he had seen so much in her childhood.

Since his retirement from office Wolseley had been busy with his personal papers, in favour of which he had put aside the completion of his *Life of the Duke of Marlborough*. At the end of 1903 was published the *Story of a Soldier's Life*. In his record of Marlborough, Lord Wolseley as a writer was at his best; in his own autobiography he is to be found at his worst. Both books were disappointing in that they broke off just where the chief character is rising to his highest level of interest. Marlborough, however, was drawn with bold yet fine strokes; his earlier circumstances are treated truthfully, yet without unnecessary unpleasantnesses; there had been much research, and

---

him for half an hour, and he told me to take my Baton and to wear the Collar of the Bath and the ribbon of St. Patrick at my formal interview with the Emperor; I was to address him in French if he did not speak English. I am to present the heir to the Crown with the Collar and Order of the Bath at a special interview. The King spoke much about the Emperor's misfortunes. The King of Roumania, he said, was a queer fellow. His wife is a poetess, and they are seldom together. The King of Servia had made, he said, a curious *mésalliance*, having married his father's mistress! Of the King of Greece he spoke very nicely; there he said I was to speak English. He asked me to write to him from each Court, which I promised to do."—W. to Lady W.

336

the utmost care had been taken to ensure accuracy ; the writer had not allowed his Protestant leanings to bias him ; the battle of Sedgemoor is a story in itself, and could not have been better told ; no reader could lay down the book without sharpened appetite for the volumes to come.

But Lord Wolseley's story of himself, which only carried him to the Ashanti War, is a very faulty vehicle. There are some delightful touches in the narrative of his early adventures ; there are many points of value to the military student ; the man's warm heart and generous spirit shine forth ; but the book as a whole is defective in construction and diffuse without being satisfying ; it suggests the holding-up to a blurred mirror what should have been a strong and arresting portrait. It may not be amiss to think that the volumes were in process of edition just when the pen was beginning to be loose in the writer's grasp, just when the sword might have begun to turn in the soldier's hand.

With the publication of his autobiography, Lord Wolseley's public career closes. In the long evening of his life there was to be nothing said, nothing done which might dull the gold of his reputation. For fifty years he had played leading parts and played them for all they were worth, and he now finally withdrew behind the scenes. At first there were frequent calls for him to come forward with his presence or his pen, but the appeals, however seductive, failed to bring him before the curtain, and in flux of time and with the noise of current happenings they died away. And in his retirement he kept silence : the loyalty which he had shown to his superiors and subordinates in the ranks he would show to his successors in office, whom he never sought to embarrass by criticism and would only now and again seek to help by suggestion. He retained to the end the command of the Royal Irish and the Royal

Canadian Regiments,[1] but after the State visit to Dublin in 1903 he pleaded to lay down his Gold Stick, as ceremonial duties were too heavy a tax on his strength. The plea could not be resisted, and the King would only devise a special pleasure for Wolseley by bestowing the Colonelcy of the Royal Horse Guards on Evelyn Wood.

The long quiet spells at Glynde and Hampton Court were varied by Mediterranean cruises and a trip up the Nile as the guest of Sir Donald Currie. These, however, brought but qualified enjoyment; Southern Europe made little appeal to Lord Wolseley, who was British to the bone. Foreign methods fidgeted him; foreign circumstances were uncongenial to him; foreign folk mystified him. The scenery alone appealed to him, and even this he would compare unfavourably with the English countryside; the hills and valleys of the Home Counties attracted him more than any Continental ranges and ravines; the Avon was always lovelier than the Arno, the Severn more stately than the Seine. Through his letters there would run a thread of scarcely suppressed complaint.

Even the wealth of his host oppressed him. " Why is it that rich men—except George Stephen—cannot refrain from alluding to their riches ? " The calls on high officials were " most distasteful operations "; the chaplains at the Continental churches were so uninviting that he " could have been more devotional in a Roman Catholic church " ; the King of the Belgians, who would come on board the yacht and who was once " a most philanthropic monarch ",

---

[1] In 1899 Mr. Borden, the Minister of Militia, asked Lord Wolseley to assume the Colonelcy of the Royal Canadian Regiment of Foot. " I never have forgotten, and shall never forget, my time in Canada or my service with Canadians." So ran the note of acceptance.

THE INNER HALL AT HAMPTON COURT PALACE, 1904.

To face page 338.

was now only " an unutterable bore as well as a sad roué ".

At the root of all the distress lay the separation from his wife. No house was really home without her ; no experience now was worth having unless she could share it ; when they were parted the hours were carefully counted until he should hold her hand again : while he is away he makes a carefully drawn deed of gift to her of all his possessions. " Every penny you can invest ", he reminds her, " will be a help to you when I go on my long last journey."

As the years slipped by, there was no great impair of physical activities, or even of intellectual grasp, but there arose a clinging mist to cloud the memory in so far as memory was applied to the happenings of the hour. Lord Wolseley would fluently relate what he had seen and done in bygone days ; he would rehearse easily what he had then read ; the events of the past stood out in bold relief, but the occurrences of the day seemed to be blotted out the moment they had taken place. As he realised his disability, he shrank more and more from general society, and especially disliked hotel life. But he was advised to winter in some sunny place ; the advice did not come amiss to Lady Wolseley, and an unpretentious, but not unpleasing, villa—Les Tourettes—near Mentone, was bought and became their home from late autumn until early spring.

There, on the 26th March 1913, without suddenness, but with no lingering of pain and weakness, came the quiet end. The last stage of the long journey was very brief and very easy. Some slight over-fatigue, a chill, a failure to respond to treatment, an apparent rally, then a relapse ; a few peaceful hours of perfect consciousness, and, his head pillowed on his wife's breast, the tired soldier sank to sleep.

The news was flashed home, and once more the

name of Garnet Wolseley leapt to every lip. All his
work and worth, all that he had dared and done,
was the theme of the hour. There would surely be
a public funeral ; Field-Marshals and Admirals of the
Fleet must bear his pall ; the doors of St. Paul's
must open to him ; he must lie with Wellington and
Nelson. Perhaps, if Wolseley could have ordered
it, this ceremonial would not have been ; the pomp
of death was always the only part of it which
he feared. He would have died so gladly—as
thousands of his countrymen were so soon to die—
with the sweat of war on his face, and the moan of
the guns in his ears ; he would have slept so quietly
in a roughly-turned grave on ground which his own
blood had helped to buy, with just a comrade's sigh
for his requiem. But King George accurately interpreted the wishes of the Army past and present, in
ordering every honour to be paid to a great military
patriot for whom he himself entertained profound
admiration and friendly regard.

By order of the French Government a section of
the Alpine Regiment stood to arms while the British
soldier was borne to the railway at Mentone ; at
Victoria Station the Grenadier Guards supplied a
bearer party, and Wolseley's old regiment, the Royal
Horse Guards, escorted his body to the War Office—
the new War Office in which he had never set foot.
Here a guard of honour of the Scots Guards was
drawn up, and here for two days under watch of
non-commissioned officers of the Brigade of Guards
there was to be seen the catafalque resting on a
carpet of purple velvet shrouded with a weight of
flowers and surrounded by huge lighted candles.

Then through the mists of a cold March morning
the cortège wended its way along a lane of troops and
through the crowded aisles of St. Paul's Cathedral,
paused for a brief service of prayer and hymn under
the dome, and passed to the allotted place in the

LORD WOLSELEY, 1905.

From a Drawing by Mr. Mortimer Menpes.

To face page 341.

shadowy crypt where Wolseley rests among his
Country's honoured Dead.

" La Guerra es la verdadera vida del hombre " :
warfare is the true life of man. Such was the motto
which Garibaldi adopted ; such might have been
the label of Wolseley's career. Military history will
assign to him his place in the gallery of Generals and
appraise at its full value his peculiar handiwork.
There had been—and certainly there were to be—
soldiers shining under showier opportunities ; to
none can be traced a higher conception of his calling
or a more consistent effort to set up the dignity—
and add to the lustre—of the profession he served.
The comrades who had been in his train from the
Red River to the Nile insisted that, given the
occasion, their leader would have ranked with
Marlborough and with Wellington—with the greatest
of English-speaking Generals. " The tragedy of
Wolseley's life was that he never met a worthy foe."
So murmured one of the group of his close followers
as they passed from paying their last tribute to the
well-loved Chief. The phrase reflects alike the
admiration which Wolseley earned from those whose
lives touched his own, and the sadness that the
grand opportunity had not come to the man who
seemed to add to every military quality the gift of
inspiring devotion in the men he led. Wolseley
passed away in no blaze of glory, in no scene of a
great military drama ; yet in truth he had met and
worsted a more redoubtable enemy than Tallard or
Napoleon. With clear brain and stout heart he had
waged war against ignorance and negligence ; he
had striven—and won—for efficiency and progress ;

he had pulled down the strongholds of endowed custom and established interest ; he had hacked his way through a tangle of prejudice and laid a path so broad and so firm that those who were to tread it would scarcely remember where and what that tangle had been. His title to fame does not rest upon victories won over Koffee Kalcali or Arabi Pasha ; as Wren's memorial is the great dome under which Wolseley sleeps, so Wolseley's monument is the British Army of to-day—the *nova creatura* of which he was the designer and architect.

As one vision inspired him, so one simple purpose drew him on ; in following it he made his every faculty the instrument of a resolute will. He was sure all the while that in time—if not in his time—there would be the great appeal to the arbitrament of the sword : to that appeal the British Army must make a full response. Had his span of life been extended for a little more than a year, he would have seen his vision enacted in terrible reality. He would have seen his country, whose honour was at stake, fling herself with something like fine reckless-ness into a fearful struggle without any thought of its duration or count of its cost. He would have marked the great military structure—for which he had been busy to clear the ground and lay the foundations—rise pile upon pile to its pre-eminence. He would have watched, with eager satisfaction, the British Empire pouring its millions of trained troops into the field, to decide the fate of those battles on which hung the destinies of the world. He would have witnessed without surprise—for he often spoke of it—monarchies overset, empires crumble, and his own Sovereign enthroned more securely than ever before. And of the issue of the world-war he would have had no doubt. In his old age there would have been the same utter trust, the same childlike belief. The God of battles, to whom he had always cried, would know that this country had her quarrel just : The All-Just would judge between England and a brutal enemy. The fight might be fierce, the warfare long, the tale of agony drawn out. But he would have been sure there could be but one end. There might be disappointment, but there would have been no dismay. And through it all the brave heart would have beat as steady as it beat high ; for the Courage which rises from sheer Faith is founded upon a rock.

BUTTON, THE ROYAL HORSE GUARDS.

343

BIBLIOGRAPHY

LORD WOLSELEY'S PUBLICATIONS [1]

Narrative of the War in China. 1862.

A Month's Visit to the Confederate Headquarters. Blackwood. January 1863.

The Soldiers' Pocket Book. 5 editions. 1869–1889.

Essay written for the Wellington Prize. 1872.

The Field Pocket Book for Auxiliary Forces. 1873.

The Use of Railroads in War. (Pamphlet.) 1873.

Military Genius. (Pamphlet.) September 1887.

The Negro as a Soldier. Fortnightly Review. December 1888.

Courage. (Pamphlet.) 1888.

War. Fortnightly Review. January 1889.

Is a Soldier's Life worth living ? Fortnightly Review. May 1889.

An English View of the American Civil War. North American Review. May-November 1890.

The Standing Army of Great Britain. Harper's Magazine. February 1890.

General Sherman. United Service Magazine. June-July 1891.

Field-Marshal Count von Moltke. United Service Magazine. September-October 1891.

The Life of John, 1st Duke of Marlborough (1650–1702). 2 vols. 1894.

The Decline and Fall of Napoleon. 1895.

The Story of a Soldier's Life. 2 vols. 1903.

---

[1] Certain of the above of which use has been made in this biography appear also in the second list.

WORKS REFERRED TO

Military Forces of the Crown. Clode. 2 vols. 1869.
History of the British Army. Fortescue. 11 vols. 1899–1923.
Lord Cardwell at the War Office. Biddulph. 1904.
Life and Correspondence of Sir J. Burgoyne. 2 vols. 1873.
Report of the Commissioners appointed to enquire into the
    System of Purchase and Sale of Commissions in the Army.
    1856.
Report of the Commissioners appointed to enquire into Over-
    regulation Payments on Promotion in the Army. 1870.
The Story of a Soldier's Life. Wolseley. 2 vols. 1903.
The Army Book of the British Empire. 1893.
The Invasion of the Crimea. Kinglake. 9 vols. 1877–1888.
Incidents of the Sepoy War, 1857–8. Sir Hope Grant and
    Captain H. Knollys. 1859.
Selections from State Papers preserved in the Military Depart-
    ment. 1857–58.
Narrative of the War in China. Wolseley. 1862.
A Month's Visit to the Confederate Headquarters by an English
    Officer. Blackwood. January 1863.
A Memoir of Lieutenant-General Sir Garnet Wolseley. Low.
    1878.
The Red River Expedition. Huyshe. 1871.
The Soldiers' Pocket Book. Wolseley. 1869.
The Ashanti War : a Narrative. Brackenbury. 2 vols. 1874.
Correspondence relative to the recent Expedition to the Red
    River Settlement, with Journal of Operations. 1872.
Life of Disraeli. Vol. vi. Buckle.
Essays written for the Wellington Prize. 1872.
Life of Sir Bartle Frere. Martineau. 2 vols. 1895.
Cetewayo and his White Neighbours. Haggard.
Life of Gladstone. Morley. 3 vols. 1904.
General Sir George Pomeroy-Colley. Butler. 1899.
Report of the Localisation Committee. 1872.
Report of the Committee on Army Reorganisation. 1881.
Military History of the Campaign of 1882 in Egypt. 1887.
History of the Soudan Campaign. 2 vols. 1889.

Bibliography

The Brain of an Army. Wilkinson. 1887.

The Crimea in 1854 and 1894. Wood. 1895.

Life of the Duke of Devonshire. 2 vols. Holland. 1911.

Events in the Life of Charles George Gordon. H. W. Gordon. 1886.

Life of the Prince Consort. Martin.

Modern Egypt. Cromer. 2 vols. 1908.

Life of Lord Granville. Fitz-Maurice. 1905.

Lord Wantage, V.C., K.C.B. By his Wife. 1907.

Thomas George, Earl of Northbrook. Mallet. 1908.

Report of the Royal Commissioners appointed to enquire into the Civil and Professional Administration of the Naval and Military Departments. 1890.

Report of the Committee appointed to enquire into the Organisation and Administration of the Manufacturing Departments of the Army. 1887.

Life of Sir Henry Campbell-Bannerman. Spender. 1923.

Small Wars : their Principles and Practice. Callwell. 1899.

From Midshipman to Field-Marshal. Wood. 1906.

History of the War in South Africa. Maurice. Vols. i. and ii. 1906–7.

Life of the Right Hon. Sir Redvers Buller. Melville. 1923.

Life of Lord Kitchener. Arthur. 1920.

Letters of Lord and Lady Wolseley. Arthur. 1922.

Some Aspects and Impressions. Gosse. 1924.

Report of His Majesty's Commissioners appointed to enquire into the Military Preparations and other matters connected with the War in South Africa. 1903.

The official papers of Lord Wolseley and a large number of the private letters used in the compilation of this biography are the property of Lt.-Col. Sir Arthur Leetham, Secretary of the Royal United Service Institution.

INDEX

Index

training : differences between the Duke of Cambridge and Wolseley regarding, 230 *et seq.*

Army Lists, 1881, grandiose scheme of mobilisation in, 226

Army Manufacturing Departments, Committee on Organisation of, recommendations of, 228

" Army Regulation Act ", 1871, main provisions of, 55 ; effect of, 56 *et seq.*

Arthur, Sir George, letter from Wolseley to, appreciative of the work done by the former's uncle, Sir Bartle Frere, in South Africa, 131 *n.*

   Letters of Lord and Lady Wolseley, edited by, 43 *n.*, 346 ; *Life of Lord Kitchener*, by, 305 *n.*, 346

Arundel, Earl of, first Commander-in-Chief, *temp.* Charles I., 287

Ashantees, the, British difficulties with, and Wolseley's expedition against, 61 *et seq.*

Ashanti, expeditions to, in 1824, 1825, and 1826, inefficacy of, 61 ; against Prempeh, 300

" Ashanti Ring ", the, nickname for officers selected by Wolseley for service in Ashanti expedition, 63-4

Ashanti War, 1873–74, Wolseley's command in, 60, 205 *n.*; causes, 61 ; plan of campaign for, 63 ; and criticism of, 68 ; organisation by Wolseley and his staff for, 64-7 ; advance on, and occupation of Kumasi, 67 *et seq.*; pleasure in Britain at success of, 72-4 ; Wolseley's return after, 72 ; in the *Story of a Soldier's Life*, 337 ; and the Press, 66, 149 ; and the use of native troops in, 124

Assouan, 186, 187, 190, 210

Atbara, Kitchener's success at, 304

Austin, Alfred, friendship of Wolseley and, 247

Austria, Emperor of, Wolseley's mission to announce accession of Edward VII. to, 335, 336 *n.*

Auxiliary Forces, the (*see also under* Militia, Volunteers, Territorial Force), Wolseley on status and equipment of, 306-7

Ava, king of, 14

Aylward the Fenian, Wolseley's description of, 130

Bab-el-Keber, the " whalers " at, 188-9

Badajos, 225

Baden-Powell, Lieut.-General Sir Robert, at Mafeking, 322 ; sketch by, 70

Bairam, Feast of, the, appointment of Legislative Council in Cyprus announced on, 104

Baker, Colonel Valentine, 60 ; defeat of, at El-Teb, 177 ; and a projected Turkish battalion in Cyprus, 99

Baker, General Sir Thomas, 64 and *n.*

Balaclava, 17, 32, 269

Balmoral, Wolseley at, 163, 165

Banca, Isle and Straits of, 21

Bantus, the, and the Natal Government, 76 *et seq.*

Baring, Captain Evelyn, *see under* Cromer, 1st Earl of

Barkley, Sir Henry, Governor of Cape Colony, and federation of South Africa, 84 ; letters from Wolseley to, on Cetewayo's war preparation, 84 ; on his progress in Natal, 86 ; reported recall of, 87 ; and Wolseley, 80-81

Barnes, Gordon's letter to, on an interview at the War Office, 173 and *n.*

Barnston, Major, friend of Wolseley, 21, 22 ; death of, 25

Barrack-square drill, Wolseley's criticisms of, 54, 230

Barrow, Major, in the Zulu War, 120

Barter, Mr., 80

Barton, Sir A., Governor of Malta, Wolseley's visit to, 93

Bassein, 14

Bastion du Mât, 270

Basutoland, 77, 121 *n.*

Batoum, 210

Battenberg, Prince Henry of, death of, 301

Beaconsfield, Earl of, and the " Army Regulation Bill ", 55 ; and India, 90 ; and the Zulu War, 114-15 ; letters from, to Lady Bradford on Chelmsford and Wolseley, 116, 126 ; to Queen Victoria on Chelmsford and Wolseley, 116, 119 ; *Life*

Index

Brown Bess musket, the, 16
Bucharest, Wolseley at, 336
Buddhist priests, Wolseley on, 14-15
Bulawayo, 314
Buller, Rt. Hon. Sir Redvers, 50, 64 and *n.*, 65, 253 ; as Adjutant-General, 254, 255, 273 ; as Commander-in-Chief, proposed appointment of, 274-5 ; as Quartermaster-General, 246 ; in command at Aldershot, 293 ; letter from Wolseley to, on newspaper reports of the Military Society of Ireland, 261 ; in the Soudan campaign, 1884, as Chief of Staff, 183, 190, 191, 196, 198, 201, 202, 204 *et seq.*, 215 ; retirement of, to Korti, 206-7 *n.* ; in the South African War, 321, 322, 330, 331 ; in the Zulu War, 119 and *n.*
Bulwer, Sir Henry, Governor of Natal, 117 ; arrival of, at Durban, 87-8 ; attitude of, to Bartle Frere, 121 ; farewell banquet to, at Maritzburg, 130 ; financial liabilities and capabilities of Natal discussed by, with Wolseley, 127
Burdett-Coutts, Baroness, 180
Burgoyne, Sir John, and the Crimean War, 31, 32, 270
Burke, Edmund, 287
Burma, likelihood of war in, 1875, 83 ; Wolseley in, 14-16 ; and his experience, 65
Burmese War, Second, Wolseley in, 12, 14-16, 146
Burnaby, Lieut.-Colonel Frederick, death of, at Abu-Klea, 200, 205 *n.*
Bushman Pass, 76
Butler, General Sir William, 64 and *n.*, 246 ; impetuosity of, 253 ; in Ashanti, 65 ; in the Red River expedition, 50 ; in the Soudan campaign, 1884, in charge of boats on the Nile, 179, 188 and *n.* ; in South Africa, 79, 86

Cadi, the Turkish, Wolseley's attitude to, 99, 100, 101
Caesar, Julius, Wolseley on, the literary ability of, 235 ; the military genius of, 37, 259

Cairo, 29, 144 *n.*, 148 ; protection of, and need for British garrison at, 155, 169-70 ; Wolseley in, 159 *et seq.*, 183, 208 *et seq.*
Calabria, H.M.S., 146
Calais, 176
Calcutta, 13, 14, 21, 22
Cambridge, H.R.H. the Duke of, 87 *n.*, 93, 144, 162, 185, 239, 257 ; antecedent offices of, and appointment of, as Commander-in-Chief, 289 ; and increased powers of, in 1888, 289-90, 291 ; compliments of, to Wolseley on Red River expedition, 53 ; delight of, in set field days, 254 and *n.* ; good wishes of, for Egyptian campaign, 146 ; his love of the Army, 234 ; and Wolseley on the loyalty and devotion of, for the Army, 234-5 ; objection of, to Roberts as A.G., 251 ; proposed new appointment for, 280-83 ; retirement of, as Commander-in-Chief, 272 ; and care of the sick in war, 237 ; and the defeat of Cetewayo, 118 ; and the office of Q.M.G., 137, 138 ; and the "Old School", 286 ; and the popularity of Wolseley, 133 ; and Wolseley at the War Office, 227 ; and Wolseley's inspection of the Guards at Suakin, 215-16 ; and Wolseley's scheme for increase of the Guards, 312 ; on need for garrison at Cairo, 169-70 ; Wolseley's Cyprus correspondence with, 109-10 ; Wolseley's interview with, and complaint of his treatment by, 140-41 ; Wolseley on his "antiquated views", 122 ; letters from Wolseley to, on the climate of Cyprus and its effect on the troops, 98 and *n.* ; on the Crimean campaign, 269-71 ; on his desire for active military service in India, 110 and *n.* ; on embarkation of the 42nd Regiment, 106 *n.* ; on the Egyptian campaign and its progress, 153-5 ; on favouritism, 183 ; on promotion by merit, 263 ; on Soldiers' Homes in Ireland, 266-7 ; on his status in South Africa, 79 *n.* ; letters to Wolseley

from, of appreciation of his work as Adjutant-General, 254-255 ; on the death of Mrs. FitzGeorge, 253 and *n.* ; on the Reserve, 139 ; on Wolseley's public utterances on military subjects and replies thereto, 230 *et seq.* ; on Wolseley's strategy in Egypt, 149 ; and his relations with Wolseley at different times, 115, 127, 165, 168, 224, 252, 253 ; differences between Wolseley and, on economies in Ireland, 256-7 ; on promotion by merit, 211, 217 *n.*, 236 ; on the Short Service System, 114, 263 ; on the Staff College and its use, 236 ; objections of, to Wolseley, as Adjutant-General, 142 ; as Colonel of the Horse Guards, 268 ; as Commander-in-Chief in the Soudan, 180 ; as High Commissioner in Cyprus, 92

Cambridge, University of, honorary degree conferred on Wolseley by, 73

Camelry, use of, by Wolseley, and the Press on, 181-2 ; Duke of Cambridge's objections to, 182-3

Cameron Highlanders at Korosko, 193

Campaign of Fredericksburg (Henderson), 236

Campbell, Sir Colin, in the Crimean War, 31 ; Indian Mutiny quelled by, 22 *et seq.*

Campbell-Bannerman, Right Hon. Sir Henry, 224 *n.*, 241 *n.* ; Army reforms of, 264, 271 *et seq.* ; and the Commander-in-Chiefship, 274

Canada, garrisoning of, 58 ; Wolseley's service in, 34-5, 39-53, 338 *n.*

Canadian Militia, the, and the Fenian invasion, 42-3 ; in the Red River expedition, 44 ; Wolseley's reorganisation of, and high opinion of, 40

Canrobert, Marshal, in the Crimea, 183

Cape Coast Castle, 63 ; sale of King Koffee's treasure at, 71

Cape Colony, and Langalibalele's rebellion, 77

Cape Mounted Police, 77

Cape Parliament, Froude's letter to Wolseley on, 85

Cape Town, preparedness for South African War at, 327 ; reinforcements of garrison at, 310, 313 *et seq.* ; Wolseley in, during 1875-76, 80-81, 88 ; 1879-80, 116, 130-31

Cardigan, Earl of, mot of, at Balaclava, 9 *n.*

Cardwell, Edward, Viscount, as Secretary of State for War, Army reforms of, 54 *et seq.*, 73-4, 133 *et seq.*, 170, 226, 256-7, 312 ; and criticisms of, and Wolseley's defence, 261 *et seq.* ; effect of, in India, 88 ; letters from, to Earl of Kimberley on Wolseley's memorandum on the Ashanti situation, 63 ; to Lord Northbrook, on Ashanti expedition, 73 ; to Wolseley, on need for a professional military man in the Government, 134 ; Wolseley's admiration for, and tribute to, 56 ; Wolseley's appointment by, as Assistant A.G., 53 ; and the younger school of military thought, 57

Carnarvon, 4th Earl of, Colonial Secretary, 190 *n.* ; and Sir Bartle Frere, 116, 131 ; and Froude's mission to South Africa on Federation of South African Colonies, 84-5, 87 ; letter from Wolseley to, on likelihood of war in Burma and offer of services, 83 and *n.* ; and Wolseley's mission to Natal, 78, 80, 82, 85

Carrington, General Sir Frederick, in the Sekukuni expedition, 125

Cavagnari, Sir Louis, murder of, at Kabul, 123

Cawnpore, General Wyndham at, 24 ; the massacre at, 21, 22 ; Wolseley's loss of kit at, 24

Cecil, Lord Edward, aide-de-camp to Wolseley in Ireland, 255-6

Cetewayo, Zulu king, 117 ; action against, Wolseley's notes for, 111, 112 ; capture of, 120 ; and Wolseley's contention of, as the end of the Zulu War, 129 ; life of, in London, 120 ; preparations for war by, 84 ; and Sekukuni, 123

Cetewayo and his White Neighbours (Haggard), 123 *n.*, 345

Index

Wolseley as ambassador to, 275 *et seq.*; Wolseley in, at Jubilee of William I., 221-2; and tour of the battle-fields of Franco-Prussian War, 222

Gibraltar, desire of Wolseley for governorship of, 138; garrison of, 312; meeting of Lord Napier and Wolseley at, 147

Gifford, Lord, winning of V.C. by, 69; with Wolseley in South Africa, 79, 86; in the Zulu War, 120

Gilbert, Sir W. S., Wolseley satirised by, in *Pirates of Penzance*, 133

Gipps, General Sir R., 273

Gladstone, Rt. Hon. W. E., 162; and Army Reform, use of Wolseley's help for, 134 *et seq.*; and a peerage for Wolseley desired by, 136 *et seq.*; and the Army Regulation Bill, 55; Government of, and the Channel Tunnel scheme, 1871, 168; defeat of, 217; praise of Wolseley by, 73; after Tel-el-Kebir, 160-61; policy of, Wolseley's opposition to, 132, 211 *n.*; and Home Rule, 268

Soudan policy of, 187 *n.*, 197, 208; and Gordon's mission in, 174-6; and his death, Wolseley on, 204 *n.*; appointment of Wolseley to command, by, 180; letter to Lord Hartington from, on Wolseley's powers in Soudan, 180-81 *n.*; opposition of Wolseley to, 168, 206 *n.*

Glasgow, Wolseley's Army speech at, 1898, 312-13

Glover, Captain, R.N., in the Ashanti War, 68

Glynde, Wolseley's life at, 334, 335, 338

Gold Coast, 300; and the Ashanti War, 61 *et seq.*; climate of, 64; and effect on British soldiers, 67; Wolseley at, 63 *et seq.*

Golden Bridge House, Dublin, birthplace of Wolseley, 2

Gomtee, River, 23

Goodenough, Colonel, in Egyptian campaign, 1882, 145, 157

Gordon, General Charles ("Chinese"), career of, 172; in China, and Wolseley on, 30;

friendship of Wolseley and, 18, 176 and *n.*, 217

mission of, to the Soudan: draft of instructions by, 174; and meeting of Wolseley and, 172-3, 174; in Khartoum, 178, 195, 196; and difficulties of communication with, 192; death of, and effect on Wolseley, 202, 204-5 and *n.*; and its avengement by Kitchener, 301

Gordon, General J., suggested as C.-in-C., India, 302

Gordon, Sir Henry, brother of General C. Gordon, letter from Wolseley to, on Gordon's death at Khartoum, 204-5 *n.*

Goschen, Viscountess, letter from Lady Wolseley to, on Wolseley's reception in London after the Egyptian campaign of 1882, 162-3

Gosse, Mr. Edmund, friendship of Wolseley and, 246, 334; letter from Wolseley to, on his tour of the battle-fields of the Franco-German War, 222-3; on Wolseley's love of books, 41; on his views on the Chinese, 29 *n.*; *Some Aspects and Impressions* by, *quoted*, 223 *n.*

Graham, Major-General, in Egyptian campaign, 1882, 145, 151-2, 157; in the Soudan, 1884-85, 177, 207, 211; Wolseley on, 205

G.C.M.G. conferred on Wolseley, 73

Grant, General, Wolseley's opinion of, and writings on, 38

Grant, Major-General Sir Hope, of the Oudh Division, 25, 26; in China, 26 *et seq.*; Wolseley on, 27 *n.*; Wolseley on his experience on the staff of, 90-91

Grant, Sir Patrick, 268

Granville, Earl, 162, 176, 207; and the evacuation of the Soudan, 215; and Gordon, 173, 176; and Wolseley's appointment to Cyprus, 91

Great Exhibition, the, of 1851, 7 *n.*

Great War, the, 171, 236, 237, 269 *n.*, 308, 342

Greaves, General Sir George, 64 and *n.*, 205, 246

Greece, King of, Wolseley's mission to announce accession of Edward VII. to, 335, 336 *n.*

359

Index

Index

Index

Index

Majuba Hill, 64, 333

Malakoff, the, 270 ; French success at, 19

Malet, Right Hon. Sir E., High Commissioner in Egypt, 149

Malta, 92, 93, 113, 147 ; climate of, 98 ; Governorship of, Wolseley suggested for, 227

Maltese, projected colonisation of Cyprus by, 95

Manœuvres, Army, institution of, in 1871, 59-60 ; and purchase of land for, on Salisbury Plain, 283 ; institution of annual, in Ireland, 259-60

Maritzburg, garrison at, in 1896, 314 ; preparations for South African War at, 327 ; Wolseley at, 76, 87, 127-9 ; and address to native chiefs in 1879, 117 ; and dinners to Bulwer, 130 ; to Lord Chelmsford, 119-20

Bishop of, 83

Marlborough, 1st Duke of, 341 ; *Life*, by Wolseley (see under *Life of John, 1st Duke of Marlborough*), truth of character as drawn in, 336-7 ; Wolseley's painstaking study of, 265-6 ; Wolseley on the military genius of, 37

Marlborough House, 163 ; reception of Wolseley by Edward VII. at, 335 *n.*, 336

Marseilles, 113

Martaban, 14

Marter, Major, capture of Cetewayo by, 120

Martinière, La, palace of, near Lucknow, 22

Mary, Queen Consort, 145, 258

Masama Station, 150, 151 and *n.*

Mason, Mr., envoy of Confederate States, 34

Master-General of the Ordnance, function of, in 1850, 6

Matammeh, military operations with regard to, in the Soudan campaign, 1884–85, 194, 196, 197, 200, 201 and *n.*, 202, 206

Maurice, Major - General Sir Frederick, 64 and *n.*, 71 ; friendship of Wolseley and, 67, 253 ; "Hostilities without Declaration of War", drafted by, 169 ; lecture by, to Military Society of Ireland, 261 ; letters from Wolseley to, on the influence

of Mahan's books, 285-6 ; on military tradition, 225-6 ; military history taught by, at the Staff College, 236 ; Wellington Prize won by, 54 ; in Soudan campaign, 183 ; on Wolseley's staff in Zulu War, 120 ; Wolseley's judgement of von Moltke to, 221-2

Mauritius, garrison of, 314

Mediterranean cruises, Wolseley's, 338

Mediterranean Fleet, the, and the Egyptian campaign, 1882, 147, 149-50

Meeah-Toon, Chief, expedition against, 15

Meeanee, 12

Meerut, 22

Melbourne, s.s., transport, 34

Melbury Road, Kensington, Cetewayo's life at, 120

Mentone, Wolseley's death at, 339-40

Meredith, George, letter of congratulation to, signed by Wolseley and others on the seventieth birthday of, 334-5

Meroe, 195, 196

Messing, Wolseley's improvements in, 229-30

Michel, Sir John, 60

Middleberg, Wolseley at, 124

Midleton, Earl of, War Secretary, 1900, 274 and *n.* ; letter from Wolseley to, on his retirement from the Commander-in-Chief-ship, 324

Military Education, improvements in, 283 ; Wolseley on, 235-6

Military Forces of the Crown (Clode), 8 *n.*, 345

Military Genius, essay by Wolseley, 37, 347

Military History of the Campaign of 1882, 144 *n.*, 150 *n.*, 151 *n.*, 345

Military Society of Ireland, revival of, by Wolseley, 261, 266

Militia, the, 75, 323 ; under the "Army Regulation Act", 55 ; equipment and status of, in 1897, 306 ; use of, in South African War, 332

Milner, Sir Alfred, 317

Minie rifle, the, 17

Mobilisation, system of, in 1897, 306 ; in 1898, 285 ; during the South African War, 327 *et seq.* ; and success of, 319

Index

Index

16 *et seq.*; in the Indian Mutiny, 21 *et seq.*
Norman, Sir Henry, 91
North American Review, the, articles by Wolseley, on the American Civil War, in, 38 and *n.*, 347
North-West Provinces (India), 22
Northbrook, Earl of,, 138, 181 and *n.*; and Gordon, 173; on the British acquisition of Cyprus, 93; letter from Cardwell to, on the Ashanti Expedition, 74
Nugent, Colonel, R.E., in Egyptian campaign, 1882, 145
Nurses, Wolseley on the social position of, 237

Odessa, 269 *n.*
Officers of the British Army, 40; promotion of, 211 *et seq.*, 217 *n.*, 236-7, 284-5; Purchase system, effect of on the efficiency of, 7 *et seq. passim*; Staff, in the Crimean War, 17; Wolseley on essential qualifications of, 42-3; and men, need of co-operation between, 228-9
Oliphant River, 123
Omdurman, advance on, 305; and victory of, 208, 305-6
O'Neil, "General", of the Fenians, 42
Operations of War (Hamley), 54
Orange Free State, 77, 86; and the South African War, 317, 318, 321, 327 *n.*
Ordahsu, engagement at, in Ashanti campaign, 69
Orders conferred on Wolseley, G.C.M.G., 72-3; K.C.B., 73; K.C.M.G., 53; K.P., 218; O.M., 335
Orders in Council, relating to:
Commander-in-Chief, functions and powers of, 1888, 289; 1895, 294-5; and Wolseley's memorandum on, in 1900, 295-6
Cyprus, establishment of Government in, 1878, 101
Egyptian campaign, calling out Reserve for, 145
Transvaal, Legislative Assembly for, 126
victualling in the Army, 171
War Office, reorganisation of, 290-91
Osborne, 310; Wolseley's visits to, 146, 248, 254

Osman Digna, 197; British operations against, 207; and engagements with, in Suakin, 177; raids of, in 1896, 302
Ottoman Government, and Arabi's revolt, 143; land rights of, in Cyprus, 107; *see also under* Turkey, Government of, *and* Sultan of
Ottoman Loan of 1855, and the Cyprus "tribute", 105
"Our only general", Beaconsfield's sobriquet for Wolseley, popularity of, 126, 133, 180
Outram, Sir James, at Lucknow, 23; Wolseley on, 24; defence of Alum Bagh by, 24, 25
Oxford, University of, honorary degree conferred on Wolseley by, 73

Pain, Olivier, bogus letter from Wolseley to, 201
Palestine, 172; Beaconsfield's attraction to, 93 *n.*
Palikao, Count, *see under* Montauban
Pall Mall Gazette, 192
Palmerston, Viscount, 58, 288; and China, 20, 26; on the Purchase system, 8
Pantechnicon, the, great fire at, and Wolseley's loss by, 24
Paris, Wolseley in, 113
Parkes, Mr., 27
Parliament and Crown, struggle between, for control of military forces, 286 *et seq.*
Patronage, military, by political chiefs, 245; *see also under* Promotion
Paxton, Sir Joseph, 73 *n.*
Pegu, 14
Peh-Tang, landing of Allied forces at, 27
Pei-Ho, River, naval and military action on, 26, 27, 29
Pekin, 26, 27; looting of Summer Palace in, 28-9; occupation of, 28
Pender, Sir John, Wolseley's yacht cruise with, 269-71
Peninsular War, 7; traditions of, 225-6
"Penjdeh incident", the, 209 *n.*
Pennyfather's address after Meeanee, 12
Persia, 250

366

Phillips, Mr., Wolseley's request for, as judge in Cyprus, 94
Pietermaritzburg, 81 ; *see* Maritzburg
Pigott, Colonel, Wolseley on, 200
Pine, Sir Benjamin, Governor of Natal, 77 *et seq.* ; and Wolseley, 81
Plymouth, 88
Poles, the, and Russia, 216 *n.*
Pondoland, 121 *n.*
Ponsonby, Sir H., private secretary to Queen Victoria, 136 *et seq.*, 147, 251, 268
Port Arthur (Canada), 46
Port Durnford, Wolseley at, 117
Port Said, 149
Portages, the, in the Red River expedition, Wolseley's description of, 48-50
Porte, the, *see under* Turkey *and* Ottoman Government
Portsmouth, 20, 72
Potomac, River, 35, 36
Prah, River, 67, 68
Prempeh, king of Ashanti, expedition against, 300
Press, the, agitation by, for Wolseley's appointment as Adjutant-General, 139 ; and relations with the Duke of Cambridge occasioned by, 140-1 ; Wolseley's attitude to the communications of officers with, 232 ; war correspondents of, 66, 149, 184 ; Wolseley on reports of proceedings of Military Society by, 261
Pretoria, 86 ; Wolseley in, 123, 126, 129
Pretorius, imprisonment of, 127
Primrose, Colonel the Hon. E., in the Soudan campaign, and death of, 182-3 and *n.*
Prince Imperial, death of, 128, 130
Prome, 15
Promotion of officers in the Army, 127, 263 ; methods of selection for, 211-2, 236-7, and Wolseley's criticisms of, 211 *et seq.* ; selection by merit, 284-5 ; and patronage by political chiefs, 245
Protestant Alliance, the, complaint of Wolseley by, 267
Provost of Trinity College, Dublin, 256

Purchase System in the Army, 7 *et seq.* ; abolition of, by the Cardwell reforms, 9, 55, 57, 134, 212 ; effect of, on efficiency, 8 *et seq.* ; incongruities of, 9 ; report of commissioners of inquiry on, 1856, 9 and *n.*
Purdon, Lieut.-Colonel, defeat of Ashantees by, 61

Quartermaster-General, functions of, 291, 299 ; Wolseley as, 130, 133 *et seq.* ; and on the post being a sinecure, 137-8
Quebec, 53
Quetta, 211

Raglan, Lord, and the conduct of the Crimean War, Wolseley's views on, in 1899, 31-3
Railroads, power of Government to take possession of, 55
Railway Corps, a, formation of, 152 and *n.*
Rainy Lake, 50
Raleigh, H.M.S., 81
Rameses III., 186
Ranger's House, the, Greenwich, Wolseley's life at, 248, 255, 257
Rangoon, 14, 15, 16
Ranksborough, Lord, 268; Gordon's friendship for, 176 *n.*
Rathmines, letter from Wolseley to priest at, on attendance of soldiers at church, 267
Rations, army, 308, 309
Rawson, Lieutenant, Wolseley's naval aide-de-camp, 157 ; death of, 159
Red Cross Society, *see under* British Red Cross Society
Red River, navigation of, by Wolseley, 52
Red River Territory (Canada) ; Wolseley's expedition to, 63, 238, 341 ; start and equipment, 44-8; description of the portages, 48-50; and the rapids, 50-1 ; satisfactory conclusion, 52-3 ; experience of, used in Soudan campaign, 179, 188 ; and Hudson Bay Co., 43-4
Redan, the assault on, 19
Regiment, the, tradition of, 225-6
Regimental titles, changes of, in accordance with Territorial basis of organisation, 138 ; and feeling occasioned thereby, 135

Index

Religion, friction due to, in Ireland, 266-7

" Republic of the North-West," proclaimed by Louis Riel, 44

Reserve, the Army, 57, 207 ; annual training of, 225; under the Army Regulation Act, 1871, 55 ; Duke of Cambridge's disbelief in, 139, 234-5 ; Egyptian campaign a test of, 152

Residency, the, at Lucknow, investment and relief of, 21 et seq.

Revelstoke, Lord, 241 n.

Richards, Sir F., 241 n.

Richmond, Duke of, announcement by, regarding Wolseley's appointment in Cyprus, 91

Richmond, Va., 36

Ridgeway, Fenians at, 42

Riel, Louis, " Republic of the North - West " proclaimed by, 44 ; expedition against, 44 et seq.; further rebellion and death of, 52

Rifle Brigade, 57, 182 ; 2nd Battalion of, in Ashanti War, 67

Riga, 216 n.

Ripon, Marquess of, application of, for Wolseley as C.-in-C. in India, 140

Robben Island, 77

Roberts, Earl, 8 ; in India, Second AfghanWar, 90 ; Indian Mutiny, 25 ; as Commander-in-Chief, 249 et seq.; Indian defence policy of, 89-90; as Commander-in-Chief, British Army, 293, 324 ; and the South African War, 318, 321, 322, 333

Robertson, Sir W., and the Great War, 292 n.

Rondebosch, Wolseley at, 81

Roon, Count von, 222 and n.

Rorke's Drift, defence of, 64 ; V.C.'s awarded for gallantry at, 122

Rosebery, Earl of, 182 ; fall of Government of, 274

Ross, Colonel, 27

Roumania, Crown Princess of, 336 King of, Wolseley's mission to announce Edward VII.'s accession to, 335, 336 n.

Royal Academy banquet, Wolseley's health proposed by Prince of Wales at, 73

Royal Artillery, the, Officers' Mess of, Woolwich, and King Koffee's treasure, 71

Royal Canadian Regiment, Wolseley's command of, 338 and n.

Royal Commissions, see under title of reference, or name of president

Royal Horse Guards, Wolseley and the Colonelcy of, 268 ; Wood as Colonel of, 338 ; and the death of Wolseley, escort provided by, 340

Royal Hospital, Dublin, 255, 256, 260

Royal Irish Regiment in the Soudan, 193 n., 198 n., 201 ; Wolseley's colonelcy of, 337-8

Royal Navy, the, see under Navy

Royal United Service Institution, the, Ashanti relics in, 70, 71-2 ; Wolseley Collection at, 29 n., 346

Royal West Kent Regiment in the Soudan, 201

Rupert's Land, 44

Russell, General Sir Baker, 64 and n., 65, 246 ; in Ashanti War, 67 ; in Egypt, 1882, 145 ; in expedition against Sekukuni, 123 et seq.

Russell, Sir William (" Billy "), Times correspondent in the Crimean War, 20, 66 ; charges against the Army made by, 130 and n.

Russia, Crimean campaign against, 269-71 (see also under Crimean War) ; and Afghanistan in 1873, 89 ; in 1885, 207 ; and Armenia, 93 ; and the Penjdeh incident, 1885, 209 et seq. and n.; Wolseley in, 171

Russian Army, the, Wolseley's opinion of, 303 n.

Russo-Turkish War, 96, 99

Sacred Carpet, the, 161-2

St. James's Gazette, 192

St. Paul's Cathedral, Wolseley buried in, 340-1

Salamanca, 225

Salamis, H.M.S., in Egypt, 150

Salamon, Saul, editor of the Argus, and Wolseley, 88

Saleh, Sheikh, 202

Salisbury, Marquess of, 83 n., 256, 325 ; third Administration of, 274 et seq.; transfer of, from India Office to Foreign Office, 93-4 and n.; and Kitchener's campaign in the Soudan, 301 ; and Lord Lansdowne's attack on Wolseley, 326 ; and

368

Index

Index

tionary Force, 181 ; difficulties of transport in, 185-6 ; Gordon and, 171 *et seq.*; the Mahdi proclaimed in, 171-2 ; withdrawal proposed, 172-3 ; and carried out, 209 *et seq.*, 215 *et seq.* ; Wolseley and defective supplies for, 227-8
command by Kitchener in 1896–1898, 301, 304-6

South Africa, military measures taken in 1879 and 1888 in, 313 *et seq.*; Wolseley in, 76-88,114-32; Wolseley on need for reinforcements in 1896–97, 313 *et seq.*

South African Federation, proposals for, by Lord Carnarvon, 84 and *n.* ; advocacy of scheme by Wolseley and Froude, 85 and *n.*, 86, 88, and by Sir Bartle Frere, 121

South African War, 225, 300, 313 ; anti-British propaganda during, and problems arising, 322-3 ; criticisms of Army administration during, 325-6 ; Kitchener and the duration of, 333 ; mobilisation for, 319-20 ; Official History and Report of Royal Commission on, 320, 327 *n.* ; possibilities of the Peace following, 333 ; précis of letters and minutes from Commander-in-Chief to Secretary of State, 1899–1900, regarding, 327-32 ; unpreparedness for, 316-19, 329, 331 ; Wolseley's views on, in 1902, 131 *n.*

Southampton, embarking port for troops in South African War, 319

Spencer, 5th Earl, 218

Sprigg, Sir Gordon, Prime Minister, Cape Colony, letter from Wolseley to, on the friction with the Boers, 314-15

Staff College, the, 261, 316 ; Wolseley's reform of, 236, and interest in, 283-4

Standerton, 122

Stanhope, Right Hon. E., Secretary of State for War, 1889, 232, 233 ; annoyance of, at report of lecture on "Barracks", 261; increase of Commander-in-Chief's powers by, 289; letter from Wolseley to, on his disinclination to accept command in India, 249 *et seq.*

Stanley, Colonel the Hon. E., *see* Derby, 16th Earl of

Star Fort, Crimea, 269

Staveley, General Sir Charles, 60, 91 *n.*

Steelpoort River, 123

Stephen, George, *see* Mountstephen, Lord

Stephenson, General Sir F., differences between Wolseley and, regarding best route to Khartoum, 179 ; superseded by Wolseley, 180, 183 ; views of, on Egyptian Occupation, 170

Stewart, Colonel James, the murder of, Wolseley on, 187 and *n.*

Stewart, General Sir Herbert, 146 ; in the Egyptian campaign, 156 ; in the Soudan campaign, 177, 184, 190, 194, 197, 198, 205 *n.* ; in the battle of Abu-Klea, 199-200, 201 ; death of, 253, and Wolseley's grief at, 206 and *n.*

Stone Fort, 52

Stonewall Jackson (Henderson), 236

Story of a Soldier's Life (Wolseley), 56 *n.*, 336-7, 347 ; *quoted* on the Duke of Cambridge, 234-5 and *n.*

Strassburg, 223

Strathcona, Lord, 39 ; and the Red River Expedition, 44, 52

Suakin, military operations with reference to, in the Soudan campaign, 1884–85, 173, 177, 186, 207, 210, 211, 215 ; Indian troops at, 302 ; Wolseley's inspection of troops at, 215-16 and *n.* ; Suakin-Berber route to Khartoum, 178, 197, 198-9

"Subalterns' Wars", nickname for Burmese Wars, 14

Suez Canal, 144, 147 *et seq.*

Superior, Lake, 46, 47

Sussex Regiment, the, in the Soudan, 205 *n.*

Swazis, the, and the attack on Sekukuni, 124, 125

Sweet Water Canal, the, 150, 157

Syracuse, 113

"System of Field Manœuvres best adapted for enabling our troops to meet a Continental Army", essay on, for the Wellington prize, 54-5, 345, 347

Taiping rebellion, suppression of, by Gordon, 30, 172

Index

United States of America, and the Fenian invasion of Canada, 39, 42 ; Civil War in, *see* American Civil War

Utrecht, S. Africa, Wolseley at, 122

Vaal, River, 322

Venice, H.M.S. *Salamis* at, 113

Vicksburg campaign, the, 38

Victoria, Governorship of, declined by Wolseley, 249 .

Victoria, Queen, 310 ; consent given by, for Duke of Connaught to join Egyptian campaign, 145 ; interest of, in troops at Cyprus, 110 ; King Koffee's umbrella given to, 71 ; reviews of troops by, after the Ashanti expedition, 72, after the Egyptian campaign, 1882, 164-165 ; views of, on the functions of Commander-in-Chief, 288-9

letters from, to the Duke of Cambridge on his retirement as Commander-in-Chief, 273 ; to Mr. Gladstone, Lord Granville, and Wolseley regarding sickness among the Guards in Egypt, 166, 168 ; to Wolseley, 211 *n.*; congratulating him on mobilisation for South African War, and reply thereon, 319-320 ; on money rewards for soldiers, 198 and *n.*; on his relinquishing office as C.-in-C., 324 ; letter to, from Beaconsfield, on Wolseley, 116, and Chelmsford, 119

and the Army, 5, 6 ; and death of Prince Henry of Battenberg, 300-301 ; and defeat of Cetewayo, 118 ; and Sir Bartle Frere, 130 ; and Gladstone with regard to a peerage for Wolseley, 136 *et seq.*; and the Guards, 311; and Home Rule, Wolseley on, 268 ; and Lord Salisbury, 217 ; at Aix-les-Bains, 210

relations between Wolseley and, 132, 146 ; in 1879, 115 ; after Egyptian campaign, 165, 168 ; his appointment by, as Adjutant-General, 141-2 ; and his candidature for Commander-in-Chiefship, 275 *et seq.*; and his declination of C.-in-C. India, 251 ; gift of Ranger's House,

Greenwich, 248 and *n.* ; and apartments at Hampton Court from, 335 ; his health proposed by, 165, 167 ; objections of, to his going to the Soudan, 180 ; his opinions on the Indian Army given to, 302-3 ; Order of St. Patrick bestowed by, 216 ; and his policy in Egyptian campaign, 147 ; support of Wolseley as C.-in-C. and correspondence regarding, 293 *et seq.*; and his Tel-el Kebir victory, 160, 161 ; visits to, 146, 181, 248, 254

Victualling in the Army, 171

Volta, River, 66

Voluntary Aid Detachments, 237

Volunteers for active service, Wolseley's predilection for, 16

Volunteers, the, 75, 323 ; equipment and status of, in 1897, 306, 307 ; use of, in South African War, 332 ; Wolseley's organisation of, 88

Voyageurs, use of, on the Nile, 179

Wady Halfa, military operations with reference to, in the Soudan campaign, 177, 181, 186, 187, 190, 191, 193, 210, 219 ; outpost at, 211

Wakerstroom, 122

Wantage, Lord, chairman of Commission on the terms of service in the Army, 261 *et seq.*

Lord and Lady, Red Cross work done by, in the Nile expedition, 237 ; Wolseley's visit to, 254

War correspondents, Wolseley's attitude to, 66, 149, 184

War Department, the, and the Royal prerogative in Army matters, 5

War Office, the, Army feeling against, in 1897, 309 ; Intelligence Department of, Wolseley's expansion of, 223-4; proposed distribution of functions at, 280 ; reorganisation of, by Campbell-Bannerman, 271 *et seq.*, 290 ; and the Admiralty, need for co-ordination of, 238 *et seq.*, 285-6 ; and the Commission on South African War, 325-6, 327 *n.* ; and the Hartington Commission, 290, 296 ; and *The Soldiers' Pocket*

372

Book, 41-2, 53 ; and Wolseley's mission to Natal, 79 *n.* ; and Zulu War preparations, 115 ; Wolseley at, 53, 54 *et seq.*, 74-5, 130, 133 *et seq.*, 168 *et seq.*, 223 *et seq.*, 252, 278 *et seq.* ; his criticisms of the organisation for war of, 292-3 ; of Q.M.G.'s department at, 106 *n.* ; his speech in House of Lords on administration of, 297-9 ; Wolseley's catafalque rests in, 1913, 340
Wardrop, Major, 207 *n.*
Warren Hastings, ordered by Wolseley, 257
Washington, 35, 40
Watkin, Sir Edward, Channel Tunnel scheme taken up by, 168-9
Wealth of Nations, The (Smith), 8 *n.*
Wellington, Duke of, 228, 341 ; as Commander-in-Chief, and views of the office of, 275, 285 ; in the Peninsular War, Wolseley on, 225 ; letter from, on our defensive weakness, 6 *n.* ; literary ability of, 235 ; on the British Army officer, 7-8 and *n.*, 11-12 ; reductions in military establishments urged by, 3-4, 5 ; retirement from politics in 1842, 6 ; Wolseley on, 259 ; death of, 13 ; tomb of, 340
Wellington, 2nd Duke of, prize for essay on Field Manœuvres offered by, 54, 64
West India Regiment, the, at Elmina, 61 ; on the Gold Coast, 65, 69
West Indies, 4
" Whalers ", use of, on the Nile, 187-8
Wharton, Lord, on the command of the Army in 1724, 287 *n.*
White, Sir George, C.-in-C., India, letter from Wolseley to, on selection for promotion, 284-5 ; in the South African War, 318, 319 ; message from Wolseley to, on political interference in the war, 319-20
" White Man's Grave, the ", name for the Gold Coast, 65
Wilkinson, Brigadier-General C. M., in Egyptian campaign, 145

Wilkinson, Mr. Spenser, articles and publications by, on need for a General Staff, 244 and *n.*
William I., Emperor of Germany, congratulations to Wolseley from, 165 ; Jubilee of, 221
William II., Emperor of Germany, 254
William III., King, and Brigadier-General Wolseley, 1
William IV., King, and the Army, 5
Willis, Lieutenant-General, in command 1st Division, Egyptian campaign, 1882, 145, 151 and *n.*, 155
Wilson, Sir Charles, in the Soudan campaign, 201 and *n.*, 203, 205 *n.*, 215 ; and the Mudir of Dongola, 192
Windsor, 312
Windsor Castle, s.s., 88
Winnipeg, 44
Winnipeg River, the, Wolseley on his navigation of, 50-51
Winton, Sir Francis de, 29 *n.*
With Essex in Ireland, ordered by Wolseley, 257
Wolseley, Brigadier-General, 1
Wolseley, Frances Garnet, Viscountess, daughter of Viscount Wolseley, 71 *n.*, 209, 248 ; in Cyprus, 108-9 ; interest of, in horticulture, 109
Wolseley, Garnet Joseph, Viscount, ancestry and parents of, 1-2 ; education and home life of, 2-3 ; entry of, into the Army as an ensign, 3, 8, 12 ; in India, 12-14 ; active service of, in Burma, 14-16 ; in the Crimea, 16-20 ; meeting of, with Charles Gordon, 18 ; voyage of, on H.M.S. *Transit*, 20-21 ; and the Indian Mutiny, 21-6 ; in China expedition, 26-30 ; in Canada, 34-5 ; in U.S.A., studying the Civil War, 35-9 ; organisation of the Canadian Militia by, and the Fenian invasion, 39-43 ; marriage of, to Miss Erskine, 43 ; and the Red River expedition, 43-53 ; made K.C.M.G., 53 ; at the War Office, and the Cardwell reforms, 54-60 ; and the Ashanti expedition, 1873, 60-73 ; honours and rewards received by, 73 ; mission of, to Natal,

Index

in Cyprus, 108-9; on King Koffee's treasure, 71; on a meal in Ireland, 259; on his mother, 92; on the Mudir of Dongola, 190 *n.*; on night attacks, 158; on the Prime Minister and Commanders-in-Chief, 218 *n.*; on his reception by Edward VII., 335-6 *n.*; on W. H. Smith, 106 *n.*; on the Soudan campaign, 196, 203; on Turkish officials in Cyprus, and Layard's attitude to, 100 *n.*, 101 and *n.*; on " Vanity ", 216-17

" Wolseley's Horse ", 1

Wood, Field-Marshal Sir Evelyn, 246, 251; in Ashanti expedition, 64 and *n.*, 65, 66; in Egyptian campaign, 1882, 145, 148, 149 *n.*; in the Soudan campaign, 181, 183, 190, 205, 206, 208; in the Zulu War, 119 and *n.*, 120, 122; as Adjutant-General, 293; as British Sirdar of Egyptian Army, 170; as Colonel of Royal Horse Guards, 338; as escort to Empress Eugénie in South Africa, 130 *n.*; as Quartermaster-General, 283; relations between Wolseley and, 253, 259-60; training of troops by, 227; visit of, with Wolseley to Crimea, 1894, 269-71

Wren, Sir Christopher, 342

Wyndham, General, at Cawnpore, 24

Xenophon, literary ability of, 235

Yakdul, *see* Jakdul

Yarrow, Sir Alfred, boats built by, used by Wolseley in the Nile Expedition, 185

Yeomanry, use of, in South African War, 332

York, H.R.H. Frederick Augustus, Duke of, as Commander-in-Chief, 3, 55, 58, 287-8

York Minster, appeal of, to Wolseley, 186

Yuen-Ming-Yuen Palace, Pekin, looting of, 28-9

Zagazig, 156, 158, 159

Zohrab Bey on Wolseley's staff in Soudan campaign, 184, 189

Zulu War, the, 129; appointment of Wolseley as Commander-in-Chief, 115; Chelmsford's conduct of, 116, 117; contribution from Natal for expenses of, suggested, 126, 127; effect of early defeats in, 114-15; success at Ulundi, 118, 119; Ulundi officially regarded as the final operation of, and Wolseley's protest regarding, 128; Wolseley's capture of Cetewayo, and plans for the pacification of Zululand, after, 120-21; Wolseley on the conduct of, 111, 112

Zululand, Wolseley's plans for settlement of, 120-1 and *n.*; criticism of, and feeling against, 123, 131-2

THE END

Printed in Great Britain by R. & R. CLARK, LIMITED, *Edinburgh.*